LIVING
INTO
FOCUS

LIVING
INTO
FOCUS

Choosing What Matters in an Age of Distractions

ARTHUR BOERS

FOREWORD BY Eugene H. Peterson

BrazosPress

a division of Baker Publishing Group
Grand Rapids, Michigan

Published by Brazos Press
a division of Baker Publishing Group
P.O. Box 6287, Grand Rapids, MI 49516-6287
www.brazospress.com

Printed in the United States of America

Library of Congress Cataloging-in-Publication Data
Boers, Arthur P. (Arthur Paul), 1957–
    Living into focus : choosing what matters in an age of distractions / Arthur Boers.
      p.   cm.
    Includes bibliographical references (p.   ) and index.
    ISBN 978-1-58743-314-6 (pbk.)
    1. Technology—Religious aspects—Christianity. 2. Attention—Religious aspects—Christianity. 3. Christian life—Mennonite authors. 4. Borgmann, Albert. I. Title.
    BR115.T42B64 2012
    248.4′897—dc23
                                         2011033946

Published in association with the literary agency of Alive Communications, Inc., 7680 Goddard Street, Suite 200, Colorado Springs, CO 80920, www.alivecommunications.com.

To
Albert Borgmann
Eugene Peterson
and David Wood
"No one I'd rather be with."

CONTENTS

FOREWORD

One of the disturbing features of contemporary culture—some think it qualifies as *most* disturbing—is the extent to which modern technology is impoverishing the way we live. Many voices have been raised in the last fifty years calling attention to the devastation being wreaked on our lives by our indiscriminate and undiscerning embrace of technology.

Arthur Boers is one of these voices. He has identified the Montana philosopher Albert Borgmann as a major prophet of our times with a remarkable ability to separate the chaff in our culture from the grain, and Boers has taken him on as a mentor. For several years he has absorbed Borgmann's philosophical analyses and concerns and in this book has written a kind of journal of his own personal "taking up with the world" (Borgmann's phrase) in ways that contribute to a life of wealth and enrichment.

In the middle of the nineteenth century, when technology was not nearly as advanced and omnipresent as it is now, Henry David Thoreau was alarmed when he observed that so many people were living lives of "quiet desperation." He responded by constructing and then living in a small cabin on Walden Pond to see if it was possible to live a life of simplicity and wealth in a culture of increasingly depersonalized and demeaning clutter. His witness to his life in that cabin, *Walden*, is an enduring monument to the fact that it is possible.

Arthur Boers in this book gives a similar witness, but in a very different setting. One difference is that since the days of Thoreau technology has penetrated virtually every area and detail of our lives. For most of us there is no escaping it, nor would we want to, for it brings many goods and conveniences into our lives. But a more significant difference between *Walden* and this book is that Dr. Boers does not radically separate himself from the world of technology by living alone on a New England pond. He has married and raised a family, he is a professor and a pastor, he owns and drives a car, has central heating in his home, carries a watch and uses a computer.

The usefulness of this book is not in its arguments or preachments (there is virtually none of that) and not in doomsday warnings and irritable complaints (these are also absent) but in its witness, the actual practices that develop into a coherent way of life, practices that any of us can embrace, practices that engage with things local, practices that nurture personal friendships, practices that maintain a close and friendly relationship with the terrain and weather in the place where we live.

It is important also to say what this book is not. It is not a book of condescending advice or a blueprint for imposing suggestions or "plans" for a wholesale renovation of a life that is out of control. Rather, it is a personal working through and reflection on the difficulties of swimming against the stream of contemporary culture and at the same time developing the focal practices that enable any one of us to revel in the good life that the Christian way invites us into.

Jesus famously said, "I have come that they may have life, and have it more abundantly" (John 10:10). Or to put it more directly in the second person, "I have come that you might live a generous life."

Despite its staggering achievements in raising our standard of living, our technology-dominated society is impoverishing far too many lives. The good life, the generous life, the abundant life has obviously eluded technology.

This is a huge irony. We live in a society that has achieved a standard of living that surpasses the wildest dreams of most of the people in the history of the world; the most conspicuous result is that far too many of us live poor, thin, trivializing lives. Advanced technology is the most prominent feature of contemporary life. It is glittering and glamorous. It disburdens us of laborious and grueling labor, promises an easier life, a more leisurely life. But there are dangers hidden in the glitter that betray the promises it offers.

So we learn to distinguish between standard of living and wealth. Standard of living simply means more money, faster cars, and bigger houses. Wealth comprises living well, having friends, exercising compassion, enjoying and celebrating goodness and beauty, and worshiping God. The concern of Dr. Boers is not to eliminate technology but to restrain technology so that it doesn't ruin our lives by depersonalizing them, disengaging us from the immediate everydayness of things and persons. For many years now, he has embraced Borgmann's passion for living a generous life. He has put the philosopher's diagnosis and concerns into practice in the context of his own life and work. This book is his personal witness to the practices that develop into a life of wealth, of generous abundance.

Most of us know far more about the Christian faith than we manage to live. There is no lack of words in the Christian community these days regarding spiritual formation, finding ways to think adequately about the Father, Son, and Holy Spirit, and receiving all the operations of the Trinity. Arthur Boers takes all this a step further. He takes what we know into our neighborhoods and backyards, our homes and workplaces. He then helps us get it all into our bones and muscles, our nerve endings and synapses as we drive our cars, use our computers, work our gardens, cook our meals, and eat together.

Eugene H. Peterson
Professor Emeritus of Spiritual Theology
Regent College, Vancouver, British Columbia

ACKNOWLEDGMENTS

Three friends in particular inform and inspire this book: Albert Borgmann, Eugene Peterson, and David Wood. I am grateful for the many ways that our lives intersect and how our friendships came to involve their spouses, Jan Peterson, Jennifer Wood, and the late Nancy Borgmann. These six people do not just talk the talk or dream the dreams—they embody the priorities, potentials, and practices of focal living.

I appreciate how Albert Borgmann gave generously of his time in correspondence, telephone conversations, and face-to-face meetings—even venturing to the Elkhart Consultation (2008) at Associated Mennonite Biblical Seminary (AMBS) with professors, pastors, writers, and activists to discuss the implications of focal living.

Eugene Peterson has been unstintingly supportive of this project in his regular pastoral inquiries about its progress, encouragement of my writing, examination of the book's ideas, reading of the manuscript, and generous foreword.

David Wood not only first introduced me to Albert's ideas but is also one of my primary faith and thought partners. We have collaborated on numerous projects over the years, and he helped facilitate the aforementioned Elkhart Consultation.

At the consultation, two people in particular contributed greatly with their expertise on Old Order Anabaptists: Donald Kraybill and Steven Nolt. My thanks as well to the event's other participants: Andy

Alexis-Baker, Nekeisha Alexis-Baker, Trevor Bechtel, Aiden Enns, Todd Friesen, Paul Heidebrecht, Lee Hoinacki, Andy Brubacher Kaethler, Gayle Gerber Koontz, Nina Lanctot, Craig Neufeld, Rebecca Slough, Karla Stoltzfus, Valerie Weaver-Zercher, and Brent Waters. The event's logistics were ably coordinated by Erin Boers.

Many people graciously talked to me about their focal practices, and they too inspired much of what follows: Ted Klopfenstein on long-distance endurance horse racing; Evelyn Kreider on letter writing; Dick Lehman on pottery; Ruth Mallory on birding; Verlin Miller on woodworking; Leroy and Winifred Saner on gardening, hospitality, and quilting; Rachel Shenk on her European bakery; Stan and Carolyn Smith on music, family life, television abstinence, bicycling, and doing-it-yourself; Don Steider on building one's own log cabin home; and Marie Troyer on quilting. Ray and Aki Epp of Menno Village, Hokkaido, Japan, hosted me for a wonderful visit where I witnessed firsthand their commitment to focal living. Another key conversation partner was Brent Graber, the go-to IT person at AMBS who blended technological expertise with theological and philosophical insights. I also talked over many ideas with our friends Kathy and Willard Fenton-Miller, all the while admiring their devotion to focal practices of cooking, hospitality, conversation, poetry, music, woodworking, and carpentry.

While I have been dreaming about this project for a long time, work on it began in earnest when my previous employer, Associated Mennonite Biblical Seminary, kindly granted me a sabbatical. Research and travel were made possible by a generous Christian Faith and Life Program grant from the Louisville Institute (funded by the Lilly Endowment). Tyndale Seminary, my present employer, also encouraged me in this book's completion, even as I was acclimating to a challenging new position.

Two people did the kind of work for *Living into Focus* that often goes unsung. Susan Murphy helped with fact and quote checking. Andy Alexis-Baker assisted with the index. I thank them both.

Margreet de Heer is a Dutch cartoonist with theological training that shows in both her humor and her insight. I am grateful that her art graces this book.

Erin Boers is a faithful and persistent, eagle-eyed copyeditor. She dedicated a good part of one vacation to scrutinizing my manuscript, and I was repeatedly astonished by what she found. "How did I miss that?" I wondered over and again. Erin also painstakingly transcribed the focal interviews. This is the third of my books she's helped with, and I can no longer imagine completing one without her.

I plugged away at this manuscript in various settings for a long time, all of them focal places, including a spring week at St. Gregory's Abbey Hermitage in Michigan and the convivial "Apart and Yet a Part" writers' retreat at the Collegeville Institute. Special thanks are due to Donald Ottenhoff, Collegeville's executive director, and all that he and his organization do to encourage writing. Final touches and revisions happened at Glad River on the banks of the South Branch of the Muskoka River.

My agent, Andrea Heinecke, a fellow hiker, believed in this project and worked hard to promote it. Thanks as well to Rodney Clapp and the good folks of Brazos for accepting and affirming *Living into Focus*. As it happens, Rodney and I first met in Missoula at another consultation with Albert Borgmann and Eugene Peterson, an event organized and facilitated by David Wood, who was then associate director of the Louisville Institute. At that very occasion I first began dreaming about this book. So it seems especially fitting that Rodney is part of the collaboration that finally makes its publication possible.

My last words are for my greatest inspirations. My deepest thanks are for Lorna McDougall, my spouse of over three decades, and our daughter and son, Erin and Paul. These three dear ones continue to teach me about and challenge me to embrace focal faithfulness. When I grow up, I want to be like them. They lead the kinds of lives that I admire and want to emulate; they show me what is most valuable and most worthwhile.

Epiphanytide 2011
Glad River
Fraserburg, Ontario

INTRODUCTION

The stress of seventh grade started me sleepwalking. Staying balanced in life has been a challenge ever since.

More than once my parents, reading or watching TV hours after I had gone to bed, looked up to find a barefooted twelve-year-old with pillow-mussed hair heading determinedly toward the back door in search of something outside. They got up, caught me by the arm, argued with me, turned me around, and insisted I return to bed. The next morning I would invariably recall a frustrated nightmare of my parents not allowing me to go where I knew that I urgently must.

When we consulted our family physician, he said my nocturnal strolling was likely a sign of stress. But, really, seventh-grade stress?

I had that year transferred from a private church school to a public junior high. The new school divided the seventh grade into sections—7-1, 7-2, 7-3—and it was no secret that these were academic distinctions. Administrators, unsure how to interpret my private school grades, took the middle road and placed me in 7-2.

I was unhappy. I wanted to be recognized as an academic achiever, and, besides, my best friend was in 7-1. I strove and studied all semester with the hope of being promoted. I worked hard every day. I prepared for everything, even the simplest spelling test. I did hours of homework each evening and on Saturdays. Thank goodness my strict Calvinist family forbade homework on Sundays, or I would never have known any break at all.

Stress has been my steady companion ever since. Along the way people have called me "workaholic" and "Type A." I am a responsible oldest child, firmly raised in a Protestant work ethic, son of a businessman and employer who expected employees to give their all. I took seriously all those hard-earned lessons that grandparents and parents told me about the challenges of living through the deprivations of the Depression, scarcities in Nazi-occupied Netherlands, and hardships of immigration to Canada with nothing but a trunk of possessions to call one's own. Not surprisingly, I have also struggled along the way with melancholy, depression, exhaustion, and occasional burnout.

Yet such strains are no longer the domain for driven overachievers alone. Our culture has a prevailing sense of being too busy, having too much to do, without enough time for things that matter and priorities that really count. Feeling worried and burdened is an unhappy reality that many of us experience, and we encounter it unrelentingly. Stressing out in seventh grade may have made me an oddball; but I'm not alone anymore.

I meet a lot of folks who are unhappy, stressed, depressed, eating poorly, and not getting enough exercise. Some weeks I feel that at least half the people who are important to me—friends and family alike—are on various medications, just to cope with life's daily realities. And this in a culture that boasts of being the most affluent and most knowledgeable in the history of the world. The simple fact, as philosopher Albert Borgmann reminds us, is "that people regularly make choices that are counterproductive to the happiness they want."[1] Study after study shows that numerous daily realities contribute to declining happiness and growing depression:

- commuting
- watching television
- spending time online
- being cut off from nature
- not having enough friendships
- living out of sync with natural and biological rhythms
- insufficient sleep
- feeling distracted

No wonder so many people pursue better living through pharmaceuticals.

Something's not working. "Labor-saving" devices make us busier. The faster computers go, the more time we give to them. As highways and cars improve, we drive farther and vehicles become increasingly expensive. Email speeds communications but eats up greater amounts of time. With the ongoing invention of "essential" devices (even energy-efficient ones), we consume growing quantities of power. I don't know about your house, but we have power strips in numerous rooms; wall outlets no longer suffice.

It's a wonder, then, that there's not an epidemic of sleepwalking these days. Or perhaps there is. Many of us sense that there's something fundamentally awry with our pace of life. Yet we don't know what choice we have or how to make a change or whether we can do anything. We impotently go through days filled with situations and circumstances and demands that feel as though they're taking us off course, leaving us unbalanced, throwing our lives off kilter. But we are as ineffective at bringing change as I was in trying to get my parents to allow me to wander the night air in my sleep. Too much of our lives are fragmented and frantic, leaving us frustrated.

Those formerly popular bumper stickers—"I'd rather be [sailing, fishing, quilting, gardening]"—were a forlorn cry for lost and displaced priorities. Putting those notices on cars made sense, as driving is a primary culprit in refashioning our lives in unhelpful ways, taking time and opportunities away from our highest and most rewarding commitments.

Pilgrims and Seekers Looking for Something More

Decades after my sleepwalking episodes, another kind of walking helped me see with a little more clarity and deeper understanding some of the issues that face all of us.

I once walked five hundred miles to attend a church service.[2] I am hardly the kind of guy that one might envision going on such a long, arduous journey. After all, for most of my life I loathed athletics. In high school I dropped phys ed as soon as it was no longer mandatory. I admired Mark Twain's rumored approach: "Whenever I get the urge to exercise, I lie down until it goes away." But in midlife, I surprised myself by starting to hike and learning the joys of doing so. Within a few years I found myself on the Camino de Santiago, the most famous Christian pilgrimage route for walkers.

My physical achievement of averaging sixteen miles a day for thirty-one days was not the most amazing aspect of the venture. Nor was it the fact that I, a Protestant minister, was on a pilgrimage, a practice normally associated with other church streams. Nor was it the unexpected reality that I, a driven, workaholic type, somehow found time for such an inefficient excursion. It was not even the reality that that route is rapidly growing in popularity. What most impressed—and perplexed—me was that many, if not most, of those "pilgrims" profess no religious faith or affiliation at all. I know why I am here, I often thought to myself, as unlikely as that may be. But what, I wondered, are *they* doing here?

On the Camino, it is customary to carry a special "passport." This identification establishes that one is an official pilgrim, authorizes one to stay in affordable hostels along the way, and—if it is stamped daily—qualifies one to receive a much-coveted certificate from the Cathedral of Santiago at the end of the journey. When acquiring this passport, pilgrims designate their motives as "religious," "spiritual," or "other." "Religious" means traditional pilgrimage priorities—prayer, penance, honoring tradition, reflection, et cetera. This was my category. "Spiritual" is vaguer, a motivation other than traditional Christian impulses but different from secular intentions or pursuits. Many in this category told me that they were "spiritual but not religious," a familiar notion in our culture. Those who labeled themselves "other" were on the pilgrimage for various reasons—the physical challenge, an opportunity to get away, an economical vacation, or a desire to hike a long distance in good company.

Although I confidently claimed the "religious" category, the "spiritual" and "other" folks intrigued me the most. There were so many of them and they raised startling and unexpected questions. Those pilgrims kept pondering the strange, unsatisfying ways that many of us live today.

Eugene Peterson, a writer who blends poetry and prophetic passion with what he learned as a pastor for some three decades, cautions that in current ways of life "the wonder has leaked out."[3] That certainly rings true to me. We are all aware of a sense of hurry in our culture. In the last church I pastored, congregants identified busyness as their key spiritual challenge and asked church elders for help. The elders agreed that this was a significant concern but then took two years to get around to addressing the issue . . . because they had so much to do! Some argue that we North Americans now in fact work longer hours and more days than we did a few decades ago. All of us agree that life feels increasingly full, hectic, and busy.

Plenty of evidence demonstrates the paradoxical reality that affluence leaves many unsettled and deeply dissatisfied. As William Greider suggests, "good times" do not automatically equal the "good life."[4] Gregg Easterbrook convincingly shows that "society is undergoing a fundamental shift from 'material want' to 'meaning want,' with ever larger numbers of people reasonably secure in terms of living standards, but feeling they lack significance in their lives."[5] As Bill McKibben observes: "Meaning has been in decline for a very long time."[6]

Surely it is no coincidence that as we become increasingly overwhelmed by demands and circumstances, our culture evinces deepening interest in spirituality. The evidence is all around. When I attended seminary in the early 1980s, I wrote a thesis about "prayer and peacemaking," but only two courses on prayer were offered. A couple decades later I taught at that school, and one could get a degree in spirituality. I now teach at another seminary, and it too offers degrees in spiritual formation. These schools reflect wider cultural trends. Consider the shelves and shelves of spiritual materials found in even the most secular bookstores now. Or films and television shows that deal with heaven, hell, angels, demons, healing, and God.

I am increasingly convinced that distracted busyness and exhausting lifestyles drive interest in spirituality today. The sense that there must be "something more" propels quests to find better ways. Folks motivated to live spiritually rich lives do not necessarily go to church, because not many Christians have offered the kind of help they need. Christian lives are just as fragmented and frantic. But seekers are looking nonetheless.

The Camino was a locus of change and transformation. Camino conversations—along the path as we walked, resting at tables in outdoor cafés, sharing tea or wine in the evenings at hostels—were often about what was amiss in our lives. We raised questions about lifestyles, jobs, relationships. We wondered about possible changes that we might, could, or would enact. We made resolutions about how we would reorient our lives. And when we contacted each other after the pilgrimage, we asked what difference the Camino made.

Frequent discussions among pilgrims dealt with vocational discernment. Marcus of the Netherlands fretted that though he had hoped his job would serve the needs of others, it actually required him to spend most of his time acting as a bureaucratic functionary. Susanne of Austria pondered new work that would allow her to live closer to family and friends. Yuki of Japan realized that her life was perilously out of balance and that her situation could only be redressed by seeking other employment. Hendrika of Belgium saw that her job did not contribute to the wider well-being of others. And I kept coming back to the fact that I felt like an exile where I lived and wanted to return to the country of my birth to be close to family and old friends. The Camino was a context for sorting and weighing priorities.

And so it was not surprising to learn of impressive lifestyle changes that fellow pilgrims made after this journey.

A Spanish factory worker that I met walked the Camino for a month and then gave up his job. He bought and rebuilt an old building in which to offer hospitality to others on the pilgrimage.

A German woman was at a time of transition and went on the pilgrimage, unsure of what was next. In a desolate area one morning she heard a flute playing. It was the host at a nearby hostel. Impressed, she ended her pilgrimage there and now tends to passing pilgrims—feeding them, bandaging feet, and offering massages.

When Jon returned home to North America, he had the resolve to take early retirement so that he could devote himself to pursuing art, something he had wanted to do all his adult years.

These folks longed to experience new ways of living. They desired to be alert, aware, and alive. They sought vigorous engagement. They wanted to find and honor priorities that could reliably guide them on routes to meaningfulness and fulfillment. And somehow the Camino helped.

Each of these folks spoke to me of the courage and clarity that came from walking the Camino. Their bravery inspired me to look carefully at my own life and its unhealthy pace. That was certainly worth the walk, a walk that woke me from automatic and unconscious patterns. I trust that sleepwalking is behind me and that more balanced and invigorating patterns of living are available to all of us.

Antidotes and Anecdotes

I know how hard it is to keep my own life balanced and sane, and I am aware that the ways I use and relate to technology often make things worse. As a family man—father and husband—I have seen the challenges of raising children with a proper regard toward television and computers and other devices while guarding precious time together as a family. As a pastor I knew that many ordinary Christians struggled to honor their responsibilities without being swamped by incessant demands and distractions from work. As a citizen and church member, I see how our communities are fraying as people get more disconnected from each other and the values they hold and espouse. These are realities for all of us. Fretting about such matters is not mere nostalgia for "good old days" that never existed. Our lives are speeding up and changing, and not always for the better. We need help, all of us.

Thus this book is written *personally*. It includes theories and analysis. Yes, theology and history and philosophy are all relevant. They certainly inform and inspire me, and we'll have glimpses of them along the way.

SEIZE OR RECEIVE
THE DAY   THE DAY

They'll help us gain clarity and discernment. It's also important to tell stories, ones that will help us see issues from a different vantage point, expanding our imagination and suggesting innovative possibilities.[7] And so we'll also speak on a small scale about big issues. I write from within my own experiences and weave in what I've learned from others who strive to live well in these challenging times.

Why do we need this book now? I keep running into people who sense something awry with life. Yet we rush on, as if sleepwalkers on automatic pilot, not knowing the right questions. Albert Borgmann quotes Canadian philosopher Charles Taylor, who sees a "narrowing and flattening" of life that results in "a loss of resonance, depth, or richness in our human surroundings." Borgmann calls this a "diminishment of our lives."[8] But it does not have to be this way.

This book attempts to get at some reasons why life for many is not as good and fulfilling as we might wish. And it offers hopeful strategies for living differently and moving forward. We are not without choices. It remains possible to live well. Albert Borgmann is one of my most important teachers on these matters, and I appreciate his counsel to me: "The best thing is knowing that there is good news: it is possible to live the good life."[9]

Part 1

FOCUS MATTERS

1

STUMBLING INTO FOCUS

In spite of my devotion to studying and working hard, already evident when I was an overachieving, sleepwalking seventh grader, many of life's most important lessons come to me accidentally, slanted and sideways, often when I least expect them.

One year I discovered—stumbled upon, really—two practices that affected me in all kinds of unexpectedly rich and life-giving ways. But I could not explain for the longest time why they were important; I just somehow knew that they were. The two seemingly unrelated phenomena were my taking up a regular practice of hiking and our family's decision to remodel the kitchen. Walking and remodeling afforded me glimmers of deeper understandings that would help me live in richer and more rewarding ways.

Learning to Move at the Speed of Life

The Niagara Escarpment dominates much of southern Ontario. Its most celebrated feature, Niagara Falls, is not its only significance. This glacially formed rocky ridge shapes cities and smaller communities on or near it for hundreds of miles. It is our region's most striking topography, the closest thing we have to a mountain, and it is visible for miles.

Its designation as a UNESCO world biosphere reserve recognizes its ecological value as a shelter for threatened forests and wildlife.

All Ontario schoolchildren study it in geography and science, but I hated those subjects. When I was twelve, the escarpment went from being a geological curiosity to a full-blown personal nuisance. Our family bought a three-acre property halfway up the minimountain, just outside the small town of St. Davids. When I rode my bike to school or to visit friends beneath the escarpment, the ride home was always taxing (even with my spiffy new three speed). A few decades later, however, I began to think more appreciatively of the escarpment.

The Bruce Trail, a natural corridor, is a lovely and often demanding route that follows the escarpment. The five-hundred-mile path—about as long as the Camino de Santiago that I eventually trod—begins near Niagara Falls and ends at Tobermory, the northernmost point of the Bruce Peninsula. For much of my life I lived near the trail, and during my sleepwalking adolescent years we were only a mile or two away. But as I said earlier, I have never been athletic or outdoorsy, and so I was not interested.

One weekend, however, when I was in my early forties, I was captivated by an article in the Saturday edition of the local newspaper, the *Kitchener-Waterloo Record*. Over the course of eighteen months, about a dozen middle-aged women had used their days off to hike the entire Bruce Trail. Within an hour I decided that I too would attempt that journey. The challenge was no small goal for me in my middle age. Long-distance walking, coping with blisters, reading maps, and layering clothing for weather would all be new to me. And there were larger lessons in store as well. In fact, some of my most important discoveries in the last few years were found on these hikes and in my growing interest in walking.

One October Saturday my family joined me for the first stage of this trail, walking with me from Queenston—site of important War of 1812 battles—to the small town of St. Davids, where I spent my adolescent years. The route on that first day was enormously rewarding and the scenery breathtaking.

Just like that I was hooked. I steadily dedicated more days off to the trail. Yet I did not finish the project as quickly as the middle-aged women who inspired me. One complication was that within a year and a half of starting, we moved south of the border. But then I worked vacation time around this priority, and within five years—the same year that I earned a Camino certificate—I received a Bruce Trail Association End-to-End Award, establishing that I was the 1,987th person who officially completed the entire five hundred miles on foot.

Why did I do it? What kept me going? Especially after the added complication of moving four hundred miles away, making it harder and harder to get back to the trail?

At first it was the same stubborn determination that drove me to work so hard in seventh grade. If I start something, I want to complete it. One of the greatest regular pleasures in my life involves making extensive to-do lists in my calendar and then having the joy of striking those things off as soon as they are completed. I do not just put a checkmark beside the line, or strike through the item. No, I take a black marker and obliterate the assignment from sight. This is a problem, as I occasionally black out the wrong line by mistake.

But while setting and achieving goals are important to me, finishing the Bruce Trail was not only about making a thick black line in my calendar. Something more profound motivated my continued effort. The many rewards intrinsic to hiking kept me moving and would not let me go.

I unexpectedly enjoyed the bodily engagement; awareness of my physical ability inspired me. At each hike's start, I experienced moments of self-doubt and asked myself: What have I gotten into? Am I able to do this? What will it take to complete this day's challenge? But those questions added greatly to my eventual sense of achievement and satisfaction. With each hike I marveled, "I can actually do this!" Such feats had been beyond imagining only a few years earlier.

Surprise at the physical accomplishment came home to me on my very first Bruce Trail hike. Our family started at the trail's official head in Queenston and quickly strolled to and past my former home of St. Davids. This was striking because as a boy my best friend was in Queenston and I never went there on my own steam. It was too far to bike, I thought, let alone go on foot. I always begged rides from my parents. But here we all were, easily covering that distance in just a couple hours. Now when I look at a map of southern Ontario, I can hardly believe that I've walked five hundred miles of it. Suddenly, a significant part of the province is familiar from the ground level because of hiking the Bruce.

One August day, David Wood and I trekked up Mt. Washington, the highest peak in the White Mountains of New Hampshire. I'd been there as a child forty years earlier when our family drove up, and I was duly impressed. But doing the physical work, encountering unpredictably raw weather and 60-miles-per-hour winds on the way (something for which this mountain is famous), and feeling leg muscle pain from physical exertion made all the difference between engaging the mountain and merely visiting it. Hiking allowed me to see my surroundings more vividly than viewing Mt. Washington's beauty through a windshield screen could (thus experiencing the ascent as though it were another television show or webcast). The slow, taxing journey meant observing and absorbing the gradual shift from lush forest to scrub above the tree line and finally to mostly bare rocks with patches of moss and leathery grass. Add to the diverse landscape the enjoyable company of a good friend and the camaraderie of other hikers that we met along the way. While Mt. Washington is known for its view of several states and even of distant Canada, when we climbed we were enveloped in clouds at the top and could hardly see ten feet ahead of us, let alone distant vistas. Had I driven up Mt. Washington, I might have felt that the excursion was a waste of time. But hiking was such a complex and rich experience that it was easily worth it, even without being able to view the famous and stunning scenery from the lookout.

In a culture shaped by technology, we expect good things to be easily, uniformly, and immediately available. Turn on the television and see something beautiful. Or heat your frozen ratatouille in the microwave. We regard children as immature for being impatient, but our gadgets train us to expect immediate gratification. Yet mountains, forests, wilderness, and other natural wonders are best enjoyed and most rewarding when we undergo their demands on us and take them seriously as they are, not as one more notch on a tourist checklist. I despair when I hear that the average visit to the Grand Canyon, this natural marvel, is only twenty-two minutes, making it a quick checklist item for quickly passing tourists.

I regret that it took me so long to make the acquaintance of the Niagara Escarpment and its Bruce Trail. A casual Saturday morning decision to hike the trail—I say this with no exaggeration—changed my life. That commitment presented me with new realities and questions that have since affected my daily mode of travel, choice of church, priorities in shopping and eating, understanding of how cities and suburbs are arranged, decisions about recreation and how many vehicles to own, and on and on. I thought I was taking on a temporary challenge; instead, the Bruce Trail slowly began to convert me. I am still surprised that I now hike; I have long had an aversion to athletics. But in recent years I discovered other rewarding sports too: walking, biking, canoeing, kayaking. And it all began with the Bruce Trail.

I should not give the impression that my approach to life shifted quickly or easily. Soon after I began hiking, I went to a conference at Holden Village, a remote, off-the-grid Lutheran retreat center in Washington's northern Cascades. I was delighted to find excellent trails near the conference grounds. Every day I set out, going greater and greater distances. As someone who never grew up around mountains, viewing the miles and miles of snowcapped peaks seemed like a fantasy. I knew that there were bears and cougars around and looked for evidence of them. I saw marmots for the first time. At the end of each jaunt, I came back fatigued and sore, longing for a hot bath. But I also felt fulfilled and even exhilarated.

In my Holden Village small group was an acquaintance named Kay. She is around my age and happens to be a therapist. Kay noticed how deeply important my walks were to me. As soon as she pointed this out, I knew that she was right. The act of hiking was knitting me together, making me whole. Once she observed that, I became more committed to regular walking.

Even with my awareness of its benefits, however, I was not yet able to articulate hiking's importance to me. Ultimately, my ideas about why hiking was so meaningful and transformative were clarified in conjunction with another practice that my family took on—something else that I knew was vital but was unable to explain exactly why.

Too Many Cooks, Not Enough Kitchen

My wife and I are not do-it-yourselfers, but we have an unfortunate habit of purchasing houses that need work. Our first house required a new roof, as did our second. We wondered whether it was our mission to keep shinglers in business. In three of our houses we removed 1970s-era wall-to-wall green shag carpeting. Another mission, apparently.

We thought ourselves clever with the third house: the roof was new, had a warranty, and looked like it would last a long, long time. The only green carpeting was on the stairs and in one hall, not too onerous to amend. The kitchen, however, was a problem.

The small, dimly lit space was easy for one person to navigate, but two adults were not able to wash dishes side by side. Cooking together was an exercise in frustration. And if someone would dare to look in the refrigerator while another family member was preparing a meal, then this was grounds for major conflict. We had too many cooks and not enough kitchen. And we knew that the problem would only get worse when our grade-school children became adolescents and needed more physical space.

Lorna began to lobby for a kitchen renovation. She's patient and I am stubborn—not to mention cheap—and so this campaign took some years to persuade me. I did not particularly like the kitchen, but having averted the cost of replacing a roof, I wanted to keep avoiding other large house expenditures. The renovation seemed like a needless luxury to me. Lorna is not only patient, but she is also persistent. So she periodically raised this possibility. And, gradually, very gradually, I was won over because—as I used to say in the premarital counseling that I offered as a pastor—"Happy spouse, happy house."

With the help of a craftsman and contractor from our church, we came up with a plan that changed not just the kitchen but also our house and, in fact, our family life. We expanded the tiny workspace to include an adjoining room that until then had functioned as a large hallway with a piano and storage capacity. At my insistence, we moved the sink from facing the wall to overlooking the backyard, adding pleasure to dishwashing. We installed warm-looking oak cabinets and atmospheric lighting.

The result was a bright and inviting room, a convivial place to be and to work, to eat and to visit. Washing dishes and preparing meals were suddenly more appealing. Lorna and I noticed that we collaborated better in the kitchen. The expanded space also included a wooden table beside an enlarged window where our family ate meals together.

When the children came home from school, they did their work at that table, while Lorna or I bustled at the counter. They invariably did not have much to say upon their arrival. "How was your day?" we routinely asked. "Okay," was the ritual response. "What's new?" came the parental rejoinder. "Nothing," was the predictable answer. But as Erin and Paul did homework, they often gradually struck up conversations with whichever one of us was chopping vegetables, doing dishes, or cooking supper.

We noticed that with the new kitchen the family enjoyed sitting together, even long after the evening meal was done. We often set aside dishes and continued dinnertime conversations. Lorna made tea and we savored each other's company. Our evenings were more focused on each other and less on the distractions of television and computers.

The kitchen had become the nucleus of our house, its heart, and suddenly our home grew a lot warmer and more enjoyable. We discovered this only by accident. Years later, Verlin Miller, artisan woodworker, told me that a house's primary room is its kitchen, a social place that is the center of activities. With our new kitchen, Lorna and I found ourselves increasingly willing and better able to host guests and get-togethers.

One of our biggest sorrows in leaving that house was letting go of the kitchen that we both loved. The next place we bought partly commended itself to us because its kitchen was large. Unfortunately, what it mostly had was "potential." This time, however, when Lorna began suggesting it was time for a renovation, it did not take me as long to agree.

As with the hiking, I suspected that there were deeper things to be learned from the kitchen. I knew that the hiking and the revitalized kitchen were important, but I still had trouble precisely articulating why.

Searching for Something More

Within six months of beginning to tackle the Bruce Trail and around the same time that we were regularly gathering with friends and family in our renovated kitchen, a philosopher helped me understand the meaning of what was happening. I realized that things true of my hiking also resonated with our kitchen experience (and later in the testimonies of fellow pilgrims along the Camino). Suddenly, many previously inexplicable phenomena made sense.

Back in the late 1990s, David Wood encouraged me to read Albert Borgmann, a philosopher of technology who has taught at the University of Montana since 1970. I quickly read two books, *Technology and the Character of Contemporary Life* and *Crossing the Postmodern Divide*. I learned a lot about how our lives are deeply affected by our use of technology. But at first I was unsure of the implications for my own life and ministry.

David, then associate director at the Louisville Institute, organized what became known as the Missoula Consultation. In March 2001 he brought in Borgmann and noted writer Eugene Peterson as conversation partners. He also invited a couple dozen Christian leaders—pastors, scholars, writers, editors, journalists—to reflect on the implications of Borgmann's work.

The event came at an intensely busy time. I was pastoring a church, teaching a graduate level course, and finishing up my doctoral dissertation. In some ways I'd not changed my harried pace much since seventh grade, I guess. But I was determined to go to the Missoula Consultation. My wife picked me up at the end of my all-day Saturday class and drove me to the airport. Once there, I discovered that a snowstorm threatened to cancel many flights. Although the weather was frightening, I arrived safely and on time. I was exhausted because of my recent schedule, but I never doubted that I needed to be part of the conversation in Missoula.

As I considered Borgmann's ideas—both in the reading and rereading leading up to the consultation and the conversations at the event—I came to a deeper sense of why hiking and a lovely kitchen were worthwhile. They are not merely privileged middle-class hobbies or luxuries. No, their implications go deeper. Rigorous, long-distance walking outdoors and creating a convivial place to cook and host were meeting needs that Lorna and I felt but didn't fully understand. These undertakings were what Albert Borgmann calls focal practices—activities that center, balance, focus, and orient one's life.

Everywhere we turn, people say that they are overwhelmed by their schedules, just too busy. Parents complain of time spent shuttling children from one extracurricular activity to another. Children are introduced to using planners in elementary school. Folks spend hours of their day commuting from behind the wheel. At every committee meeting at work or church or in the community, the lengthiest discussion usually comes at the end of the agenda when the group attempts to determine a common time slot for the next gathering. One writer I admire describes our lives as being marked by "pathological busyness, distraction, and restlessness."[1]

This unsettled sense of being harried, hurried, and harassed is not just anecdotal. Statistics suggest that North Americans may in fact be working longer and longer hours. Our lives are congested with demands and expectations. Every era has its own particular obstacles and challenges to the spiritual life. Busyness is a significant one these days. We live in a culture to which Exxon Speedpass's promise of "Less Stop. More Go" appeals.

As we have seen, even while people are preoccupied with stress and busyness—"hurry poverty" or "time sickness"—there is also an astonishing and steadily rising interest in spirituality. I grow increasingly convinced that our emerging fascination is intrinsically related to our frenetic lifestyles. People feel distracted, disoriented, dissipated, and despairing. They sense that there is something more, and their deep yearning is a response to the mad pace of their lives.

Albert Borgmann argues that our contemporary culture—with its emphasis on putting technology and consumerism and devices at the center of our lives—shapes our characters, our families, and our friendships. In fact, he would contend that the forces of technology and consumerism too often deeply *deform* us. Yet at the same time he holds out alternative ways of living, favoring a lifestyle that he calls "focal." He's been talking and writing about these things for a long time, and recently, popular literature is taking up similar concerns with such titles as *Hamlet's Blackberry*, *The Shallows*, *Alone Together*, and *The Tyranny of Email*. Consider, for example, this *New York Times* headline: "More Americans Sense a Downside to an Always Plugged-In Existence."[2]

Focal living, as advocated by Borgmann, helps us identify and perceive the "something more" that people seek. When our existence seems shallow and unfulfilling, he commends focal concerns that "center and illuminate our lives."[3] Focal things and focal practices move, teach, inspire, and reassure. Focal living poses a telling contrast to many realities of our lives today that merely "lead to a disconnected, disembodied, and disoriented sort of life."[4]

Finding the Focal

Borgmann's "focal" terminology sounds promising, but what does it mean? *Focal* is not a long word—only two syllables. We sometimes use *focal point* metaphorically to describe something that is of central interest, our highest priority, or the main thrust of an argument. *Focal* has to do with being focused and centered on what is meaningful.

A simple but revealing question for any of us would be to consider what the center of our home is. The kitchen? The living room? The porch? Many houses that I visit have their primary room oriented toward a television—perhaps a large, on-the-wall plasma screen—or some other "entertainment center." The "family room" is often organized for watching television, surfing the net, or playing virtual games, not for engaging other members of the family, let alone neighbors or guests. In our 2007 interview, Borgmann contended that television is of moral importance: "When I teach my ethics course I tell these relatively young people that the most important decision that they'll make about their household is first whether they're going to get a television and then second where they're going to put it."

The word *focus* comes from the Latin word for "hearth"—a wood-stove or fireplace, an essential item for comfort and even survival in many climates. A hearth—as its name implies—is often at the *heart* or center of a house. A lot of attention goes into maintaining a hearth, keeping it in good and safe working order, supplying it with fuel. Especially in cold weather, people and pets will cluster around this spot. When our family went to an off-the-grid cottage each summer, my children loved to have me make tea and start a fire each chilly morning. They snuggled in sleeping bags, sipped their steaming drinks, and sat mesmerized by the flames.

As Borgmann notes, hearths have always had symbolic power.

> In ancient Greece, a baby was truly joined to the family and household when it was carried about the hearth and placed before it. The union of a Roman marriage was sanctified at the hearth. And at least in the early periods the dead were buried by the hearth. The family ate by the hearth and made sacrifices to the housegods before and after the meal. The hearth sustained, ordered, and centered house and family.[5]

He shows that even though we no longer invest fireplaces and wood-stoves with explicit sacred meaning, we surround them with "precious things of the family's history," including photos of loved ones.[6] A friend once lived in a small, inner-city Chicago apartment with a fireplace that no longer functioned. He put special objects—a piece of art, pottery, a lovely feather, a fetching rock—on the mantelpiece and called it his "altar." The symbolic power of such devices is so compelling that many houses now are outfitted with gas fireplaces to draw people cozily together in front of the flames. One can also get DVDs or programs to turn television sets or computer screens into mock fireplaces.

Lorna and I visited Albert and Nancy Borgmann in their chalet-style home where they lived for around four decades. It is perched on a slope above the Rattlesnake Wilderness Area just outside Missoula, overlooking several mountain ranges. Although they did not design the house, it was easy to see one of its important attractions. At the center of the main floor is a massive fireplace constructed from local stones. It stands at the junction of the kitchen, dining area, and living room. There is not a television to be found. Even though he is over seventy, Albert still chops, hauls, and supplies the wood for the hearth.

The attraction of such centers—woodstoves, fireplaces—is not only symbolic but also practical and functional. One February when I was a teenager, our family went overseas to the Netherlands and stayed with my grandmother in her small row house. Like many Dutch domiciles in the 1970s, her home did not have central heating but was furnished with a *haard*—Dutch for "hearth"—in the main room, a combination living and dining room. Fed by piped-in fuel, its flames barely visible through the screen, it was the sole heat available. The rest of the house was shut off and thus cold and damp. When going to bed, one hustled as quickly as possible through chilly bathroom ablutions, tossed on several layers of bedclothes, and climbed between clammy sheets, waiting to warm up. In the evenings, the family stayed close together in the living/dining room reading, talking, visiting, studying, or watching television. That *haard* was a technological device that pulled people together and gave families and friends a focus.

Other devices have similar potential.

When I walked the Camino early one summer, having enough water was a priority but almost never a worry. Every village we passed through had a prominent fountain, and usually the water was drinkable. By fountain I do not mean one of those white porcelain sinks we find on the walls of hallways in schools, churches, and public buildings here in North America. Those often offer only a dribble of liquid and make you wonder what germs you might be risking when you use them. Rather, in Spain the fountains are impressive brick or stone structures six feet high or taller. They draw on local springs and pour out a steady stream. The fountains usually collect and retain their flow in a large basin or a small pool. The accumulated water was suitable for laundering—I occasionally used one that way after a long day's hiking—but it had other purposes too. Once I ate lunch in a small village, perched on a wooden bench outside a café. I watched as a dozen cows casually strolled down the main street, drank from the village fountain, and then turned and headed back up the road, presumably toward their home.

Those fountains were gathering and resting places for pilgrims. Snacks were shared. Maps were compared and routes discussed. Counsel was offered about the route. Blisters were tended. Faces and feet were rinsed and cooled. Encouragement was given to one another.

The fountains were also crucial to village life. We often saw elderly men sitting nearby, as they obviously did day after day, swapping news and gossiping, visiting and holding court. But, alas, the importance of such focal places is passing even in Spain. Richard E. Sclove writes about studies done in one Spanish village after it benefited from the arrival of running water.

> With pipes running directly to their homes, [villagers] no longer had to fetch water from the . . . fountain. As families gradually purchased washing machines, fewer women gathered to scrub laundry by hand at the village washbasin. Arduous tasks were rendered . . . superfluous, but village social life unexpectedly changed. The public fountain and washbasin, once scenes of vigorous social interaction, became nearly deserted. Men began losing their sense of easy familiarity with children and donkeys that formerly helped them haul water. Women stopped gathering . . . to intermix scrubbing with politically empowering gossip about men and village life. In hindsight this emerges as a crucial step in a broader process through which [villagers] came to relinquish strong bonds—with one another, animals, and the land—that had knit them into a community.[7]

As a child, I noticed how many Bible stories took place beside water wells. I assumed that this was all just a curious coincidence. Crucial events in Hagar's life occur near a well (Gen. 16:7–14; 21:15–19). Abraham's servants conflict with another group over a well (Gen. 21:22–34). Future wives were met at such locations—for example, Rachel (Gen. 29) and Zipporah (Exod. 2). One of Jesus's most famous encounters and conversations occurs at a well in Samaria (John 4).

What I did not perceive before walking the Camino is that in the Bible wells were not just devices for procuring water or aiding laundry, as important and crucial as those functions were. Fountains and wells helped people gather and connect. But what happens when they are gone or no longer used? It is not an idle accident that malls often have fountains; they try to capture something of the purpose of older fountains. In the Detroit airport, a delightfully animated fountain shoots seemingly random jets of water several feet through the air. People, not just children, often stop and watch for a time. I am not aware, however, of strangers conversing there, let alone people finding potential life partners.

We celebrate no longer needing to haul water. When I visit Haiti, I marvel at those who carry heavy buckets for long distances on their heads. I am not suggesting that we return to that kind of drudgery. There are benefits to piping in water. We no longer do laundry outside in cold liquid, and our clothes do look better. But we don't know, Borgmann points out, how to recognize the "cultural and social losses" in such changes.[8]

Adopting technology often deeply affects our relationships and interactions. Maggie Jackson notes that even in the difficult and tedious labor of taking care of homes and families, whenever we do work together, "we're creating the glue that binds us to the humans we love." She is concerned that relationships may be thinning out so that we are "roommate families" rather than having intimates with deep, intense interactions with each other.[9]

Though some have opted to live "off the grid" and find the lifestyle rewarding, my point is not that we should abandon contemporary technology and naively take on previous hardships and all become—using familiar biblical terminology—"hewers of wood and drawers of water" (Josh. 9:27). Nor do I believe we should pine after the "good old days." Rather, my hope is that we consider which hearths can hold us together, which wells can help us drink in abundant life.

Bringing and Holding Families Together?

Every once in a while a billboard boasts, "The family that prays together, stays together." I loathe that expression. I am leery of reducing Christian faith to a slogan, especially if it rhymes. Religion is too rich and too important to be used as a commercial. And, of course, families praying together inevitably staying together is not only a misguided claim, it's a bald-faced lie. Statistics show that religious faith is not in and of itself a guarantee that families will not break up.

I am also uneasy because this proclamation feels vaguely threatening and oppressive. On a scary note, I remember how a friend was repeatedly abused by the head of her household, who was also in charge of the family's worship. They prayed, but theirs was not a healthy togetherness. There are dangers in imposing prayer.

In spite of my uneasiness about the slogan, I do see a sliver of merit in the claim that "the family that prays together stays together." Even though it is wrong and misguided on many levels, it points to a very real need and concern, a loss that many feel keenly. Less and less do we find that there are interests or activities or priorities that bind us and build us up together. As Robert Putnam pointed out some time ago, we're all "bowling alone" now. As a consequence of the decline of civic-minded community organizations—bridge clubs, service organizations, charities, and, yes, bowling leagues—people are increasingly disconnected.[10]

One might say that our social disconnections are *technologically enhanced*. Central heating displaced hearths so that individuals can now disperse and disappear to separate spaces in our houses. Such heating decentered home life. And other technologies also gut opportunities for relating to one another. Having air-conditioning and television inside the home has meant that we no longer linger outside on porches—cutting us off from visiting with family members, neighbors, and passersby. Television supplants visiting and hospitality. As a pastor visiting homes, I often had to ask people to turn off the television as we tried to talk.

Not long ago, when families watched television, they did it together. I have good memories of watching TV with my parents and sister and various housemates along the way. Granted, there are better ways of spending time together, many of which our family enjoyed (meals, barbecues, church, vacations). But now our homes have so many screens—from multiple television sets, to desktop and laptop computers, to various kinds of MP3 devices—that even that formerly common activity, as unsatisfying as it may have been, is disappearing. Family members watch television programs separately, isolated in their different rooms.

What now holds the potential of helping families or friends, communities or neighborhoods grow together? Borgmann is the thinker who has best helped me come to grips with these matters, and thus throughout this book you will see that I am often interpreting, appropriating, and applying his ideas. Borgmann recommends commitment to focal practices, focal things, focal places. This commitment, he demonstrates, is a key way to begin living lives that are rich, fulfilling, and meaningful. This can be key to living the good life.

Focal living does not need to be about huge endeavors and initiatives, but about reclaiming priorities that are ignored or threatened. Activities suggested by Borgmann—eating meals together, sharing tea, playing board games, making live music in a group, hosting neighbors, exercising hospitality, hiking, cooking, reading together, gardening—are all small, normal, easy to do.

Now that our children are out of the house and we look back and name the best memories, some of those are once-in-a-lifetime events and experiences: their births, their accomplishments and graduations, trips to Scotland and the Netherlands where their grandparents once lived, their struggles with major life decisions. Yet we also recall many mundane and daily occurrences: eating meals, conversing over tea, going to the playground, hiking as a family, entertaining guests, hosting visitors from overseas. Those prosaic practices stitched us together as a family and formed each of our characters. They were convivial and life-giving.

My friend Nelson grew up as one of the younger members in a large farm family. He told me recently that they never went on vacation, at least not the days or weeks away that most of us associate with that term. There were several reasons: their farm needed careful daily tending, they could not afford expensive travel, and his thrifty parents never were convinced of the need for vacations. But once a year they would all go on a daylong excursion. Nelson began anticipating it months in advance. They would get up early in the morning and be gone until late at night. It was usually a trip to a nearby large city to visit a zoo, museum, or historical site. And they would have the unmatched luxury of eating in a restaurant, something rare for this large family. When Nelson recounts this, he glows with the good memory. He also tells how full his family's life together was; not ever being able to take a multiday vacation was not a deprivation. He did chores, wrestled and argued with brothers, played games with the family, and spent time outside. There was no television, and children developed an extraordinary breadth of hobbies, from woodworking to amateur radio to launching rockets. Nelson's parents delighted in the children's diverse interests, and helped them buy cameras or rockets or shop tools or artists' paintbrushes. Even though the whole family worked hard, there was a sense of Sabbath and creative play. There is no question that the person Nelson is—a gifted man of talent and character—was shaped by small practices in his family of origin. It is no surprise that his own family now, his spouse and children, together value meals, hospitality, reading aloud to one another, games, intellectual pursuits and engagements, poetry and art.

When I thought of hiking as *only* a hobby or of our congenial kitchen as *merely* a luxury, it was easy for me to overlook their importance. But when I understood that they were focal practices, I began to take them more seriously, to be committed to them, and to make sure that I made space for them in my life.

Displacing Focal Priorities

When we allow devices and machines to reside at the center of our lives, we displace values and practices that once enriched the quality of how we live. We end up serving our gadgets instead of using them as tools to support our priorities. Technology itself becomes the center and purpose of how we live. For example, automobiles take up more of our lives as we make increasingly lengthy commutes and feel the need to earn greater amounts of money for their purchase, upkeep, repairs, and insurance.

In seminary courses on personal spirituality, I encourage students to adopt a slightly rigorous daily "rule" of prayer and Bible reading to reflect on what that life is like for one semester. They submit proposed guides to me at the beginning of the course and then hold themselves accountable to their commitment. One year, a graduate student in the last semester of her degree seemed particularly stressed. No wonder, really, as she was newly married, holding down a job, and supervising the student residence where she and her husband lived. Something had to give, and so she decided to cut down her television watching to *only* two hours a day. I am not sure how she found the time for that much TV, but, on the other hand, the average North American watches close to three hours daily.

We must pay attention to what is supplanted by our habits of technology usage. As Borgmann points out: "What concerns or distresses one about technology is its tendency to destroy or displace things and practices that grace and orient our lives."[11] Vital priorities and values often get shunted aside by how we choose to use technology.

Television displaces family time, volunteering, prayer, and even Sunday and Wednesday evening worship. In the 1950s and 1960s the *Wonderful World of Disney* and *Ed Sullivan* lured many away from Sunday evening church attendance. My friends Stan and Carolyn Smith occasionally owned a TV, but Stan told me that they found the set often messed things up: "You start to build your life around [the television] instead of anything else that you think is important." When I asked *what* was important, his list included: friends, church life, exploring outside, and doing things as a family.

What else is displaced by our use of technology?

Traveling via car displaces the exercise of walking to perform essential tasks. The unintended results of dependence on cars are several. We don't enjoy our surroundings in the same way. Our neighborhoods are no longer places to get to know other people. We live on blocks characterized by roads designed to move vehicles swiftly and efficiently.

I regularly visit churches with technologically enhanced worship bands prominently displayed on a stage. The lectern or pulpit is below the dais. A flat, blank screen is usually the most visible object in the room. Drummers are encased behind clear acrylic walls and singers resembling famous entertainers hold microphones. Without exception, the sound of the lead singers' voices and the instruments dominates.

In such settings it is difficult to hear the congregation sing. I look around, noticing that half of the people around me stand silently. Congregants may clap and raise hands, but many do not open their mouths. Even when nearby neighbors do sing, I cannot hear them. In this kind of contemporary worship—driven by amplified music, bands, microphones, and videos—congregational singing is overwhelmed and displaced by gadget wizardry. Technologically enhanced instrumentation and sound equipment has threatened to dislodge—instead of encourage—the voice of the church. Congregational song, an endangered focal practice once accessible to many different people, classes, and ages, can be unwittingly supplanted.

As devices and commodities move into the center, focal things and practices become peripheral. In an interview with David Wood, Borgmann observes that when several hours of screen time "come into our lives, then something else has to go out. And what has gone out? Telling stories, reading, going to the theater, socializing with friends, just taking a walk to see what's up in the neighborhood."[12] For example, he notes:

> Once a television set is in the house, the . . . decision whether to read a
> book, or write a letter, or play a game, or tell stories, or go for a walk, or

sit down to dinner, or watch television no longer really ranges over seven possibilities. The presence of television has compressed all alternatives to one whose subalternatives [are represented] in the question: What are we going to watch tonight?[13]

People who watch television programs are less engaged with their communities; they are less likely to volunteer for good causes, go to church, or visit other people.[14] While watching television contributes to loneliness, people tend to compensate for that loneliness by watching more television, a perpetual and unhealthy spiral.[15] Similarly, online activities displace direct time spent with colleagues, relatives, and friends; they isolate and contribute to isolation, in spite of the "promise" of online communities.[16] A University of Washington study showed, for example, that just having a television on—even if no one is watching it—correlates with a marked decrease in conversations and interactions between children and adults.[17] Likewise, people who spend a lot of time on social networking sites tend to be less socially involved.[18] In spite of these troubling consequences, we persist in making such technological devices central to our lives.

When my wife was a nurse at a new elementary school, its innovative principal, Ray Gyori-Helmuth, initiated a creative way to connect with surrounding neighborhoods before the school year started. On the Sunday afternoon before classes began, school staff—and their spouses—would tour the area on bikes. This would provide a firsthand glimpse of how and where pupils lived. And it would be a friendly way for staff to greet students. A fun time was had by all the bike riders as we chatted and laughed with each other. In two hours of riding, however, we encountered only four students. Afterward, we realized that most were inside, savoring the AC and perhaps watching television or playing video games. There were that day—if you'll pardon the pun—virtually no students to encounter.

We're all good at naming the conveniences technology provides. We're not so good at recognizing its inconveniences, displacements, losses, and intrusions. Sherry Turkle wisely contends: "We have to love technology enough to describe it accurately. And we have to love ourselves enough to confront technology's true effects on us."[19]

It does not have to be this way, Borgmann urges, and he proposes an antidote. By putting focal practices and focal things at the center of our lives—making them focal priorities—we counterbalance the potentially negative effects of technology and consumerism. Devices take their proper place only when we show devotion to what matters most. So it is important that as we diagnose the shortcomings and hazards of how we live that we also consider focal practices that point us in other, more life-giving directions. As Borgmann told me, it's not a matter of complaining about devices. We're not trying to take away good things; rather, we're trying to make time for the cultivation of "something much better."

Embarking on a Focal Pilgrimage

Embracing focal living is not about oughts or shoulds. There are many ways to incorporate focal priorities. Seeing how others live out such commitments is *suggestive* and *disclosive*. Pay attention to the focal practices of others and you will see something and think, "I do that," or "I could do that," or "That reminds me of doing such and such."

At the closing session of the Elkhart Consultation with Borgmann in 2008, Todd Friesen, pastor of a suburban Mennonite congregation, observed:

> As I think about returning to our congregation in Chicago, I think in terms of my own strategy. I want to work intentionally to affirm the areas in our congregation where we are already engaging in focal practices and don't even know it.
>
> Many in our congregations are not aware of the deeper meaning of what they're doing. One gift we can give them is to show them, this is really significant. Instead of saying, "Why don't you do this?" [or] "Why don't you do that?" take some of the things that we're doing and talk about why they're so meaningful and talk about how they're making space in our lives for what the good life really is and use that as an opportunity to talk about the good life. It's already happening here, but let's do it more, and push it out and hopefully draw in others who haven't made this space yet in their lives.[20]

A good pastor, Todd celebrates positive things already happening among his congregants.

One year, I set out to interview a dozen people and ask them about their focal practices: baking, quilting, bird-watching, woodworking, endurance horse riding, carpentry, letter writing, et cetera. Some people I knew well, some not very much at all. On the whole, they are regular folks. They might be gifted in their particular passion but were not famous. I was aware of them usually by word of mouth, through friends or acquaintances. Most of their focal practices are things I either could never do (I just do not have the skills) or would never do. But I wanted to learn more about how their priorities helped them thrive. I wanted to get acquainted with ordinary folks who lived nearby, the kind of people who are likely in your neighborhood too. I wanted to test Borgmann's ideas and see how people have come to understand similar ideas on their own. I had a feeling that there was much to learn.

Two things in particular impressed me.

First, exploring one focal practice often led to speaking about many others. When I spoke to Leroy and Winifred Saner about their commitment to gardening, conversation also moved easily, quickly, and naturally to their family memories of cooking, hospitality, quilting, butchering, photography, woodworking, and picture framing. Those activities are intrinsically related. Each focal practice resonates with others.

The second thing that struck me is that many folks were surprised that I wanted to talk with them. They are not famous, do not necessarily lead organizations, have not written books. These salt-of-the-earth people wondered why I would be interested in their simple practices of letter writing, carpentry, or quilting. But as we talked about what they were doing, each became excited and animated about their ability to articulate why a particular activity was so important to them. When I explained Borgmann's notions of focal practices, something clicked. My interviewees suddenly had new ways of expressing what they already knew to be true about the richness afforded them through their respective practices.

But Would I Know a Focal Practice if I Saw One?

As I talk about focal practices, people ask how to recognize whether or not something or some activity is focal. Washing dishes? Playing golf? Watching NASCAR on television? Online gambling? Video games? I used to try carefully and deliberately to categorize each example but found that doing so doesn't adequately respond to the real issue.

Figuring out whether an activity is focal can be complicated and require discernment. To some extent we need to decide for ourselves. Some things we cannot answer for each other. When I was a teenager I used to ask my parents, "Yes, but how did you *know* that you loved each other enough to get married?" Though their marriage flourished, they never had a satisfactory response to my question. Ultimately, I would have to figure that out by myself. There are some obvious qualities that go into a marriage: affection, humor, compatibility, shared interests, common values. And my parents and other couples I know modeled many of these. But a couple might have all of them and still not quite click. Or maybe they click for no reasons apparent to anyone else. Ultimately, each of us must sort some things out for ourselves.

This is not to say that anything goes. It is clear that some activities are focal—eating meals together, playing musical instruments, hiking, church singing, gardening. Other activities clearly are not focal—casino gambling, viewing pornography, drug abuse, drinking to excess. Figuring out the extremes is easy.

But even potentially worthwhile activities can be misused or trivialized or idolized. And many other activities fall into gray areas. It is not productive to sort out all such categories, especially not on a case-by-case basis. It is more useful to gain a broad understanding of focal priorities. To Borgmann's way of thinking, focal concerns are objects, activities, or practices with three characteristics: commanding presence, continuity, and centering power.[21] We need to unpack those terms in order to understand and appreciate them.

2

AWE AND INSPIRATION

One summer day, four middle-aged men set out in a canoe to raise money for Wilderness Wind, a Mennonite camp and retreat organization that encourages, outfits, and facilitates trips in the Boundary Waters Wilderness of northern Minnesota. Our Paddle-a-thon goal was to take a canoe on a thirty-mile round-trip in one day. That was a dozen miles farther than I had ever canoed before in a single day. But our team managed to achieve its daunting goal during thirteen hours of all kinds of weather—bright sun, blue skies, dense fog, and steady rain—and in spite of numerous rugged portages that slowed us down. There were other obstacles too. One of our party stumbled and fell just before the trip began, at sunrise, and he hobbled his way through the day, even on those dreaded portages. When we got back that evening he went to an emergency room and only then did we learn that he'd broken several bones in his foot.

Toward the end of the day, weariness had settled into muscles through-out our bodies. My arms ached as I mechanically kept plunging the paddle back into the waves, stroke after stroke, too many to count.

In the final hours of paddling, many motorboats raced by, carrying up-ended canoes on their roof racks! Vacationers had canoed out into the wilderness as far as they could for the day and were being picked up and given a speedboat ride home to lodges where they were staying. I admit to some envy as I looked at those zooming boats. But had one of those vessels offered a ride, we would have declined—and not just because the Paddle-a-thon rules stipulated that we go the distance under our own power. Rather, we knew that it was important to encounter the water and its challenges directly. We had to supply the energy, not mechanical engines. We recognized the value in our exertion. The late Bill Mason, Canada's most famous canoeist, used to speak of keeping wild places "undiminished." He preferred "primitive" travel modes like hiking and canoeing. Motorized transportation, he argued, eats up miles and makes surrounding scenery small and insignificant. "You've seen it all; yet, you've seen nothing."[1]

The first characteristic of focal things, practices, and priorities is what Albert Borgmann calls "commanding presence." They take energy and effort; they make demands on us. They can be tough taskmasters as they require discipline, attention, and focus, thus helping us to grow in *character*. They are beyond our control or our ability to manipulate or consume.

When I hike, I take up a focal practice. While strenuous, it engages me with focal places (forests, wilderness, mountains). Preparing a meal is a focal practice that requires the discipline of working with food. When my children first learned to play piano and then other musical instruments, they spent many hours practicing scales, mastering theory, and rehearsing particular pieces. A commanding presence often involves a lot of repetition, but one trusts that the repetition has merit and will bear fruit.

Alas, as a result of our lifestyles, it grows harder and harder to see why focal practices might be worthy priorities:

> As the pace of life increases, Americans are becoming more likely to avoid activities that require patience, learning, discipline, and total commitment. Instead, they choose activities . . . that lend themselves to their hurried lives and to the endless parade of new technology. People are content to learn to play the stereo, not the piano.[2]

I understand the difficulty of choosing focal practices in the face of so many potential entertaining and easy distractions. I grew up watching lots of television. It was not until middle age that I began to explore long-distance walking.

I have read many marvelous books where people pay tribute to favorite focal practices: running, cooking, mountain climbing, bird-watching, sailing, horseback riding, kayaking, canoeing, gardening, fly-fishing. When such testimonies are especially eloquent, they may even lure us into trying those activities ourselves. I enjoy reading about pursuits that are not my own even if I do not intend to try them. The passion people feel for their chosen activities is inspiring. Several qualities of commanding presence are evident in the ways people describe their focal practices.

While such activities are rewarding, they are also demanding. They can be difficult and taxing. They do not necessarily come automatically, smoothly, or easily. Japanese novelist Haruki Murakami says that he is naturally constructed and designed to be a runner, but then discusses how hard he works and trains all year to stay in shape, to prepare for marathons, and to remain spiritually and emotionally balanced. He continually has to figure out how to keep himself motivated, keep himself going, keep himself running, even though he knows that he loves what running brings to his life.[3]

Intriguingly, the skills demanded and the energy expended in focal activities increase enjoyment of those activities. Edward Abbey writes: "All things excellent are as difficult as they are rare. . . . If so, what happens to excellence when we eliminate the difficulty and the rarity?"[4] Of course, the level of challenge makes rewards all the more rewarding. Thomas de Zengotita claims that "hardship" and "intense discomfort" help us encounter reality "and, after a while, you feel more real yourself."[5]

Commercials for ready-to-bake cookies and pizzas rightly assert that working together with one's children in the kitchen is more fun than buying something off the store shelf, makes the house smell pleasing, and gives opportunities for family interaction. No matter what commercials assert, baking cookies or cooking meals oneself—with all the trial and error involved—is far more satisfying than purchasing frozen dough, slicing off pieces, and baking them into a predictably reliable result.

Furthermore, focal activities are beyond our control, another aspect of commanding presence. Read an honest and inviting book on gardening and you will hear of trials and tribulations, weeds and bugs, uncooperative weather and nuisance animals. Gardeners and farmers are in suspense every year about how crops will fare; there are no guarantees. Focal practices do not predictably produce foreseeable results. Yet unforeseen and unanticipated developments are crucial.

Sometimes walking causes blisters. On certain days there is not enough wind to sail. Or there may be too much wind and too many waves for kayaking. The dough may fail to rise when we try to bake. Who knows what might go wrong when we set out? That's not only or merely the price we pay. It turns out that the best undertakings of our lives—marriage, family, raising children, pastoring, teaching, writing—never turn out exactly as planned.

I recall one hike a few years ago, where forty-miles-per-hour winds buffeted my companion Ralph and me, making the chilly air feel subzero. It was Easter week and we were on the Bruce Trail but had not calculated on winter getting in one last bitter April lick. We gingerly picked our way over icy, snow-covered rocks, aware that we were only a few feet away from a cliff edge that plummeted straight down to a rocky shore far below. The cold bit into our exposed faces, and sometimes we had to force ourselves to keep going. As someone who reluctantly discovered hiking, I might well have wondered why in the world I was doing this. This could not be a good time, could it? Well, actually, it was. Later that day, we found a cozy restaurant. We sat near the fire in its hearth, absorbing its warmth, watched the play of orange light and shadows, enjoyed a hearty beef stew, and savored a cold local beer. We thought about our small achievement, talked about our friendship and our families, felt invigorated by the challenges of the day, and remembered how beautiful the slippery rocks and battered trees were.

Edward Abbey wrote of a particularly difficult desert hike, a nearly disastrous and potentially fatal misadventure, where he almost got permanently lost, without food. He summarized how he felt at the end of the day, when his future was still uncertain: "No matter. I stretched out in the coyote den, pillowed my head on my arm and suffered through the long, long night, wet, cold, aching, hungry, wretched, dreaming claustrophobic nightmares. It was one of the happiest nights of my life."[6]

Unpredictability is a crucial aspect of the rewarding nature of focal practices. If one knows that each hike will be enjoyable, then there will not be the same satisfaction. Our culture—relying on devices and gadgets—expects guaranteed results. Press this button and get that effect. Many of our favorite machines and gadgets—remote controls, computer mice, cars, air-conditioning—are about giving us the power to affect surroundings, to make circumstances comfortable, to know what to expect. Yet, as regular travelers to the Boundary Waters Wilderness Area will tell you, a significant aspect of why one's time there is so rich is because you never know what the weather will be like, what will happen, which animals you might see. Every year that I went to the Boundary Waters I hoped to see a moose. But it was always a wild moose chase, and I have yet to see one. Even so, the animal's elusiveness is one allure of those trips.

Finally, commanding presence points to a greater reality that deserves our attention and even awe, reminding us about our true nature and place. We are humbled.

> Awe is triggered by experiences with that which is beyond our control and understanding—that which is vast and requires accommodation. This experience, at its core, centers upon the recognition of the limitations of the self; in Confucian thought, we feel a deep sense of modesty. Around the world awe has a modest physical signature seen in acts of reverence, devotion, and gratitude: we become small, we kneel, bow, relax and round our shoulders, curl into a small, fetal ball.[7]

Alas, those opportunities are easy to miss. During one season of my life I walked regularly along the Detroit River to deal with depression. I was having trouble motivating myself to get regular exercise, even though I knew it was good for me. But I noticed that there were numerous cans strewn along my route, each one worth a five- or ten-cent refund. I began bringing a plastic bag and picking up cans as I went. Cleaning up the environment is good, but, bizarrely, I gradually began measuring the worth of my walks quite literally by how much money I earned that day (usually less than a dollar a trip). Once, I was walking along with my head focused on the ground, so determined was I to earn every last possible cent, and I happened to glance up and noticed that the sun was setting. The blazing orange disk was streaking the entire sky and made the normally muddy river look like a golden torrent. The view was a commanding presence, one that I had almost missed because of my penny-pinching preoccupation.

I still go off course in other ways. My wife and I are fond of the beauty of rocks. We have them in the yard, around the garden, on coffee tables, in bowls, and on bookshelves. We even stockpile them in our garage—in case we run out, I guess. We love their wildness, unpredictability, colors, and surfaces. I sometimes pick up rocks while hiking, canoeing, or kayaking. If I am not alert, I can spend my whole journey focusing on finding "good rocks" to take home, not taking in the simple glory of what is around me.

FOCAL ACTIVITIES

It is easy to get distracted. One paddling buddy had a GPS for the first time and brought it on a Boundary Waters canoe trip. He spent most of the journey in the bow of the canoe, with his head down, studying the machine in his lap, hardly paddling. He seldom looked up at the surrounding blue waters, leviathan-shaped granite boulders, hardy pine trees, cloud-filled sky, lonely loons, or soaring bald eagles.

A friend of mine attends a liturgical church where Communion is celebrated every Sunday. One morning a fellow member moved toward the altar while talking on his Bluetooth phone. His multitasking efficiency could not spare even a few moments. He was getting lots done, I suppose, but somehow he missed the point of the celebration and his murmuring interfered with those around him who were trying to worship. That story reminded me of the Dutch cartoonist who, listening to me talk about focal living, drew a caricature of the Last Supper. People sit around the classic table but are not exactly focused; one disciple watches television, another works on the computer, still another chats on a phone, and Jesus looks at his oversized wristwatch!

At a worship training workshop we were warned against allowing pauses or "dead air." People must be provided with incessant activity and stimulation or they will become bored, we were instructed. I am reminded of a community where I worship regularly. First, there is a long period of singing accompanied by many instruments and singers at the front. As the leader stands up to read Scripture and pray, the musicians dismantle instruments, drink from water bottles, and shuffle off the platform. It is difficult to listen to the Bible reading when parties move around. That is why I admire liturgical churches that precede Gospel reading with a procession. The congregation stands and watches, each person turning his or her face and entire body in the direction of the Bible and the reader. The focus is clear and undivided.

It is not hard for those who are religiously or spiritually inclined to realize the worshipful connotations of "commanding presence." Worship involves encountering, facing, and meeting God. This transcendent experience is beyond control or manipulation, one calling us to conversion and transformation. How those experiences can overwhelm and overcome us is succinctly conveyed in Charles Wesley's great hymn, "Love Divine, All Loves Excelling," which includes the phrase *"lost in wonder, love, and praise."* True worship will evoke reverence, appreciation, vitality, awe, and commitment to virtue and truth.

The Scriptures are full of descriptions of commanding presence. In Psalm 29, for example:

> Ascribe to the LORD, O heavenly beings,
> ascribe to the LORD glory and strength.

> Ascribe to the LORD the glory of his name;
> worship the LORD in holy splendor.
> The voice of the LORD is over the waters;
> The God of glory thunders,
> The LORD, over mighty waters.
> The voice of the LORD is powerful;
> the voice of the LORD is full of majesty.
> The voice of the LORD breaks the cedars;
> the LORD breaks the cedars of Lebanon.
> He makes Lebanon skip like a calf,
> and Sirion like a young wild ox.
> The voice of the LORD flashes forth flames of fire.
> The voice of the LORD shakes the wilderness;
> the LORD shakes the wilderness of Kadesh.
> The voice of the LORD causes the oaks to whirl,
> and strips the forest bare;
> and in his temple all say, "Glory!"

God is the ultimate manifestation of commanding presence—glory, strength, holy splendor, majesty. Note that the psalm proclaims that these attributes are reflected in natural wonders too, including thunder and mighty waters, cedars and wilderness, oaks and forests.

Meals and Commanding Presence

There are more modest examples of commanding presence. A basic but essential focal practice is making and sharing food. Because of the ubiquity of fast food and microwaves, we sometimes forget how complex putting together a meal is—raising or procuring food, preserving and storing it, preparing it, chopping it into appropriate sizes and spicing it, and finally, serving it.

There are exalted times when we realize the profound meaning of food taken together; think of the Christian celebration of the Lord's Supper, or Eucharist, or the Jewish observance of Passover. Or consider the tea ceremony.

Many etiquette guidelines remind us of the commanding presence of meals. As a country girl my mother was invited to a city class-mate's birthday party. She was delighted to see that Dutch crepe-styled pancakes—among her favorite foods—were being served. She promptly rolled one up with her fingers and ate it by hand, the custom in her family. She was mortified when others laughed at her; they knew how to eat properly with a knife and fork. She resolved then and there that her children would know too. That she taught us well. But in university I was eating dinner at the home of an upper-class friend and at the end of the main course was surprised when his mother circled behind me and adjusted my knife and fork to the more proper "twenty past four" position. I had let them lie randomly on my plate, as was our family custom.

The point of table manners—whether hats, utensils, being excused, or leftovers—was not to invent rules to separate the classy from the trashy. Etiquette reminds us of the eminent worth of a meal as an end in itself, a focus, a focal practice. Rules of etiquette—"most of them having to do with neatness, cleanliness, and noiselessness"[8]—transform meals into rituals, even works of art. Pausing before one eats, offering thanks to God and to one's hosts (marking the meal as a ritual), giving an encouragement to others at the table (*bon appetit, buen provecho, eet smakelijk, guten appetit*), making a toast, and taking time to savor food all reinforce a sense of commanding presence.

Margaret Visser reminds us of a basic dinner rule: "Refrain from other pursuits while it is in progress. No one will knit, watch television, or read a newspaper."[9] That is because the meal ought to be one's priority, one's focus. When I was a child, TV dinners catered to one major temptation. Now there are additional distractions, including cell phones. I am so grateful when I visit people who refuse to answer the phone during a meal because meals are a commanding priority.

We hollow out other meal occasions as well. I once attended a church general convention where Communion was celebrated at the close of the event. The service included feeding several thousand delegates and was accomplished within ten minutes. People were eager to move on to catch buses for the long ride home. Rather than feeling worshipful, it was ecclesiastical fast food. Churches can now purchase single-serving, portable, hygienic Communion sets. Small plastic cups containing grape juice on the bottom and a wafer sealed on top are encased in an easy-to-remove and throwaway plastic cover (embossed with the image of a grain of wheat). One can quickly take Communion without risking germs, without the bother of pouring juice or wine or preparing bread ahead of time. We might even add a sacramental act of passing waste-baskets up and down the rows to take care of the accumulated garbage.

Ironically, one such product is called "Remembrance" ("A Versatile New Resource for Celebrating Communion"). But what does it call to mind and remembrance? Meaningful meals at table with those near and dear? Bread baked lovingly by parents? Food raised sacrificially by farmers? Faith ancestors risking their lives to share the Eucharist? The hermetically sealed packets are about the size and shape of coffee creamers one gets in fast-food restaurants. When I use the product, the only remembrance I have is how food can be degraded into cheap and meaningless—but convenient—fuel. With such a thin celebration, other meals are indeed evoked, but are they ones we wish to remember? Looking at these plastic-encased elements, I hear a disembodied voice asking: "Would you like fries with that?"

We deepen awareness of a meal's commanding presence when we lay out the table as nicely as possible. This does not necessarily mean fine china and elegant furniture. One of the happiest, most memorable dinners Lorna and I have ever enjoyed was with a couple that we had met only a few months earlier but who would become lasting friends. We were all recently out of school, and none of us had much money. We ate our first supper together at a rough wooden construction spool that Kathy and Willard had adapted for a picnic table. We were behind their house under the El tracks of our inner-city Chicago neighbor-hood, trains regularly screeching past. That meal—much of it made with food grown in Kathy and Willard's backyard—was a gesture of invitation and hospitality.

It was a modest occasion, a down payment on a rich and long-standing friendship. The meal commanded our attention and deserved our focus. But the fact that it set the stage for a friendship for many years to come leads us directly to the second important aspect of focal practices: they connect us to others and other realities.

3

FOCAL CONNECTEDNESS

A battered violin hangs on Diane's living room wall. It's beaten up and scratched. She tells me that it belonged to her Romanian father and came from the old country. It's one of the few mementos that she still has from him; he died decades ago while only middle-aged. The violin is a focal thing. When Diane looks at it, she remembers him playing it for her when she was a child. Hanging an old violin on the wall, even if one cannot play it and even if it is not exactly lovely anymore, makes perfect and obvious sense. But I cannot imagine that my son—as much as he loves me—would ever decide that my old stereo receiver is beautiful or meaningful enough to be displayed.

Focal practices and focal things affect us on various levels. They link us into a rich network of people and ecosystems. This is their second primary characteristic and quality. Albert Borgmann uses the terms "manifold engagement" and "continuity" to describe the kinds of connections focal practices create. What does he mean?

Borgmann explains that focal realities touch us within at different levels and connect us outwardly in many ways too. Two people who love canoeing write of the benefits of being self-propelled on the water: "It is during times like these that we feel most in balance: physically fit, emotionally fulfilled, intellectually challenged by weather, water and navigation conditions, and spiritually close to all that sustains our lives."[1] And they are surely right. Body, feelings, intellect, spirit, and soul are all involved and interwoven. Activities that link emotions and spirit and brains and bodies contributes to happiness. Robert Kubey and Mihaly Csikszentmihalyi write: "Truly rewarding experiences . . . almost invariably require concentrated involvement and interaction with complex information. The things that give people 'natural highs'—playing music, a close game of tennis, an intense and meaningful conversation with a friend, a job well done—all require that we pay attention, that we look, listen, and act with care and skill."[2]

This not only has implications for how we feel inside our bodies, minds, emotions, or spirits but also how we relate beyond ourselves too. Focal reality engages us externally as well as internally, drawing us out of self-preoccupation. Jesus spoke this way when he told us that living out the greatest commandment requires multifaceted engagement with God: "You shall love the Lord your God with all your *heart*, and with all your *soul*, and with all your *mind*, and with all your *strength*" (Mark 12:30, emphasis added). Often people make the mistake of assuming that religion is only about some disembodied aspect of our spirits and that matter and bodies and physical reality do not count. But that is not the Christian testimony.

Anyone who has loved another—family member, spouse, child— knows that truly rewarding affection is not confined to one narrow aspect of our being. We do not just love with heart or mind or physical attention. Love stirs our feelings. Love engages us intellectually; at some level and in some way we can name reasons why we care so much for the other. Love has concrete bodily implications: we demonstrate it by providing food or working or tending to needs or being physically affectionate. Love sparks our imaginations and helps us see ourselves and the wider world in new and more vital ways. That's why literature, music, and poetry are inspired by this basic human yearning. While they sometimes work out well, online and virtual romances are risky and often unfulfilling because they do not engage on multiple levels; they run the hazard of being a passing fancy, an unsubstantiated crush, a thin attachment.

Gardening puts one in touch with the earth and the weather but also with the food we eat and farmers and other growers who advise us on best practices. When my spouse bakes bread there are all kinds of robust connections—with people who taught her how to bake, those who shared recipes with her, good bread that she's eaten, those who receive and appreciate her baking, farmers who grew the grain. But when I thaw a frozen microwave dinner I am in no explicit relationship with anyone; the continuity is thin. Rachel Shenk, a self-taught baker, loves to ponder the connected significance of bread:

> Bread is a staple through all cultures. Plus it has a huge history. I visited Pompeii when I was young. They found loaves in the ovens there. I thought, "Oh, wow, that's so cool." To think that you're a part of this huge strand of people having done this forever and ever. And to know that all over the world there are people doing this exact same thing.

Focal reality draws us out and helps us encounter others. When our family moved from Waterloo, Ontario, to Elkhart, Indiana, our son Paul changed high schools. He had the good fortune to be befriended by several teens who wanted to start a band and needed a drummer. Paul had learned piano and trumpet, but neither of those skills was directly useful for the new challenge. So he took up drums. Lorna and I often went to hear this young punk group. Their connectedness was rich and complex. They were engaged with each other—they attended the same school, socialized frequently, and rehearsed regularly. They worked hard and enjoyed themselves. Live music challenged them intellectually, moved them emotionally, tested their physical endurance, and was an expression of their passions and faith. They were connected with friends, relatives, and schoolmates who came out to hear them. They were tied to those who had taught them how to play and to their parents, who made them take lessons in earlier years. They had a tangible bond with folks who created their guitars and drum kit. They relied on those who had written and performed music in the past. And on and on. Paul also felt a link to the paternal grandfather he was named after because my dad drummed in a band in the Netherlands as a teenager. While I enjoy music on an iPod, listening to that device offers nowhere near the depth, complexity, and interrelatedness of hearing my son—or indeed anyone—produce live music.

Focal practices root us widely. Verlin Miller is an artisan woodworker who lovingly designed and built his own house. As we sat in his home, admiring handmade furniture and cabinets, he spoke of how he'd been influenced by the farm where he was raised, Franciscan and Benedictine and Anabaptist spiritualities, Shaker and Amish craftspeople, artisans in Denmark and Japan, a Mennonite seminary professor who built his own hermitage, and the architectural genius and maverick Frank Lloyd Wright. They were all present with Verlin in his do-it-yourself house.

Rich interconnectedness has many implications. I'm concerned that images projected on overhead screens in worship literally have no depth and are completely dependent on the vagaries of lighting and power sources. As soon as the energy is cut, the pixels disappear. Let us appreciate instead the rich complexity of quilts and pottery and tables and flowers.

Our school's chapel has four lovely tapestries at the front. These were commissioned for the school and created by Reet Mae, an artist inspired by her father, a painter. She collaborated in this project with her daughter, also a painter. For over two years, up to thirty volunteers gave over two thousand hours to planning the pieces, finding materials, sewing, and quilting. The panels depict creation, pain and promise, redemption, and fulfillment. In them one can see Canadian life, rural and urban. Trees, waves, water, plants, grapevines, mountains, and wind are evoked. The figures in the panels allude to South American tribespeople, a Kosovo refugee, a Nepalese poppy picker, a Bosnian soldier, and a group of Saudi Arabian women. As Mae depicted suffering, she thought of her aunt who was exiled while pregnant to a Siberian labor camp. The banners are silk, some of them painted, and done in earth tones; they incorporate thousands of wooden and glass beads sewn throughout. In an interview with our school's former president, Mae said that the banners were intended to be "uplifting, inspiring praise and worship." They are focal in every sense of the term. Yet this stunning gift is now overshadowed by other objects. Invariably the room's focus is two overwhelmingly large screens (not to mention cables strewn across the dais to support various electronics). Every time I am there, I feel a sense of loss. I wonder how many people who regularly worship in that space—as often as two or more times a week—know or appreciate what is on the walls.

Worship practices, rituals, and symbols engage us by being *multivalent*. They convey many meanings at various levels. The water of baptism, for example, suggests relief from thirst, refreshment from heat, cleansing from sin, but also danger, death, and destruction. Bread, fire, and light have multiple allusions. Worship at its best may move us emotionally, inspire us intellectually, encourage us spiritually, and engage our senses.

My church is full of immigrants from the West Indies, Sri Lanka, and Hong Kong. Congregants take worship seriously and come in their finest clothes: handsome suits, brightly shined shoes, gorgeous saris, lovely dresses, and striking hats. Worship is a focal practice with commanding presence, of course, and demands beautiful and appropriate attire. One of my favorite parts of the service is when people move forward to take Communion. I catch a vivid glimpse of the kingdom of heaven as people from around the world gather at the table. In each service we are joined with those celebrating at that moment and those who celebrated in the past but also those who will celebrate in the future: "I tell you, many will come from east and west and will eat with Abraham and Isaac and Jacob in the kingdom of heaven" (Matt. 8:11).

The Lord's Supper binds us not just with people who receive elements but also with farmers and food, creation and creatures. It connects us to the past, the present, and the future: "Christ *has* died, Christ *is* risen, Christ *will* come again," we proclaim with conviction. Psalm 29, mentioned in the previous chapter, shows the manifold engagement of worship by addressing "heavenly beings" and citing waters, thunder, cedars, flames, and fire. Focal practices are never thin.

But we frighteningly distort and hollow worship. I watched a famous "Christian" television talk show where hosts invited viewers to get bread and grape juice from their kitchens so that we would be able to celebrate the Lord's Supper. Now there are churches experimenting with "online Communion." As Gordon Mikoski notes:

> In the digital age, it may be the case that the classical debates about the presence of Jesus Christ in the Eucharist have been inverted. The question with which we may now have to wrestle is not "In what way is *the Lord* present in the Supper?" Instead, the question is "In what ways are *we* present?"[3]

Some churches practice "virtual baptism"—pastors Skyping to a candidate who dunks him or herself in a bathtub. It's hard to think of anything lonelier or more disconnected.

While shut-ins benefit from worship broadcasts, the risk is that others will prefer the ease of receiving services at home and become isolated and disconnected. One friend began pastoring a church that had a vibrant radio ministry. This was obviously beneficial for those who were too old, infirm, or ill to attend church. A no-brainer. Yet Pastor John noticed declining attendance over the years. Congregants liked being able to listen to the service over breakfast and not having to dress up. On rainy days, even more people elected to stay home. He persuaded the church to drop the broadcasts; a valid ministry had been distorted into a convenience, one detracting from discipleship. Worship needs to connect us deeply and root us widely.

My father never showed his emotions easily. I learned from others—never directly from him—that he had been beaten by his own father. His military experiences in Indonesia after World War II left him with nightmares that plagued him until the end of his life. But, again, he never said much about this. When my sister died at seventeen, for the first year after her passing he had trouble uttering her name. He was struggling; he expressed his grief differently than my mother and I. I was told only after he died that years earlier he cried every time I left home to go to university. He was a complicated man, not given to sentimentality or to revealing tender feelings.

Yet in worship he regularly got choked up. There was a hymn that we sang in those days, "By the Sea of Crystal," that affected him deeply. It is about John's book of Revelation vision of saints gathered by a glassy sea to praise God. The first verse says:

> By the sea of crystal, saints in glory stand,
> Myriads in number, drawn from every land,
> Robed in white apparel, washed in Jesus' blood,
> They now reign in heaven with the Lamb of God.[4]

As I say, this came up regularly, and so through repetition it accrued new and deeper meanings. It first affected my father after the death of his father. He could see his own dad—as flawed as that man was—standing on that saintly shore. A few years later, his beloved mother-in-law died. And some years after that, his daughter was gone, and then she entered into the picture. Singing one hymn drew my father into

Christian tradition and theology, touched his heart, and helped him to grieve painful losses.

Missing Connections

Resurging interest in farmers' markets and other deepening commitments to eating locally (some people consume only food that comes from within a hundred-mile radius) are ways that people address a gnawing sense of disconnection. Growing numbers of folks see the value in being directly acquainted with farmers and producers. My wife, Lorna, makes a priority of visiting such markets. She likes knowing the names, quirks, and personalities of our food producers. She appreciates being aware of the geography and conditions of where our food comes from. And we are also better off knowing the true cost—and worth!—of what we eat.

In northern Indiana and far beyond, the name Dick Lehman is synonymous with beautiful pottery. An immigrant friend of mine has trouble, because of her accent, pronouncing his name. But, on second thought, her rendition—"De Clay Man"—works pretty well. Lorna and I cherish a number of his pieces ourselves.

Dick recalls customers' meaningful encounters. One day a woman spent an hour looking for a mug. Repeated offers of assistance were declined. She picked up every mug that she could find, hefted it in her hand, and lifted it to her lips as well. Finally, she settled on one. Turns out that she'd driven a couple of hours to the studio. She'd had a Lehman mug for years. She liked how it fit her hand and her lips, but eventually it broke. Dick recalls: "She said life wasn't as good without it." It was worth the investment of the drive, time, and energy to find another.

He also recalled when a young woman came to acquire fifteen different mugs. It was common for soon-to-be brides to make such purchases for wedding attendants. When Dick asked if a wedding was the occasion for these gifts, she began crying. Between tears she explained that she was already married, but her marriage was dissolving after a long struggle. She and her husband wanted to thank and acknowledge all the people who were helpful in their unsuccessful efforts to keep their marriage together—and they wanted to do so through a marriage dissolution ceremony. The mugs were gifts for this occasion.

Eight years later the same woman returned to the studio to buy another collection of mugs. Dick did not recognize her and as a result of the earlier experience had stopped asking leading questions about weddings. She said, "You may not remember me, but I am the woman who bought mugs for a marriage dissolution ceremony. I'm happy to tell you that I am going to be remarried. I could think of no better way to celebrate the occasion with friends than to purchase mugs for our attendants."

Continuity and Connectedness of Meals

I love surprises, but my wife, well—not so much. Nevertheless, I was able to catch her off guard—and delight her as well—for her fiftieth birthday party. Our young-adult children and I took her to a favorite restaurant. Unbeknownst to her, the place was filled with three dozen folks who came from as far away as four hundred miles. There were siblings and friends, relatives and people who had known us for decades, and members of our current church and previous congregations. When Lorna and I talk about that meal, even now years later, the thing that we most often recall is the joy of looking up and down the long table and seeing people that were important to us, folks that we had loved over the years, sitting together, some meeting for the first time, enjoying each other's company, laughing, and becoming acquainted. It was a small glimpse of heaven.

Meals engage us internally, of course, by satisfying our primal need for food. Eating is one of the few basic urges that humans ritualize. Other urges are often cared for in private, out of sight. But meals do more than address physical desire. Our taste buds savor the results when a cook has cared to tickle our tongues and caress our sense of smell. Our intellect is inspired by the creativity of a concoction. A pleasingly arrayed plate or carefully set table may arouse aesthetic gratitude. And food touches memories. Both my wife and I have certain preferences for comfort foods that connect us reassuringly with long-ago childhoods. I love revisiting the chunky applesauce that my mother used to make from apples from our own trees, and Lorna enjoys buttery mashed potatoes that recall special gatherings at Thanksgiving and Christmas. Certain tastes help us vividly relive childhood scenes that we might otherwise forget. Many of us are passionate about food and have all kinds of memories associated with it. A great discussion starter is to ask people to describe one of their most memorable meals.

And, of course, meals invite external engagement as well. At its most basic level, eating a meal connects us to the food itself, the farmer who grew it, those who harvested it, people who transported it, and on and on. A traditional grace goes like this:

> Gracious God, we thank you for this food.
> Bless the hands that prepared it.
> Bless it to our use and us to your service,
> And make us ever mindful of the needs of others.
> Through Christ our Lord we pray. Amen.

Food links us concretely with the soil and rain and sun, the earth and the weather, which make food possible. Margaret Visser spends a whole book exploring the origins of one relatively simple meal and notes: "All the continents on earth and a good many countries are represented in the ingredients for this particular dinner."[5]

The traditional rule of not doing anything else while eating leads to attentiveness to food's commanding presence (as we saw in the last chapter) but also ensures that we properly appreciate those at table with us. This is no small thing in a culture where fewer take meals together and where meals may be interrupted by phones, instant messaging, or texting. We've known our friend Francine for decades and always admired her hospitality. She recently told us that she's reluctantly and regretfully stopped inviting relatives for dinner because they persistently text at the table. Awareness of others during meals goes back a long way. Words such as *companion*, *company*, and *compañero* (Spanish) all suggest people with whom we share bread. (*Pan* is Latin for "bread.") In many cultures, Visser notes, eating together is what defines a family.[6]

An old-fashioned word, *conviviality*, connotes warm, lively times of socializing, and it is best visualized as sitting at table with others. The table is the place where we gather family and friends. We review the events of the day, catch up on each other's lives, mark a transition together. One of the most common ways to mark an occasion is to have a meal, a banquet. Some churches do not often celebrate the Lord's

Supper, but their potlucks may have a sacramental quality. A former congregant used to say, "*Potluck* is church language for 'party'!"

Some of my happiest moments on the Camino were at the end of a day, dining with pilgrims. Years later, I still recall where and with whom I ate. I liked—even loved—the food, but I was most grateful for the company. As Christine Pohl writes: "A shared meal is the activity most closely tied to the reality of God's Kingdom."[7] No surprise, then, that so many New Testament stories—parables about banquets, feasts in homes, the last supper, miracle feedings—revolve around food. One acquaintance likes to say, "If you can read the gospels without getting hungry, you're not paying attention."

Trends in our culture show that people eat together less and less, and while eating they pay attention to technological media. With harried schedules, we may dash in, blast something with the microwave, wolf it down, and take off for the next activity. Then another family member comes along and does the same thing. One UCLA project showed that many "dine together only 17 percent of the time, *even if everyone is at home.*"[8] I know households where the day's main meal is taken with family members balancing food on their lap—or on a TV tray—and focusing on a screen rather than each other.

Years ago I was delighted when friends found a new gadget: a simple, plastic cup holder to hang from a car window enabling one to bring coffee. Now vehicles are actually designed for eating while driving. Built-in cup holders are a norm. The glove compartment door may fold down to serve as a tray. Some cars have refrigerated spaces just for food! Eating meals while driving is now common because people spend long hours commuting or hurrying between engagements and commitments. Americans may consume as much as one-fifth of their meals—even up to two meals per day—in cars.[9] Food-related collisions also grow more common.[10] The multitasking solution of eating and driving is becoming as hazardous a combination as drinking and driving. The food industry caters to this by developing handier packaging to encourage people to eat while behind the wheel.

In our immigrant family, it was not uncommon for us to jump into the car after church or after Sunday lunch and just set out with no particular direction in mind. After a time of roaming, one parent would say, "Hey, we're near so-and-so's house. Let's drop in." This was perfectly acceptable behavior. There would always be coffee and goodies available for surprise guests. If the visiting went well, it might last until evening and soup or bread would be stretched accordingly. On the Sundays we stayed home, we often heard doors slamming in the driveway and that was the first hint we had that we were receiving guests. This was normal and routine. People were prepared to offer spur-of-the-moment hospitality. Yet gathering with friends and extended family is also increasingly difficult now. Lorna and I find that we have to invite people six weeks or more in advance to be able to eat together.

When Lorna and I were preparing to move back to Canada to be near family and old friends after having lived in the States for seven years, one colleague, John Rempel, had us over for a farewell dinner at his home. It was a pleasant summer evening, and we ate outside in his backyard gazebo, attended by a mother cat and her kittens, who lived four doors down. We noticed the slow breeze, the sound of crickets, the gradual sinking of the sun, and the sudden appearance of fireflies. The meal involved herbs John had grown himself and vegetables that he purchased from an Old Order Mennonite farm family, one we often bought from as well. We ate bright red tomatoes and sweet carrots, locally grown. The German-style potato salad was a recipe from John's family. We all enjoyed the tender lamb, and both John and Lorna laughed as they recalled eating tough, chewy mutton when they were children.

We talked about our lives. All of us had things to say about parents, especially John, as his mother had died the previous year. We recalled other meals that we had eaten together at John's table and ours, in restaurants, and with other friends. We conversed about our current involvements: course prep, travels, moving arrangements. We discussed future plans of study and work and eventual retirement. We remembered how our friendship had begun, expressed appreciation for our relationship now, and voiced our hopes and intentions for staying connected even when we lived far apart. Past, present, and future were all there; connection and continuity abounding.

4

FOCAL CENTERING
AND ORIENTING POWER

Years ago, I traveled to Paris as a fervent, young Christian who doubted the merit of many other Christian traditions, especially Catholicism. And I was not interested in architecture either. After a month in Europe, I'd had my fill of old museums and churches.

Yet on my first day in that famous city, happening to bike past the cathedral of Notre Dame, I argued with myself about whether to visit. Yes, it was a famous location, but I'd seen quite a few of those by then. And, really, what could a "Catholic" place offer? I eventually decided to drop in for a visit. It was a "must-see" tourist site after all. From the moment I entered the doors, I was dumbfounded. I shocked myself by exclaiming aloud, "Oh . . . I want to be a Catholic!" Here was a robust tradition that had much to teach me. I savored the beauty, having no idea that in the years to come I would grow in my appreciation for liturgy and sacraments.

The third and final quality of focal realities—things, places, practices—is that they have centering or orienting power. They help us experience and be in touch with something greater than ourselves. They teach us about our deepest priorities and most important values. They call us to something larger, more purposeful. They reveal and disclose vital truths that help ground and direct our lives.

I have already noted how the Camino was a place where many walkers became accidental pilgrims reflecting on their lives, asking vital questions about vocations. The Camino, with its churchly heritage and associations, obviously reminds us of God. But even many people there who were not believers per se found courage for life-changing decisions. Numerous folks were in a liminal state: recovering from illness, mourning a loved one, grieving a broken marriage, pondering a change of vocation. Walking the Camino helped them make significant transitions.

I had parallel experiences while hiking the Bruce Trail. In some ways, that project was a whim sparked by a local newspaper article. But over and again I realized that something deeper was working on me during those occasions on the path. I recall one Bruce Trail jaunt in particular. After a semester of teaching at a new school, I felt overwhelmed. My stress was not just caused by the pressures of a new vocation, but by giving up my life as a pastor and the costly move my family made to enable me to teach. I was depleted. So I went for six days on the trail.

On that journey, I felt myself relax, the tensions streaming away. I decompressed from the strain of months of intense work and an emotionally draining agenda. I grew more centered. I paid attention to the beautiful surroundings. During daily prayers, I heard familiar Scripture texts in fresh ways. I was clear about priorities for each day. Suddenly I did not feel so torn by conflicting expectations. I was climbing out from the burden of being overwhelmed.

Time on the trail helped me reevaluate how I had lived the last months. I could see clearly that many focal concerns (reading, writing, prayer, family) had not received proper attention for some time. I resolved to live differently, "to pay attention to the deepest thing [I] know," as Douglas Steere evocatively described prayer.[1]

What particularly struck me about my six days on the trail was how closely they resembled my time on monastery retreats over the past decades. I dare not live without regular visits to the monastery. Occasionally, when too much time passes between retreats, my spouse reminds me of my need before I am aware of it. I grow difficult to live with, and she helpfully suggests, "Isn't it time you visit the monastery again?" During such excursions I can almost predict the following themes that invariably arise, and they all have to do with centering power.

First, I relax, start to breathe deeply, and slowly release tensions and stress. I gain helpful perspectives now that I am at a distance, no longer in the midst of things. Then, I see how my life started to get out of balance. (Sadly imbalance seems a regularly recurring state for me.) Finally, I gain clarity about how to address my latest conundrums. I go home with new resolve that will carry me for some time, although I eventually and inevitably need another retreat, to be centered once more.

Many people I interviewed talked about centering power. They told of how their well-being, mental health, and sense of balance depend on focal practices.

Ted Klopfenstein, now in his early eighties, has been involved with horses all his life. He is passionate about endurance horse riding and only recently stopped when a horse "fell on him" and broke Ted's neck. Even so, he speaks with reverence about horse travel.

> You don't have to go to church to worship. You can worship any place. I've had intense worship periods by horseback. One time I was riding up the Rocky Mountains, up Thompson's Pass, and it was so spiritual. I'm up there and my friend from Illinois, she's crying. I said, "What's the matter?" She said, "Oh, it's so beautiful, I can't stand it." That's worshiping. Not worshiping nature but worshiping the Creator of nature. Because everything we have is created.

Ruth Mallory told of the connection between birding and faith: "I've had experiences that I describe as God kissing my cheek. It wraps you in worship." Rachel Shenk the baker says that bread has a "spiritual aspect" because it's used in religious services, helps people survive, and also "feeds the spirit." Don Steider is the handiest man that I know. He built his own log home after finding and lumbering all the wood for it himself. He speaks reverently of wood as both one of his "channels to God" and a means that helps him better understand God.

Centering and orienting power does more, reminding us of what we most need to prioritize, helping us decide and discern between many available options. Albert Borgmann told me:

> We're overwhelmed with offers all the time. They come in the form of advertisements mostly. They come in comparisons with what other people do—"Should we do that too?"—what we read in the paper and so on. Orientation is to know what to take and what not to take. And if you have a focal practice that centers your life then that focal practice allows you to make those choices.[2]

I don't know about you, but I often need that kind of reorientation.

In one period of my life, I indulged in a decadent urban habit that I'd heard about but never tried. It was neither drugs nor gambling, neither alcohol nor sexual promiscuity. For one reason or another—probably just timidity—I have never been caught up in any of those particular thralls. My vice was more intellectual.

During a time of disillusionment about my experience at the hands of a Christian institution, I stopped attending church for half a year. I slept in on Sundays and then savored that ultimate urban indulgence, the weekend paper. Over a long, leisurely breakfast and several cups of coffee, I slowly and deliciously waded through national news, editorials and op-eds, book and movie reviews, and even the color comics. And I spent a lot of time and energy on a most un-Sabbath preoccupation—studying ads for sales and clipping coupons. I basked in those slow and lazy Sunday mornings, their quiet and leisure. In my bitterness back then, I did not miss church at all, I'm sorry to report.

Finally, for various reasons, I decided to visit a church. On Pentecost Sunday, no less. I planned to hate the experience. I resolved that I'd try it once, and then return to Sunday morning newspaper cocooning. Nevertheless, I was unwillingly smitten by that church service. I soon became a regular churchgoer once more. And wouldn't you know it—God's humor is always at work—this was also the very place that called me to be a pastor. In fact, in little over a year I was part of the ministerial staff.

For the next decade and a half, Sundays were largely absorbed by my role and duties as a pastor. I do not recall pining even once for those truant days when I had nothing more to preoccupy myself than a fresh Sunday morning paper.

Peak, Flow, and Unitive Moments

There are junctures and epiphanies in life that offer to teach what we most need to know, where we need to focus our lives and invest our energies. Such moments cannot be manufactured or forced, but arrive unexpectedly, as a gift, a grace. When I was a seminary student in my midtwenties, my wife and I drove with a friend across southern Michigan on our way home for Christmas. On a rural back road suddenly everything was suffused with a mysteriously glowing light. All three of us fell silent. Something strangely wonderful was happening. We remained very, very quiet. Everything around us—the old road, the bare maple trees, the fallow fields—inexplicably shimmered. The sky was lit up. We had never seen anything like it. It passed soon and we kept driving. Afterward we all agreed that something unusual had happened, but none of us knew what it was.

At the Missoula Consultation, Albert Borgmann commended his listeners to pay attention to "the moment of grace where things are properly centered in a way that we don't have to unsay it or surpass it at a later moment."[3] These kinds of experiences are beyond our control and usually fleeting. Yet they sustain and encourage us.

Essayist David Weale helps students identify such occurrences by asking:

> Had they ever been swept away by a song or piece of music? Had they . . . stood at night and gazed up at the stars, and experienced a mysterious connection with objects millions of light years away? Had they ever been "in the zone" while participating in a sport, which took them beyond their ordinary level of awareness and competency? Had they ever experienced such a deep solidarity with other members of a choir or team or audience that individual personalities dissolved into a single identity? . . . Had they ever become so absorbed in a task or hobby that time disappeared? Had they ever, during extremely difficult or sorrowful times, been filled suddenly with the deep certainty that everything was going to be fine? Or had they ever had their hearts momentarily melted by an unexpected gesture of compassion?[4]

There are various theories about moments in our lives when time stops and we are fully present. Abraham Maslow described "peak experiences." Virginia Woolf wrote of "moments of being," which one author summarizes this way:

> Now and then . . . from the confusion of everyday life, a clarity emerges, and we see the connections between one thing and another, between one person and another, between one place and another. In such moments, we become aware of how rich is the tapestry of life we wander through. We understand that the world is our home.[5]

Mihaly Csikszentmihalyi explores a sense of "flow." Runners claim their own kind of "high." Psychiatrist and spiritual director Gerald May speaks of "unitive experiences." Barry Lopez, one of today's best nature writers, also describes sensations "characterized as an awareness of unity with the divine, or as a release from the routine coordinates of life, as a greatly expanded sense of the present, or as a religious experience without the symbols of religion."[6]

None of these terms is precisely equivalent. "Flow" usually occurs when absorbed in activity, good work, or rewarding practices—perhaps Van Morrison or some other exemplary musician in the middle of a concert. On the one hand, flow does not happen without effort, exertion, and deliberation. One might think of Scottish Olympic athlete Eric Liddell's famous line in the film *Chariots of Fire*: "When I run, I feel God's pleasure." On the other hand, "unitive experiences" are more likely in moments of silence and stillness.

Nevertheless, all these authors agree that there are points of particular significance in our lives. Something feels altered, different; time passes without our awareness. We forget about ourselves. These kinds of phenomena, however described, involve a sense of wholeness, satisfaction, reward, accomplishment, clarification, and having a glimmer of what matters most, what is most important, what are our highest priorities, being involved in something larger than ourselves. Often we do not realize what is happening while in the midst of such times. As soon as we pay attention or think too self-consciously, the moment disappears. All the terms—unitive, optimal, flow, peak, zone, being—convey a sense of significance, purpose, and perhaps even ultimate worth. These are times, as fleeting as they may be, when we recognize our deepest priorities. In moments such as these, we experience pleasure, profound well-being, grateful contentment, and a deep sense of purpose and joy.

It could be getting harder to encounter such moments. Gerald May observes that unitive experiences (feeling at one with oneself, God, and the wider world) may be "more accessible" in "so-called primitive cultures" and were far more common in the past. Westerners are often "less available or open to such moments" because of "preoccupations with willful thinking, planning, and doing."[7] Yet even we are not completely cut off and hopeless. On most days there are numerous opportunities. Unfortunately, we are largely oblivious: "Extremely brief unitive experiences happen to most people numerous times each day, but . . . they go unnoticed."[8]

We have noted the pronounced spiritual searching and hunger in our culture. Something is missing, awry. Boston University philosopher Erazim Kohák argues that blindness to God's presence is exceptional. Humans, as a species, throughout the millennia and all over the globe have been worshipers of the Holy. The awareness of God's presence is and ever has been the most persistent specific trait of our species.[9]

Bill McKibben's take is this: "In ancient forests . . . there are no atheists."[10] This reinforces my hunch that today's spiritual questing is related to how we live. Again, the point is not to be naively nostalgic for "the good old days." Rather, the longing for flow or peak experiences or moments of engagement point to a sense of yearning for something that we need but that has substantially and significantly dwindled, if not disappeared. Like Joni Mitchell and the Woodstock generation, we still want to get "back to the garden."

It is possible to draw the wrong conclusion from peak or unitive experiences, focal moments or flow. We might see their satisfying stimulation as an end in themselves. If I decide that an "athlete's high" is my primary reason for getting exercise, perhaps I could just find a pill that would give me the same rush, without all the effort.

Ruth Mallory described with great joy a visit to the shores of nearby Lake Michigan, "We live close to it and every time I visit, I wonder, *why don't I come more often?* I was up there recently and the sky was so beautiful." She had gone with another avid birder; they were hoping to see a species that would have been a "lifer" for Ruth, one that she's never seen before. When the bird did not show, her companion apologized for the failure and inconvenience. But Ruth would have none of that. "I said, 'It doesn't matter; I got to be on Lake Michigan.'"

By noting life's significant moments, we claim courage to prioritize practices and places that engage and invigorate us. Jesus talked about his practice of "abundant life." Discerning reflection on what gives us life will help us to live fully and well.

Psalm Reorientation

Several years ago, I moved from the pulpit to the podium, from church to the classroom, and became a professor. Now, aside from my baptismal commitments as a Christian and my obligation as a church member, the demands on my Sunday mornings are far different. I still attend church. That no longer is negotiable. And I have also taken up the Sunday paper once more, but differently.

For one thing, somewhere along the way I stopped receiving daily newspapers. We could not keep up with all that reading in our hectic lives. If, everyday, I want to pray, spend time with family, exercise, and read something worthwhile, then there is often no room for what the media deem a priority. I've heard that Hegel once observed that the daily newspaper displaced morning prayer.

Surprisingly, a Sunday subscription costs about the same as subscribing to the daily paper. I've been baffled by how much pressure the local paper exerts to persuade me to go back to their daily fix. When I sheepishly tell sales representatives that I recycle most of their periodicals, they are undeterred. As a writer, I would not welcome hearing that most of my hard work is not even read but goes straight to the recycling bin. But I suppose that paper purveyors have a particular agenda: revenue from ads, ads, and more ads.

There were other reasons to cut back on newspaper intake. What reporters found pressing and urgent was not always so. The latest crises and deadlines sometimes rang false. The preoccupation of the moment was often forgotten within a day or two or eclipsed by some other pseudo- or virtual predicament. I need time to sort and sift. Events often are not best understood immediately. They develop and unfold. First reactions are usually not particularly revealing, and definitely aren't worth being preoccupied with. Being aware of every crying and pressing headline of each and every day does not necessarily make me a better Christian, family man, professor, or citizen.

With the weekend paper I would be informed, but not in a reactive way that sways with every teapot tempest. A little time would have passed—even if only a few days—for assimilation and analysis. By now perhaps some false alarms would be exposed. Maybe the important but underrated story would emerge.

Thus on Sundays I still rise early, as I do most days, but without pressure or obligation to exercise or get ready for work. Rather, I head outside and enjoy the street's rare silence. I breathe in air as I fetch the fat paper. In the early morning light, I read the latest news, summaries of the week, book reviews, editorials, and features. (There are no comics in this paper, and it comes from a city far away, so even if the ads tempted me they are irrelevant.)

There is much that I love about this habit. But it has its difficulties and challenges. The leisure of this practice often stands in contrast with what I read. Wars and bloodshed. Hard-heartedness and mean-spiritedness. Environmental destruction and callow greed. Disastrous decisions and blind behavior. The news does not get prettier just because I only take one dose a week. Perhaps it is even more densely unpleasant that way.

I often find the experience dispiriting. I become angry and disillusioned, despairing and depressed. I feel frustration and horror. All in the luxury of my comfortable chair. If the newspaper was all I read on Sundays, my spirit could not survive, let alone thrive.

There is a psalm that always brings me up short, whenever I read or, better, pray it. Psalm 73 (the *Book of Common Prayer's* version here) powerfully conveys what I experience Sunday morning as I ponder the paper.

It begins with a confession of praise.

> Truly God is good to Israel,
> to those who are pure in heart.

Then the psalmist promptly confesses liability and weakness, the error of his ways.

> But as for me, my feet had nearly slipped;
> I had almost tripped and fallen.

The issue is clear. He spends too much time dwelling on the situation and behavior of others, especially those who apparently do not live and act in the light of God.

> Because I envied the proud
> and saw the prosperity of the wicked.

He goes on in careful detail to list what he hates about those who "suffer no pain" and who have "bodies . . . sleek and sound."

> In the misfortunes of others they have no share;
> they are not afflicted as others are.

Up to this point, mostly I am noncommittal as I hear the psalmist; I am not yet identifying too closely with him. But soon his words strike a nerve. He begins to list not just the affluence of others but also the despicable ways in which they live.

> Therefore they wear their pride like a necklace
> and wrap their violence about them like a cloak.
> Their iniquity comes from gross minds,
> and their hearts overflow with wicked thoughts.
> They scoff and speak maliciously;
> out of their haughtiness they plan oppression.
> They set their mouths against the heavens,
> and their evil speech runs through the world.

It's not hard to find such ugly realities in any single Sunday paper. Sometimes discussed matter-of-factly, sometimes glossed over, and all too often detailed with admiration. Of course media literally empower "evil speech" to run "through the world."

The psalmist, a true believer, despairs at what he sees because of its evangelistic implications. People observe the prosperity of the wicked, he tells us, and conclude that God is not aware and does not even know. Then he admits that the problem is not just the spiritual well-being of others. The injustice tempts him too.

> In vain have I kept my heart clean,
> and washed my hands in innocence.

He is enticed to give up, to lose heart and faith. Here I resonate. As I read the newspaper, I want to cry out with psalmists and prophets and the Apocalypse of John: "How long, O Lord, how long?" I recall my friend, a committed Christian peace activist who has lived sacrificially for decades and says regularly with a rueful grin and self-deprecating laugh, "I've lost pretty much every battle and cause I've struggled for over all these years." Like the psalmist, my friend and I can be tempted to despair. In the end, the Sunday paper is measly and meager fare for sustenance and faith.

The low point of the psalm surely is where the author admits his incomprehension, his stupefaction before realities that do not compute.

> When I tried to understand these things,
> it was too hard for me.

But in the very next verse, that is reversed.

> Until I entered the sanctuary of God
> and discerned the end of the wicked.

In worship he recovers his bearings, getting reacquainted with God's truth and ways, God's will and desire. He finds himself and God once more. Worship rouses him from the nightmare.

> Like a dream when one awakens, O Lord,
> when you arise you will make their image vanish.

Suddenly he sees what is true and important. He is freed from desperation and despair.

> When my mind became embittered,
> I was sorely wounded in my heart.
> I was stupid and had no understanding;
> I was like a brute beast in your presence.

All because of worship and prayer. Suddenly he sees and knows his place before God, the God who will not let him go or abandon him.

> Yet I am always with you;
> you hold me by my right hand.
> You will guide me by your counsel
> and afterwards receive me with glory.
> Whom have I in heaven but you?
> and having you I desire nothing upon earth.
> Though my flesh and my heart should waste away,
> God is the strength of my heart and my portion for ever.

This last confession strikes me as particularly astonishing. Even in illness and death, he clings to conviction about God. That sustains and grounds him. He needs nothing more.

I no longer settle for the Sunday paper alone. I do immerse myself in the latest bad news, cynical and pessimistic analyses, and the usual horrors of "all the news that's fit to print." But then I head to church for the tonic of a different perspective, a glimpse of a greater reality.

I prefer to walk to worship, enjoying the fresh air, exerting my body, and taking my time to approach God's sanctuary. Once there, I am reoriented to God and God's reign by singing God's praises in the company of the faithful, hearing Scriptures read and expounded, praying about essential things, being bonded with fellow believers, remembering that we are not alone, honoring "the better part," and giving offerings to God. I am caught up not just in a vision of God's reign but in my experience of it as well. I know it once more. Worship has a way of relativizing and putting into perspective all that I have encountered in the paper that morning, as bad as it may happen to be on that particular day.

It was once popular to quote an aphorism, supposedly penned by Karl Barth, about reading with the Bible in one hand and a newspaper in the other. I've decided to read the Bible a lot more than the newspaper. Possibly even more important is being inspired by God's Spirit through Scripture-saturated worship. There we find our place before God and understand our call in this world. There we are formed to live hopefully and to minister to the aching needs all around us. Again from Psalm 73,

> It is good for me to be near God;
> I have made the Lord God my refuge.
> I will speak of all your works
> in the gates of the city of Zion.

Worship is the central focal practice. It reminds us of what's valuable, what's lasting, what endures.

The Orienting Power of Food

When my daughter was ten, she became a vegetarian. I cannot recall what prompted her decision, but I soon discovered that many of my acquaintances' children were vegetarian as well. When my son was a young adult, he elected first to be vegetarian and then moved a step further to become vegan. He too is part of a growing network.

Food is an essential way for people to express their values, to live by their convictions, to uphold what they consider most vital and important. We see it in the slow food movement, which offers alternatives to fast food and convenience. And we see it in books such as Barbara Kingsolver's *Animal, Vegetable, Miracle* or Michael Pollan's *The Omnivore's Dilemma* and *In Defense of Food*, which celebrate growing and knowing your own food and eating moderately and mindfully. All these emphases remind us that food has centering and orienting capacity. Food points us in the direction of what matters most.

The ability of meals to ground us is powerfully portrayed in the 1987 Danish film *Babette's Feast*. This Academy Award–winning movie recounts a story, written by Isak Dinesen, taking place in the remote Jutland coastal area of Denmark in the late nineteenth century. There a Lutheran minister had established a rigorous Christian sect in a small village. After his death, his two daughters, Martina and Philippa—named after Martin Luther and Luther's good friend Philipp Melanchthon—carry on his work. They gather the dwindling community of the faithful for prayers and Scripture study, and bring food and spiritual comfort to the aged and ailing in their town.

The sisters act in joyful compassion, believing in what they do. But their setting is desolate, the congregation is getting older and growing smaller; to the viewer it is hard to see beyond the sisters' somber, sober existence. Besides, the congregants have mounting regrets about how they have lived, let each other down, and even betrayed one another over the years. Gatherings are often disrupted by quibbling and quarreling, bitter memories and recriminations.

Into this challenging setting arrives a middle-aged Catholic woman, a refugee from France, whose husband and son were killed in upheavals in her native land. A letter of introduction says simply that she "knows how to cook." The sisters take her on for housekeeping and feeding the hungry, even though they cannot afford to pay wages. Babette learns how to make their spartan fare of fish and ale bread. She prepares burbling brown stews that—as viewed in the film—look nothing short of repulsive. She serves faithfully for over fourteen years. She proves a canny housekeeper, and the sisters discover their money stretches further because of Babette's care with the purse.

Martina and Philippa decide to have a special evening to celebrate the hundredth anniversary of their father's birth. They want a modest supper with coffee. But Babette for the first time makes a request of them: she would like to host a French dinner party. In the meantime, she has won a staggering amount of money in a lottery and insists on paying for the meal. The sisters reluctantly acquiesce. Babette orders specialties delivered from France, including a live turtle, a crate of quails, and bottle after bottle of vintage wines and champagnes.

The ascetic sisters worry about the lavish preparations. They convene a secret meeting of the faithful and confess that they have erred. They worry that the food Babette is readying may be evil, perhaps even a witch's offerings. So the disciples all promise to help the sisters. While they will eat out of polite obligation, no one will comment on the quality of the repast. They resolve not to enjoy themselves.

The day arrives. Babette has been busily working in the cottage kitchen, over an open fire, an artisan tending her craft. A village boy assists her. The time and energy they spend remind us that this is a meal with *commanding presence*, the first quality of focal practices.

There will be caviar, cheeses, foie gras, pastries, and fresh fruit—a cornucopia as was never seen before in this remote Scandinavian location. The table is laid with fine linen cloth and napkins, china plates and bowls, crystal goblets and candle stands. Yet as the group gathers, they remind each other that food is not important and that they have lost their sense of taste. They must not be taken in by the temptations of plate or palate.

Twelve people convene, echoing the group that gathered with Jesus at the last meal. One is a visitor to the community, a successful military officer who once lived in Paris and is not aware of the covenant to avoid commenting on the food. He cannot hide his astonishment at the wonders of this great feast or at the equally perplexing fact that no one else seems surprised and appreciative. It reminds him, he says, of a famous Parisian chef that he once knew who was the "greatest culinary genius" in France. He is unaware that she is now in the kitchen. He marvels at what they are served, but the villagers pretend not to understand and offer non sequiturs whenever he compliments the food.

Yet as the meal progresses, all eat with growing satisfaction, even gusto, in spite of their prearranged promise not to enjoy themselves. They drink the wines not just because of thirst but because they obviously appreciate the taste. Lips smack. And people begin to smile. The sisters also gradually relax and are evidently happy.

Gradually, people recount memories. The general speaks of gourmet dining in France. The group recites Scripture passages, recalls sermons and teachings of their founder, and remembers with appreciation his achievements. So the meal connects them to faith, forebears, Paris, youth, and the past. In other words, it evidences *continuity and connectedness*, the second aspect of focal practices.

And healing commences. Old foes confess ancient sins and grievances against one another and forgive each other. Blessings are offered. During the meal, partakers are freed from regrets about past choices and paths. All begin to see and to trust that grace was at work in their history, in spite of hardships and sorrows along the way. There are songs and prayers, tenderness and blessings. They ponder the meaning of their lives, trace God's providence, recommit themselves to each other and their faith. In other words, they enjoy *centering and orienting power*, the final dynamic of focal practices.

Babette stays the whole time in the kitchen, tending to the various courses, and sending in the village boy to wait on guests. She remains anonymous, serving the well-being of the congregation. By the end, the sisters realize that the meal was a gift, not a dangerous compromise, and they thank Babette for her good work. Ever since the lottery they had had some sadness, knowing that Babette would soon leave because of her recently won wealth. But now they are astonished to learn that the entire sum of ten thousand francs was spent on just one meal. They hardly know what to make of such a lavish gesture, an extravagance that leaves Babette impoverished. But Babette has no regrets: "An artist is never poor," she says. Philippa then blesses Babette with a promise: her artistry will be practiced and celebrated in heaven itself.

In this meal, we see, then, all the qualities of focal practices—*commanding presence, connectedness and continuity,* and *centering and orienting power.* These aspects of focal practice pose a strong contrast to the many factors that lead to off-balance and off-kilter lives. They point to richer ways of living.

Testifying to What Gives Life

In Unlearning Consumerism, a spiritual disciplines class, my students were leery when I assigned them to bring in something precious to them. Some wondered whether the assignment was a trap. In a course that sought to undermine consumerism, would they be chastised for showing and telling about something material that had special worth or value to them?

But they diligently followed the assignment. One person brought in Muslim prayer beads. She'd been a development worker for many years in a Muslim country in Africa and cherished this connection with people there and worried about resentments directed against Muslims after September 11. A middle-aged student showed us the precious journal kept by his father in the mid-1940s, just a few years before the student was born. The students' stories were all met with wonder, awe, laughter, joy, and amazement. A few even brought tears to the eyes of the tellers.

As it happened, it was early spring. An organic gardening activist brought her watering can. Two students displayed bright and colorful bouquets from their gardens. We marveled at the beauty of those flowers. We heard stories about their care and harvesting. The bulbs had been received from friends and then had been split and passed on to other people too. One student showed a painting by her husband, a young artist of great talent. She considered this his greatest work, so that alone made it worth admiring. But she also spoke of his hopes to support himself through art and how he had sacrificed years of artistry to earn enough money to pay for her seminary education.

All these students responded eloquently to a simple homework assignment. Without ever hearing Borgmann's theories, they produced and testified about focal objects.

When I interviewed Ruth Mallory, she was in her early eighties and had been birding for a couple decades. Birding changed and reoriented her: "It's been a door that's led me into discovering who I really am and discovering who God is and discovering my true spiritual home. It's only been in my senior years that I've come to know what really gives me joy, what my passions are, and what worship is meaningful to me." Birding, she said, helped her "to feel okay about who I am."

Marie Troyer is the cheery secretary of a church where we once were members. One of her passions is quilting. Her sister teases that Marie and fellow quilters are part of a cult. What the sister correctly perceives is that quilting has clarifying, centering, and orienting power. Marie told me that quilting helps her to focus, to quiet down, to put things in perspective, to deal with challenges, and even to help her move beyond depression. It brings peace and is its own reward. "It even," she said, "gives my life purpose." She never thought that she'd be able to talk in front of a group, but when the church asked her to speak about quilting, she was articulate and confident. Not a traveler, she nevertheless went on a mission trip to Mongolia to share quilting with women there and returned to speak publicly about her experiences.

My friend Nancy is a creative pastor of an unusual congregation, a country church in an isolated midwestern hamlet. A number of the parishioners are old-timers, having attended the church for decades. They are the usual array of people you might expect in a rural setting: farmers, merchants, factory workers. Another portion of her congregation fled to this setting, almost as refugees from big cities and stressed-out lifestyles. They chose to live off the land or by the work of their hands or by using other skills.

One year during the Easter season, Nancy asked various members to talk briefly during the sermon time about "whatever gives you life." Richard came in overalls and rubber boots and spoke about the joy that he finds in farming and how he hears God through the growth of crops and the well-being of animals. Kathy, who loves poetry, read an evocative piece that she wrote about the annual return of sandhill cranes. Willard brought freshly cut wood and gave a sermon "without words." In silence, he built a footstool, then seated a member of the congregation on the stool and washed his feet. Nancy reports: "This is still the most remembered sermon in the last five years. We use the footstool weekly in worship."

The voices of these testifiers were passionately intense. Not only did their practices give them life, but also in some ways the parishioners felt born to participate in and talk about the activities they loved; such commitments helped them feel whole and balanced, centered and deeply happy. The entire congregation listened quietly and attentively. No one fell asleep. Although not everyone was a farmer or birder or carpenter, congregants recognized significance in what was shared.

When Nancy told me about this series, I responded with delight: "Why, they are all talking about focal practices!"

These presentations were, in a sense, what Christians once called "testimonies," even though the presenters did not use explicitly religious terminology. They eloquently demonstrated the centering and orienting power found in important and significant activities. They were not just talking about hobbies and diversions. They were naming experiences that they could not imagine living without. They are fortunate to have made these discoveries.

But, here's the thing—how many people do you and I know who could offer such testimonies? We have, Albert Borgmann says, "left behind and lost forever, it seems sometimes, the world that once was 'charged with the grandeur of God.'"[11] How much of your life or mine is centered on focal priorities? What is it about our lives today that makes living with a clear sense of direction particularly difficult?

Part 2

LOSING OUR FOCUS

5

GOING ON THE ALERT

I spend far too much time in airports.

I expected a recent trip to be straightforward. I needed to take three flights and knew that I would travel for the better part of a day. I brought along ample reading and work to keep meaningfully occupied and to avert fretting while underway. I arrived in plenty of time at the first airport and was optimistic about what was ahead. Silly me.

Bad weather delayed not only my own flight but also several before and after it. The gate area gradually filled with people, and their rising anxiety was palpable. There were not enough chairs in the room; many sat on the floor or hovered over those who were seated. Knowledge that in two days it would be Thanksgiving, making this the year's busiest flying week, increased the tension. While it was only noon, passengers were already being recruited to stay the night.

My flight did eventually leave, but it touched down two hours late, just in time for me to miss my connection on another airline in a neighboring terminal. I could see my jet on the runway, but that did me little good. Although I bought all my tickets from one airline, I was booked on jets from two different companies. Now I was in limbo, or, perhaps more accurately, purgatory; neither airline was willing to be responsible for me.

I stood in line for thirty minutes at the airline in charge of my second flight. They referred me to the first airline with the hope I could catch an alternative. So I waited at one of that airline's gates. The staff there insisted that I needed to leave the secure area and go to a ticket counter in another terminal. Doing so, I saw that the wait was over an hour long. Ticketing agents informed me that I could stay overnight—at my own expense—or try flying with the first airline, but I would have to line up elsewhere. Confused? So was I. I proceeded to still another terminal. While attendants there helped me quickly, I stood at the counter for forty-five minutes as they argued with the other airline about who should pay for my new ticket. (They also tried unsuccessfully to locate my baggage.) They finally gave me a ticket twenty-five minutes before a flight was to leave from a fourth terminal.

I ran as fast as I could. No doubt my haste and perspiration made me look suspicious. At security I was pulled aside for extra scrutiny. When I pointed out how late I was, they matter-of-factly said that I could just catch a flight the next day. They scrutinized my books and, happily, concluded that it was okay for me to read mystery novels. Once through, I ran again. I managed to catch my flight, which boarded late, and we then waited on the runway for two hours. By the time we arrived at the next airport, it was midnight. So I missed my final flight home and remained overnight in a pricey hotel nearby—at my own expense, of course.

That was the second time in a row that flying had gone awry for me. My experience highlighted how airports resemble our lives. I spend considerable time running, scurrying, and hasting to no apparent end. I do not spare enough time to carefully discern or set priorities or align actions with my values. I hardly know whom to ask to help me figure things out. In much of my day-to-day experience, I feel isolated and alone, cut off from the people and places and priorities that I most esteem.

I used to marvel at the extensive cell phone use in airports. Now I understand. People would rather be somewhere else. Most calls that I inadvertently overhear are not profound: "I've just arrived at the airport"; "My plane is late"; "I should get there in so many hours." Airports are not places to be, attend, or dwell. They are only a means to an end. And so passengers long for contact and turn to mobile devices hoping to find it.

Becoming ALERT

Today, many challenges and a good deal of our uneasiness have to do with how we relate to and rely on rapidly evolving technology. But what is technology? Edward Tenner matter-of-factly describes *technology* as "modification of the natural world."[1]

You and I use technology every day. Even when I try to "get back to the basics" and head to the wilderness, I am immersed in it. Gear and clothes—often surprisingly fancy and expensive—are crucial. I carry insect repellant, sun screen, ibuprofen, and binoculars to enhance both my journey and my comfort. I have a life jacket for safety, a Gore-Tex hat for shade from sun and protection from rain and to retain body heat in the cold, and a nifty water bottle to prevent dehydration. Canoes too are amazingly sophisticated and technological, both in their design and in the materials used in their construction. I like Kevlar canoes, not because I am fascinated with high-tech material, but because they are light and easier to carry on demanding portages. In the wilderness, we are more aware of how vulnerable we are and how crucial proper equipment is for both comfort and safety. Without exaggeration, the right technology can make the difference between life and death.

Make no mistake: we need technology. There is no human culture or civilization without it. Cooking, growing food, clothing, and playing music all involve technology.

Sometimes our understanding of specific forms of technology evolves. Trains adversely affected natives and natural regions out West in the United States and Canada. But now many locals are train aficionados. Alain de Botton reminds us that though windmills were once loathed (condemned for theological and aesthetic reasons), they eventually became a cherished part of Dutch heritage—not just on postcards but even celebrated in great works of art, especially Golden Age painters.[2]

Nevertheless, the impact of technology on our lives warrants careful consideration. It is easy to find ourselves in the predicament Martin Luther King Jr. long ago described: "We have allowed our technology to outrun our theology."[3] We're not so good at carefully weighing the price of technological progress.

The issue is not technology itself but the reality that we often do not reflect on how we are affected and formed by our use of it. I am not opposed to technology. No one is. Not even the much-maligned, so-called Luddites, nor the romanticized but misunderstood and occasionally mocked Amish. All of us can name many benefits brought to us by technology. Several of my own family members have been seriously ill, and medical know-how and amazing machinery both relieved their pain and prolonged their lives. So, yes, there's much to celebrate in technological advancement.

However, we should learn to see the full impact of the ways we use technology. Some technological solutions may make problems worse. Communication devices were supposed to bring us closer to family by allowing us to work at home; instead, they often detract from time and attention for spouses and children. Computers and cybercommunication were going to help us become paperless, but we consume growing quantities of paper. Machines grow quieter, but we use more of them and so add to the noise. Devices are increasingly energy efficient, but we employ so many that we end up using more power than ever. While computers and online connections get faster, the time we spend on them keeps going up. The better we are at responding to email, the more we are inundated by it. While it gets easier to assemble meals and food becomes convenient, our society shows greater problems with obesity. People feel safer because of cell phones, but then, without much wilderness savvy and bolstered by an optimistic sense of the connectedness afforded them by their cell phones, they end up taking needless risks.

One problem inherent to a discussion of the dangers of technology is that we make issues too big and distant. You and I will probably never be faced with the choice of whether or not to use nuclear weapons. Occasionally people we know deal with once-in-a-lifetime quandaries about how much medical intervention to approve for loved ones or even whether or not to withdraw life support. We have concerns about technology that include surveillance, consumerism, identity theft, and increasing amounts of dangerous waste and pollution, among other ecological problems. The geographer Jared Diamond details looming environmental issues: destruction of natural habitats, loss of wild foods and wild species, erosion of farmlands, diminishing access to major nonrenewable energy sources, freshwater depletion, toxic chemicals, invasive alien species, atmospheric gases, population growth, and growing human impact on the environment.[4] Author Ronald Wright observes, as he reflects on previous "crashed civilizations," that "our present behavior is typical of failed societies at the zenith of their greed and arrogance."[5]

Still, there are also closer-to-home, deeper, more mundane—possibly less-obvious—issues at stake. Technology affects not only decisions about how to start lives or end them, but it is also intertwined with all aspects of our lives. How we deal with it affects our character as individuals, communities where we live, relationships both close and distant, and the quality of our lives. It often drives decision making in automatic and unconscious ways. We may use devices without considering the consequences of new possibilities or how they relate to our values. Most of our decisions about technology take place in a personal sphere.

Too often our interactions with technology follow a predictable trajectory: because it is available we use it, then we think it is normal, and finally we expect or even demand that others employ it as well. At one school where I taught, teaching faculty were alerted that they would have a new online course management system. The professors were not consulted, just informed. The teachers liked the previous system that they had only recently learned. Not only did the previous system work well, but it was also free. The new system was unwieldy for teaching purposes, but other departments had purchased it for database management. Those departments, however, were not directly connected to teaching. Now everyone in the institution was obliged to use it. A possibility became an expected norm, even when the norm did not make pedagogical sense.

Using cell phones—even hands-free models—impairs driving much as alcohol does. It makes collisions more likely (annually causing as many as 2,600 traffic deaths in the US, not to mention 300,000 accidents). Yet people continue to drive and talk on phones. Many phone companies resisted legislation to restrict talking on mobile phones while driving.[6] In the past Christians supported temperance movements, but I am not aware of any Christian group that campaigns against talking on the phone while driving. I do not hear the topic addressed in church. (The only cell phone behavior we question is usage during worship.) Yet it's not unusual to see congregants on phones while driving into or away from the church parking lot. What are we to make of such behavior?

Are we deliberately choosing the ways that we want to live, or are we just carried along with the bad habits of wider society?

A grandfather told me about the toddler granddaughter his wife cares for a few days a week. When their grandchild visits, the granddad loves going home for lunch. He arrives at the door and the little girl runs with great eagerness to see one of her favorite people. But one day when he came home with anticipation, his granddaughter was nowhere to be seen. She was watching a children's video. He went into the TV room to find her, but she was so captivated by the screen that she did not even acknowledge him.

Walking home from work, I saw something that at first impressed me. It was late in the afternoon, early in the summer, and the sun shone warmly on my back as I headed east across a broad field of Indiana prairie grasses toward a busy road. A few cars and SUVs sped by, briskly moving north and south. Approaching from off to my right, I saw a thirtyish man pedaling his bicycle. He had a racer's hunched-over posture and his legs were pumping steadily. He was—very sensibly—wearing a helmet. Since I lived in an area where not many people walked or bicycled (and where one could not even find sidewalks let alone bike paths), I looked with appreciation at someone engaging in this self-propelled, environmentally friendly means of travel. He was pulling one of those fancy trailers that carry children. As I stood at the side of the road waiting to cross, the bicyclist passed me. I could see a toddler sitting in the back, appearing content. He too was wearing a state-of-the-art helmet.

I did a double take and wondered why the father rode one handed. This seemed careless, given that he was not only on a bike but also pulling a load—a valuable and vulnerable one at that. I saw that his other hand was curled up to his ear; he was talking on a cell phone. All this on a busy road with no shoulders and thus no room for errors.

It is hard to compute how many things are wrong with this picture. While this father invested in expensive technological gear—state-of-the-art bicycle, streamlined trailer, protective helmets—he was riding single-handed, an iffy proposition at the best of times. Worse than that, he was holding a gadget with the other hand, and could not easily grab the handlebar should he need to. By conversing on his phone, he was distracting himself from the wobbling bike, road conditions, rate of traffic, and communication from his little son or other vehicles on the road. On the one hand, he looked safety conscious. He had purchased useful protective gear. On the other hand, he was indulging in risky and dangerous behavior that could quickly and irrevocably affect him, his son, and passing drivers.

I often see a small child walking hand in hand with a parent whose other hand holds a phone—ignoring the child. Many worry about how technology use affects children and adolescents, but "parents' use of such technology—and its effect on their offspring—is now becoming an equal source of concern to some child-development researchers."[7]

Given such examples, let us set big technological dilemmas aside. While important, they can also be red herrings. Many of us overlook that simple day-to-day choices—about cars, microwaves, cell phones, email, internet, television, dishwashers, communication options—have great and detrimental impact on our quality of life. If we do not pay attention to these effects, then chances are that devices will shape us in ways that we would not consciously choose.

How do we begin to get a handle on what ought to concern us?

Six aspects of how technology affects us need vigilance. Whether we're talking about relatively old-fashioned twentieth-century cars, televisions, or radios, or whether we pay attention to more recent devices (and who can predict what's next?), these areas need special, constant, and devoted care. They warrant discernment. The realms of concern in our technologically dominated lives today are as follows:

- ATTENTION: What is the primary and ongoing focus of our awareness? Screens and virtual relationships? Family and neighbors? Voyeuristic television "reality shows"? Nature and our surrounding environment? Is our capacity to pay attention, dwell, and be aware diminishing? Are we so overwhelmed with information and stimulation that our ability to respond is affected? Are we moving from receptivity to expecting to control what we perceive?

- LIMITS: What guides our sense of what is appropriate? Do we have the moral strength to recognize when something is beyond the pale and that we need to say no? Or does technology, which makes more and more things possible, including voyeurism, pornography, and gambling, also make all things permissible? Which taboos are worth guarding? How does technology free us from moral constraints and accountability? What is the relationship of technology to addictions? How does technology reinforce addictions? How is technology itself addictive?

- ENGAGEMENT: How are we coping with life and its challenges? Do we approach our day and those we love with calm anticipation, eager to be and work together? Or do such rushed and harried attention spans lead us into being demanding and curt? How does technology speed encounters, making conflicts and misunderstandings more likely? Does planned and perceived obsolescence contribute to eroding commitments?

- RELATIONSHIPS: Do our lives include rich networks of loved ones, supportive friends, caring confidants, and casual acquaintances? Are there people who know us in our fullness, care about our hardships, and challenge us to grow in virtue? Or are our lives characterized by growing isolation and loneliness, our relationships dispersed and fragmented? What are the implications of having relationships increasingly mediated by technology while opportunities for face-to-face conversations decline and in-the-flesh friendships decrease? How does technology reinforce casual approaches to relationships, ones that are easy to enter or exit but do not necessarily sustain? What kinds of communities are created by our technology use?

- TIME: Do we have a sense that there is enough room in our lifestyles for the things that truly matter—work and play, rigor and rest, love and laughter? Or are we too busy to live according to our deepest and highest priorities? Do distracting demands and pressures lure us away from our highest values? How does engagement with technology make us busier? And how does technology erode and displace opportunities to pause and determine, reflect on, and honor ultimate priorities?

- SPACE: How well connected are we with the geography and places where we are located? Are we rooted in neighborhoods, connected to the earth and our environment? Or is much of our life lived abstractly in "virtual" reality?

This is no arbitrary list. These were relevant concerns earlier last century when people encountered cars and radio and television for the first time. In fact, these were the kinds of questions that various "Old Order" religious groups (Mennonites, Amish, Brethren, Quakers) asked. I have heard people mock Old Order resistance to "progress," but those groups correctly and perceptively anticipated many looming issues and problems. Such questions are just as relevant today as technologies multiply and rapidly grow more complex. Everywhere I go—previously as a pastor, now as a teacher, writer, and speaker—I hear from folks struggling with these issues. People face dilemmas but are not quite sure how to work with them. They look for direction but do not have a sense of where to go. We have not figured out how to think and talk about such matters.

People of faith have always asked these types of questions and raised these kinds of issues: Where do you look with your eyes, listen with your ears, focus with your minds and imaginations? When do you say yes and when do you say no? How do you relate to others—people, objects, nature, God—in a way that trusts that things move at their appropriate pace? How do you love others, God, nature, and yourself? Where do you invest yourself and your time?

These areas of concern are not completely and neatly separate. They affect and interact with each other. Where I pay ATTENTION influences where I look (LIMITS), whether I am enamored of those who are speedy or appreciate that important matters might go slowly (ENGAGEMENT), how much I prioritize friendships (RELATIONSHIPS), when I choose to listen, pray, or be silent (TIME), and how I relate to physical surroundings and location (SPACE). Each of the six realms is related in many ways to all the others. They are intertwined.

You may have noticed that the areas—ATTENTION, LIMITS, ENGAGEMENT, RELATIONSHIPS, TIME, SPACE—form an acronym: ALERTS. I am the first to admit that this might feel forced or corny, even gimmicky. Still, this is a helpful way to frame our thinking about the issues at hand. This list of six covers key concerns about how we relate to technology on a daily basis.

Code Orange

"ALERTS" terminology has downsides, to be sure. It can convey a sense of peril and panic. Used that way it can undermine ATTENTION (we pessimistically and unrealistically focus on dangers), LIMITS (if we worry about matters that may never happen or are not our concern), ENGAGEMENT (we foster a sense of anxious unease), RELATIONSHIPS (we look at others suspiciously or cling to them insecurely), TIME (we are unable to relax and allow new and imaginative possibilities to unfold), and SPACE (we begin to mistrust all places as potentially hostile and retreat to the supposed safety, security, and predictability of virtual reality instead).

Ever since September 11, Americans have been steadily counseled to be on alert. Each time I go to the airport, I hear announcements from the Bureau of Homeland Security, warning that the "Current Threat Level" is Orange or "High Risk of Attack." It has been at that same level for years. There is only one higher category of risk.

There are two problems with a state of constant alertness. The first is that it facilitates less-measured responses, such as the rush into Afghanistan within a month of September 11 that led to a war that may well be irresolvable (in spite of expensive and impressive military technology). Amazingly, the war effort has taken longer than World War II. The invasion of Iraq also proved costly, and its benefits are likewise unclear.

The other problem is that if one always needs to be on alert, is constantly attending to a high "Orange" attack risk, after a time one no longer heeds warnings at all. It's the familiar story about crying wolf too often. Airports constantly broadcast the same Current Threat Level, and so we no longer listen or take them seriously.

Code Orange is not a call for discernment. If the airport risk changed to a lesser threat than orange, no doubt security requirements would not be altered. Will there ever be a time when it is okay to accept packages from strangers, leave bags unattended, or keep one's shoes and belt on through security checks? What do such standards and their counsel really mean?

Seeing Yellow

Yet alertness is a key stance in daily life. We teach our children to be watchful ("Look both ways before crossing the street"), and that skill is useful throughout their lives. Watchfulness is also a significant posture in Christian understandings of how to live and pray. Think especially of Bible texts and themes associated with Advent.

When I first learned to drive, I was taught that defensive driving was one of the most important skills to acquire. Defensive driving means paying careful attention to conditions around you and being observant of the behaviors of others nearby (pedestrians, drivers, bicyclists).

Learning to drive is a good example of watchfulness in another way. Driving is a realm where we encounter a familiar technology that invites alertness and discernment. As children, we learned about traffic lights. We knew how to color the three signals—red, yellow, and green—and what they meant. Red and green are the clearest. They unambiguously tell us that we must stop or we may go. If we get them wrong, other drivers—with horns and hands, voices and fingers—remind us of our duties and obligations. Or if our incorrect actions are observed by police officers, we risk fines.

The most intriguing signal, however, is the yellow light. It means "pay attention," "be alert." Unlike other signals, the yellow light always calls for judgment. Do I stop or proceed? (Except in Chicago, where it was a goad to speed up and go for it.) Sensible drivers see a yellow light and need to make a decision. Is this light leaving me lots of time to get through the intersection, or is it about to turn red immediately, cueing cars to begin crossing from my left and right? Are the roads dry enough that I can brake safely, or will an abrupt change of speed send me skidding on the rain, slush, or ice? Are cars behind me going too quickly to stop if I bring mine to a halt? Sometimes we make bad decisions about yellow lights—for example, when we rush them just because other people are doing so or purely on the basis of hurry.

A yellow light is always a call to pay attention, be alert, make a choice. There is no simple rule for how one ought to behave. It is not always appropriate to stop when the traffic signal goes amber, nor is it always appropriate to keep going. It depends on a number of factors beyond our control, unpredictable, ever shifting, and changing. It's a surprisingly complicated exercise, with no clear right or wrong.

Dealing with technology is like paying attention to yellow lights. I know people who for good reason refuse to drive and others who in good conscience have several motorized vehicles. I manage to live without a cell phone and consider this a wise choice for myself, but my wife uses one with good purpose. Some believers that I admire have never owned a television—or got rid of one after years of watching it—but

others make wise use of their televisions. There are no clear dos and
don'ts here, no absolute rights and wrongs. TV or not TV is not, as it
happens, the question.

But just because there are different good choices does not mean that
these choices are unimportant or that all options are equal. I once mis-
calculated a left-hand turn during a yellow light and not only was my
car totaled, but I was fined and earned demerits on my license as well.
The stakes can be high.

Thus this book makes a case for giving special consideration to matters of ATTENTION and awareness, LIMITS and taboos, ENGAGEMENT
and patience, RELATIONSHIPS and community, TIME and the pace of
life, and SPACE and how we honor place, whenever we are faced with
discernment about technology.

Jesus once commended his followers to be clever as serpents and
innocent as doves. We require both attributes when we think about
technology. At times our unexpected queries may sound overly critical,
but asking questions can help us to discover how to live well in and
amid technology. There truly are serious issues at stake, with perhaps
more dangerous implications than many of us realize; yet there are also
ways of understanding and interpreting these issues that can help us
cultivate good lives amid the complexity. We have options and agency
to live differently, even to live focally. We have more control than we
realize.

6

ATTENUATED ATTENTION AND SYSTEMIC DISTRACTION

One happy childhood memory is when my father brought home a new TV. Not just any television, mind you, but our first color set. TVs were different then, and not only because color was relatively new. The console my parents bought was typical: a big, solid unit. It had four sturdy legs and was encased in a substantial wooden cabinet. It was too big and unwieldy to move by oneself. There were no remote controls either. One chose an episode and stuck with it through all the commercials, usually only getting up to change the station when a program was over. Not that it mattered much; we had only a few channels to choose from anyway. Most television watchers now would not have much use for the unit that my parents splurged on four decades ago.

The much-anticipated set arrived on a Friday afternoon. We quickly hooked it up to the antenna. That evening we watched it for hours. My father was there, even though he normally worked six long days a week. My mother was present, though she was a conscientious housekeeper who usually had a lengthy list of pressing but unfinished tasks. My little sister—always the most relaxed family member—certainly joined us. And I was there. I undoubtedly had a stack of homework to do, but I also have always been the family member most prone to television addiction.

My sister and I watched Saturday morning cartoons. All four of us stayed put Saturday afternoon and evening as well. Our family was highly committed to weekly church attendance, but I vaguely recollect that we opted for Sunday morning television viewing instead that week. We had no company and went nowhere Sunday afternoon because we all wanted to savor the new set. That weekend we ate in front of the television, even though we were normally devoted to sitting down together for meals that began and ended with prayer.

We were, in short, mesmerized by this machine and in the following years spent many hours in front of it. The TV was located strategically in the northeast corner of our living room, with the couch and comfortable chairs positioned for easy observance.

Mostly, I hardly remember what we watched. Yet one Sunday evening show attracted our devotion, *Mutual of Omaha's Wild Kingdom*, a

THE BLESSINGS OF TECHNOLOGY

nature program. With it we traveled around the world to observe and learn about exotic animals. In conversations that our family had with other families about our color television, we always said the same thing: "We especially like nature shows." We argued that this was grounds enough to justify the expenditure. What we learned about animals and saw in scenery made our color television worthwhile. TV was helping us love and appreciate the outdoors.

Now I am not so sure. Those documentaries taught me that truly exotic wildlife and beauty is elsewhere, far away. I picked up that it is too hard to get there myself. I saw that it is easier to let someone else do the work so I could watch it on television. I may even have learned that nature is not worthwhile unless it is portrayed on TV.

As I've recounted, when I was in my midforties, I began hiking the Bruce Trail. My first hike was enormously rewarding and the scenery breathtaking. While the day was cold—it was late October—the Niagara River sparkled in the sunlight. Large, old trees towered overhead. I marveled at gargantuan limestone boulders that threatened to break off and plummet down high cliffs. I was awed by lovely glades.

What struck me most about the beauty of these vistas was that they were within a mile or two of where I lived my teenage years. They were there all along, but I had never seen them; my movements outdoors back then were confined to an automobile. My views of nature were through screens: outside it was the car's windshield, inside a television. Ironically, I spent hours captivated by glittering color-TV nature images but did not walk a mile or two to engage the bountiful beauty in our own backyard. There was definitely something wrong with this picture. It just took me a few decades to figure that out.

Screening Our Attention

One of the most significant challenges of contemporary technology is how it shapes our awareness, where it attracts our attention, and the ways that it sometimes—perhaps even often—draws us away from the things we value most.

Driving in vehicles means seeing everything through a screen, a windshield. One is not aware of outside weather or temperature. We can even heat seats. One does not smell the scents of the air, fields, and flowers while driving. Everything rushes past as fast as if we were watching it on television or the world wide web.

How many "screens" come between us and reality? How does reliance on technology obscure or distort imagination and perspectives, awareness and mindfulness?

A primary purpose of screens, of course, is to separate us—the literal meaning of *screen*. Windshields shield us from elements of wind and rain, snow and sleet. They may be tinted to protect us from sun. They also grant an illusion of being isolated from surroundings, making it psychologically easier to pitch trash out the window or act rudely toward pedestrians or even shave or apply makeup while driving. TV and computer screens teach us how to be a disconnected audience. Like my father, who used to curse people he saw on televised news, we can talk back at the images without consequence.

One way to think about where we pay attention is to remember an old theological word. "Idolatry" is a problem of directing reverence and regard in the wrong direction. Similarly, the monastic practice of "custody of the eyes" reminds us to use caution in where and how we look. It requires us to be careful with our gaze: not staring at people, not being distracted by every noise or intrusion, leaving others to their privacy, and of course focusing on matters that are appropriate, edifying, and inspirational. We easily spend too long looking the wrong way at the wrong things, much to our own detriment. The psalmist writes scathingly about idols that "have mouths, but do not speak; eyes, but do not see: and ears, but do not hear; noses, but do not smell . . . hands, but do not feel; feet, but do not walk." And then he observes that idolaters are like their idols, and "so are all who trust in them" (Ps. 115:5–8). What we gaze upon forms who we become.

Our lives are shaped by our focus. The direction of our attention not only shows values, but it also forms character. Simone Weil made much of the importance and potential of loving awareness. It was during her leisurely recitation of a seventeenth-century poem that she suddenly and unexpectedly had the experience of being possessed by Christ. From then on, Weil was a mystic. Her daily discipline included reciting the Lord's Prayer with complete concentration; this often led to further mystical experiences.[1]

As we consider technology and how it affects awareness, there are three areas of concern. First, it often decreases capacity to pay attention, to dwell. Second, the quantity of information and stimulation it delivers can overwhelm and thus interfere with our ability to respond. And, third, it teaches us to expect to be in control of what we think is worth noticing or heeding.

Television and Systemic Distraction

Technology may first of all decrease ability to slow down, pay attention, pray, or contemplate.

Television, for example, draws our awareness via glittering images that are easy to access and that addictively hold our gaze by altering rapidly. The camera fades in and out, swiftly shifts scenes, closes in on a character and then the character's face, and may then move to another part of the world entirely. Television's way of depicting stories is much different from watching a live play, an activity that invites us to focus deliberately. Jerry Mander calls television's shifts in perspective "technical events." They alter "natural imagery" and are "intended to keep your attention from waning as it might otherwise. The effect is to lure your attention forward like a mechanical rabbit teasing a greyhound."[2] Technology grows increasingly sophisticated, and TV producers now work harder at providing startling and dramatic perspective shifts. Television programs, commercials, and films are all speeding up. Research shows "that virtually everyone in the television industry ardently believes that the audience attention span is growing shorter, and that to hold the audience, . . . editing must be even faster paced and present more and more exciting visual material."[3] As communication and digital technologies develop and complexify, they employ increasingly hyper ways of attracting and holding our gaze.

It is growing common for television channels to broadcast ads for other shows during programs, embed brand-name goods within scenes, or float teasers across the bottom of the screen. Some cable stations simultaneously show news-film clips, headlines about other news, weather, time, stock market reports, and camera views of traffic. Viewers heighten the intensity by channel surfing and multitasking.

This all contributes to what some call "continuous partial attention." (We'll give more consideration to this in a later chapter when we look at multitasking.) Our focus shifts from one item to another, never settling anywhere too long. I dare not count up how often I start surfing the internet and come to myself later wondering where the minutes, if not hours, have gone. Not for nothing does one friend speak scathingly of the "world wide waste of time."

A key human capacity, one that has always been understood as crucial to spiritual life—the ability to pay attention—is being attenuated. The effect can be to make our awareness lazy. We are susceptible to distraction and bore easily—"Been there, done that." Conversation partners—even family members—might not be as clever as scripted sitcoms or talk show comedians. Life does not move as quickly as YouTube videos. And the natural world is not as accessible as the documentaries about it.

There are spiritual stakes here. William McNamara vividly described contemplation as "long, leisurely, loving looks at the real."[4] Weil wrote: "Prayer consists of attention. It is the orientation of all the attention of which the soul is capable toward God."[5] Robert Farrar Capon says that a human's "real work is to look at the things of the world and to love them for what they are."[6] We are risking the quality and rich potential of spiritual life.

The priority of careful observation is contradicted by our "systemic distraction" culture.[7] We live in an age of technologically induced and reinforced attention deficit disorder. Maggie Jackson bluntly writes, "We are on the verge of losing our capacity as a society for deep, sustained focus."[8] It is sobering to be reminded by Mihaly Csikszentmihalyi and Eugene Rochberg-Halton that most psychological pathologies "are characterized by 'disorders of attention'" and then to consider how our attention may be misdirected and malformed by technology.[9]

One year, I visited different churches each week, ones within walking distance of my home. Many—no matter the denomination or tradition—used PowerPoint, overhead screens, and loud, amplified music bands. The most sophisticated churches projected nonstop videos, often of nature scenes. Many showed announcements while taking offerings; these resembled commercial ads. I had plenty of questions about what I saw: Were these media consistent with the proclaimed Word? How do such formats shape believers? Was the use of technology in keeping with worship traditions? How were appropriate technologies discerned and chosen?

I found it discouraging and dispiriting when I discovered this in church after church. Yet as I kept visiting, I also added more sympathetic ponderings. Maybe this is now the only way to reach out, connect, attract attention. Perhaps many people are now incapable of contemplative, slow-moving worship. I am unsure. And I am also deeply uneasy.

Making L.I.A.R.S. Out of Us

Many of us feel overwhelmed by information, data, and images—all of which leave us stressed, tired, and anxious. We have a hard time knowing what is true or trivial, vacuous or vital, essential or ephemeral. And we are often debilitated by what we learn, unable to take it all in, let alone act on it or respond meaningfully.

Growing numbers of commentators note our current *information overload*. Our sources of data expand exponentially. We are bombarded with facts, ideas, and demands from email, faxes, pagers, cell phones, blogs, and tweets. Michael Posner writes:

> Information via the Internet doubles every three months. More information has been produced in the past 30 years than in the previous 5,000. The Sunday *New York Times* contains more information than the average 18th century [artisan] acquired in a lifetime. We are adrift, trying to stay afloat in an endless ocean of constantly repeated facts, news, data, numbers, statistics, reports and surveys.[10]

Tom Vanderbilt notes that the more info one is faced with, the less respect and attention one gives.[11] Walter Kirn claims that "researchers estimate that the average city dweller is exposed to 5,000 ads per day, up from 2,000 per day three decades ago."[12] We are inundated. It becomes hard to know what is important, what is a priority, what is crucial. As we add distracting technologies into our lives, the flood grows. The truth, as Csikszentmihalyi and Rochberg-Halton remind us, is that we all have limits to our ability to pay attention; it is a "finite resource. At any given moment we are incapable of focusing on more than a few bits of information at a time."[13]

While we may feel better informed, there are consequences. Information overload affects us, our communities, and our society. We cannot take in everything that comes our way, and this adversely influences decision making. Messages arrive faster than we are able to process, and this increases the difficulty we have for discerning choices.

Ruth Conway notes that the "flood of information" often leaves us apathetic and distanced from issues and struggles in our own lives and backyards/communities.[14] Even when one feels emotion, there is often no active way to respond. "Newsworthy" events may be so far away that we assume we cannot do anything about them. Marva Dawn, relying on Neil Postman's work, speaks of "L.I.A.R.," which stands for "Low Information-Action Ratio." Because we as media consumers receive news of problems we can do little about, we become calloused or debilitated by everything that we hear and know.[15]

We are unsure what is true or trustworthy. Photos and films, voices and music are easily manipulated, managed, altered. Aware that some information is unreliable, we may become suspicious or dismissive of everything we hear or encounter. We no longer know whom or what to believe or—let's face it—where to give our attention. Perhaps that's our preference. An ad for Samsung says: "Reality. What a letdown. Announcing the stunning Samsung DLP TV."

There is yet another aspect to our ensuing lack of initiative and action. I have noticed when working with social justice groups, for example, that there is often a preoccupation with whether or not we get media coverage. Efforts are primarily judged as worthwhile if the newspaper, radio, or television showed up and announced it.

I'm in Charge Here. Not.

Finally, many technologies of the last hundred years—whether cars that drive us wherever we might choose, remote controls for televisions or sound systems or PowerPoint programs, multiwindow options on computers, or search engines for the web—give us a sense of the ability and right to control what we take in and see. We assume that if something does not keep our attention or amuse or please us, we can just go ahead and change "channels."

Professor David Ehrenfeld tells an illuminating story about teaching:

We have rearranged tables and chairs in a semicircle . . . to . . . allow all twenty-five students to see and hear each other and me. Class is in session; I am talking. Two students sitting together . . . —a thirty-year-old man with a pager on his belt and a twenty-year-old woman—are speaking to each other and laughing quietly; they see that I am looking at them, and they continue to laugh, not furtively or offensively but openly and engagingly, as if I weren't there.

What is going on, he wonders?

Is there chalk on my face? Is my fly open? Have I repeated myself or unconsciously misused a word or inverted a phrase?

He concludes that there is a new "passive and casual rudeness" in our culture. "When my students were laughing, it didn't occur to them that I would be bothered—at that moment they were treating me as if I were a talking head on television."[16]

When I teach, numerous students have their laptops open. They tell me that they may be checking email, surfing the web, texting, shopping, or even playing games. Some students neglect to mute sound effects when their computers run. Concert halls—and sometimes churches—regularly instruct people to turn off electronic communication devices, but teachers do not necessarily have that much authority.

The problem is not merely that students' behavior shows the distractibility of people in possession of such devices. Nor is it the fact that their behavior distracts others (by the clicking of their keyboard, for example). The issue also involves intrinsic incivility. Those students do not mean to be rude; they are just oblivious. They do not understand that their behavior may be questionable. Accustomed to being in control of when they watch or listen—to television, iPods, podcasts—they are no longer aware that interacting with others nearby might have different demands and expectations. Now when you teach or speak, perform or preach, you must try to hold the attention of folks who are used to being dazzled by technical wizardry or they will be bored or dismissive and just start looking elsewhere. They can easily turn their gaze to readily accessible gadgets in their hands or pockets, on the tables or walls.

Ehrenfeld's students treated their class like one more technological entertainment occasion. Any teacher or speaker knows that the audience also needs to "perform," but the students exercised no responsibility for how well the class proceeded. Their behavior showed a lack of regard and empathy for fellow students and their professor.

Abundant desktop windows, gadgets, and remote controls train us to think that we always deserve to be in charge. We grow casual about being distracted and are encouraged to divide our attention. Been there, done that, so let's move on and look elsewhere. Many devices are celebrated for giving options for communicating, but they also enable us to ignore those we prefer not to deal with: leaving messages when we know no one is home, screening phone calls, ignoring emails, unceremoniously "unfriending" people on Facebook.

We have all been at a party and noticed new acquaintances scanning the room, looking for someone more interesting to converse with. Steven Levy says that we now live in "a never-ending cocktail party where you're always looking over your virtual shoulder for a better conversation partner."[17] We cannot build deep and lasting relationships if we turn away from others the moment they become boring, irritating, or challenging. Neither cocktail party practices nor television-viewing habits are helpful for growing in friendship, intimacy, and love.

Increasingly, people may be physically present but transacting business with someone else at the same time via technology. The issue is not only etiquette and civility; "the more distracted we become, the less able we are to experience the subtlest, most distinctively human forms of empathy, compassion, and other emotions."[18] Christine Pearson, coauthor of *The Cost of Bad Behavior*, writes about a study of over nine thousand workers and managers in the United States. The study firmly established that workplace incivility is rising. She notes that "when people disappear from formal or informal meetings via their electronic devices, their colleagues interpret it this way: 'You are less important to me than my cell phone/PDA/laptop/latest gizmo.'"[19]

There is also a theological challenge. When we put our own particular priorities at the center of everything, it becomes harder and harder to acknowledge God or any factor that might be beyond our control and prediction. We noted above that this ATTENTION alert is connected with a nasty, old-fashioned term: *idolatry*. We think of idolatry as bizarre practices involving fire and sacrifices, gaudy statues, and frenzied dancing. But the concept is still relevant because it involves, among other things, attributing too much importance to the wrong priorities. Idolatry can mean thinking something is more valuable or powerful or fearful than it truly is.

The greatest joys in life are finally and ultimately unpredictable, beyond our control. A central and key Christian conviction is that God cannot be forced or manipulated into doing anything. God is beyond our power and predictability. Another way to explain idolatry is to say that it is a misguided attempt to make God conform to our will.

We all encounter joys that come undeserved and unbidden. The beauty of sunsets and sunrises exists partly in the fact that we never know what to expect. They are momentary, fleeting. As much as we appreciate great artists, no painting or photograph can ever capture the lovely, breathtaking wonder of the sky being streaked once more with the latest palette of bright red and burning orange and deep purple.

Some people urge us to consider "designer children," choosing gender, height, intelligence, hair color, physique, interests, athletic abilities, et cetera. But a parent's deepest joy is to receive and welcome a child in all its unexpected mystery and to make room for that child's potential to grow and unfold. We are called to learn how to love this mysterious other, just as each of us longs to be received and loved for who we are and as we are.

I have been married for over three decades. The most meaningful gifts my wife and I offer each other are not necessarily ones I would have predicted or chosen. Marriage has helped us grow, but it has not always been fun or easy for either of us. Most growth as a couple occurs when we do not see eye to eye—when we need to learn new ways to work and live together. Sherry Turkle discusses those who advocate manufacturing robots that we can love, ones that embody our preferences, ones that we might even marry to overcome loneliness and have as sex partners.[20] But such options only reinforce selfishness, self-centeredness, and solipsism—and would still leave us lonely.

Those who practice spiritual disciplines over time know that commitment to prayer is a fundamental stance that profoundly challenges the spirit of our age. It calls us to pay attention to realities that are only slowly revealed (rather than easily drawn and captivated by hyperactive images on both TV and the web). It makes us wait for meaning to emerge and unfold (rather than settle for sound bytes). It helps us dwell in mystery (rather than chase instant solutions). It encourages us to engage in practices that show no immediate benefits (rather than dash from task to task). It invites single-minded attention to the things of God (rather than distracted multitasking). It requires staying still and doing similar practices over and again, even when they seem repetitious (rather than questing unrelentingly for the new and dismissively writing off the familiar as "been there, done that"). Being people of prayer and contemplation, worship and compassion, means that we submit ourselves and make room for what Ursula Franklin calls the "unprogrammed and unprogrammable events."[21]

Learning to wait and be patient is a spiritual discipline. Simone Weil recognized this when she titled her mystical classic *Waiting for God*. The Hebrew Scriptures remind us of the priority of waiting for the Lord (for example, Pss. 25:3; 27:14; 37:7, 34; 40:1; 62:1; 130:5–6). Isaiah promises: "Those who wait for the Lord shall renew their strength" (Isa. 40:31). Such counsel reminds us of our dependence on God and our subservience to God. Judeo-Christian traditions also celebrate God's patience. In the parable of the prodigal son—sometimes called the parable of the waiting father—the left-behind parent longingly looks for the return of his son (Luke 15:20). We do not just wait for and on God; God waits for us too.

Counterbalancing Attenuated Attention

We need not settle for attenuated attention. Winifred Gallagher makes a case for choosing our focus, insisting that we have more control than we realize: "If you could just stay focused on the right things, your life would stop feeling like a reaction to stuff that happens to you and become something that you create: not a series of accidents but a work of art."[22]

We have options. Let me suggest a couple examples, one a contemporary focal practice and one with a long spiritual legacy. You may know of others.

Bird-Watching

A simple way to slow down, pay attention, be receptive, and experience wonder is to take up a pastime once associated with British women of a certain age in sensible shoes. I recommend Jonathan Rosen's *The Life of the Skies: Birding at the End of Nature*. Birds, he notes, are largely invisible to many people today but are now our primary remaining access to nature and the wild. "Looking at birds, I feel, for lack of a better word, whole." This, he asserts, is not merely a hobby. "It's a natural, inevitable part of my engagement with the world."[23]

Ruth Mallory became serious about birding late in life, but not too late for it to shape her life. By now, she's visited every continent—except Antarctica—because of her passion. When we talked, she was eighty-two and had 1,873 birds on her life list. This was not just activity for the sake of a fulfilling retirement. "It's only been in my senior years that I've come to know what really gives me joy." She loves to be out in nature. There, Ruth's spirit is fed. She told of a time when she was birding in West Texas with a friend. There was a spectacular sunrise and "this huge concentration of cranes take off in a flock over this pond where they're mirrored in the water. Just the whole experience wraps you in worship." And birding feeds her intellectually. Learning to identify birds by sight and sound, she told me, "keeps brains active."

As she saw how deeply healing it was to be in nature, she also began to ask herself what she needed as a worshiping Christian. She found herself drawn to liturgical practices that honor silence and beauty. Both birding and worship nurture her contemplative urge. "I began to find my own spiritual home through all those experiences," she told me. It was the birding, Ruth said, "that opened the door to getting in touch with who I really am and to feeling okay about who I am." It also reoriented her theology. While she had long heard of God as a judge eager to mete out punishment, her passion for birds helped her be "in touch with God's creation." There she saw God's "abundance, love, creativity." When she thinks of all she and her husband spent on birding travels, she says: "I've always felt God smiling on me and delighting in these trips. God delights in my delight in his creation."

When I hear how bird-watching filled her late decades with grace, I wonder what would have happened without her discoveries—if not, in other words, for the birds.

Praying with Icons

Orthodox Christian traditions employ religious icons to aid the faithful in becoming quiet and centered, praying, and paying attention. Those who are not of this tradition might be unaware of how we are formed by images. Orthodox theologian Anthony Ugolnik worries about our culture: "In a world replete with the images that shower down upon us from billboards, pour from the television screen, adorn our cities and public parks, and inhabit our entire interior landscape, the religious image has little power of itself to claim its own dominion over the imagination."[24]

Ironically, *icon* now refers to computer screen symbols representing a document, file, program, or command. While religious icons are visual, their resemblance to what goes on our screens ends there. In contrast to images composed of pixels, icons are layered literally and figuratively. An actual icon is created painstakingly and prayerfully, as the iconographer slowly applies gesso, egg tempera, various pigments, and even gold leaf. Centuries of tradition lie behind the themes of icons and how people are portrayed. I love Henri Nouwen's *Behold the Beauty of the Lord: Praying with Icons*. He not only explains the tradition but also invites us into it by including lovely color reproductions of four famous Russian Orthodox works. "Gazing," he writes, "is probably the best word to touch the core of Eastern spirituality."[25]

Both practices—bird-watching and praying with icons—invite us to take action and initiative. Sometimes birding happens unexpectedly, perhaps even by grace: once I saw a wild turkey in our suburban backyard, and I have seen snowy owls and snow buntings while driving. But even so, discipline was involved. One cannot see what one does not notice or prioritize, if one is not paying attention at some level. I would not have recognized birds along the road or in my backyard if I did not have at least some birder disciplines. Birding and icon-praying demand that we take steps. No couch or screen potatoes here.

Furthermore, both practices are beyond our control. We cannot alter or affect them by pressing buttons on a remote or flipping a switch. There is never a guarantee that the birds we seek will show up when we look for them or that an icon will speak to us. Both experiences may feel at times dry and unrewarding. No glitter or glamour here.

And, finally, birding and praying with icons both demand being slow and single-minded. You stay still for a time. You focus carefully. You concentrate and resist distraction. And you wait for reality and revelation to unfold and flower in their own way and at their own pace.

It is possible for us to embrace practices that heighten our attention.

7

ELIMINATING LIMITS AND ENDANGERING TABOOS

My neighbor Donnie was the first person to teach me about pornography. I was twelve years old and we had just moved to the rural area where I would live all my adolescent years. He was eleven, his home just up the road, and there were no other boys my age, as far as I knew, within a mile or two. So it was natural and inevitable that during my first spring break in the neighborhood he and I met and became casual friends. Because of his two brothers, older teenagers, Donnie knew things that I never dreamed about, even though he was younger than I.

One day, I found a beat-up magazine in the ditch near our house, apparently tossed out of the window of a passing vehicle racing down the secondary highway. Curious, I picked it up and suddenly became even more curious. The cover was gone, and the pages were rain soaked, but this issue was filled with pictures of women in their underwear. The photos were black-and-white, and I did not know what to make of them.

I knew that this was not something to share with parents. So I walked over to Donnie's house and showed it to him once we got up to his room: "Look what I found," I said casually. "My brothers have magazines like this," he told me. In their room we found the stash in the closet, under their gym clothes. We quickly noted what was there and moved on. I did not understand why anyone would possess such things. I don't know what happened to the magazine I found. I probably left it behind at Donnie's. My curiosity, slight as it was, was satisfied.

One of my friends is a Coptic Orthodox priest. His tradition takes confession and spiritual direction seriously. In the 1990s, he told me regularly about preadolescent boys in his congregation who talked to him about struggles with temptation. They were about the age I was when I found that magazine in a ditch, but they were regularly exposed to pornography on the internet and were getting daily unsolicited email invitations to view inappropriate materials.

John Palfrey and Urs Gasser write evenhandedly about technology. They are not needlessly alarmist. But they offer disturbing observations about online pornography. For one thing, many youths spend most of their online time "without adult supervision."

A Google search using even a remotely naughty word turns up many varieties of pornography, just a click or two away and free for the viewing. There are hundreds of thousands of adult sites on the internet, which doesn't take into account the large number of explicit amateur videos. One expert claims that nearly all young kids come across pornography online while doing their homework.

Some children seek out pornography, but others—large numbers—see it unintentionally. There are two crucial differences between preinternet and contemporary pornography. One is what Palfrey and Gasser call "ubiquity"—the fact that it's all around us—and the other is that it is so easy to access.[1]

Integrity Theft

Many people argue that technology is neutral. It all depends, they say, on how you use it and who is using it. But there is little question that television has become increasingly risqué and suggestive and that the internet takes pornography to previously unimaginable levels. The overwhelming influence and direction of much technology is not neutral. This should not surprise us. Peter Nowak amply illustrates in *Sex, Bombs and Burgers: How War, Porn and Fast Food Shaped Technology as We Know It* that much of technology is driven by an explicit agenda.[2] Many of our greatest advances are brought to us by purveyors of porn, junk food, and violence.

Technology often frees us from moral constraints. A major achievement of the automobile was liberating youths from local supervision, making it easier to experiment with drugs, alcohol, and sex. A primary factor undermining churches' capacity to hold members accountable is that it is now easy for members just to uproot and drive to other churches. Automobility broke down the ability of families and communities to hold certain standards. Daniel Lohrmann, a computer expert and unabashed technology lover, suggests that temptations and threats to our values—what he calls "integrity theft"—reached new thresholds in our era: "PCs, mobile computing, cell phones, BlackBerries, and the millions of things we can do on the Internet have forever changed the scope and sophistication of the battles that we face in the twenty-first century."[3]

It was once easy to be sheltered from pornography. Obviously some people—Donnie's brothers, for example—had access. But they had to work at acquisition, going out of their way to purchase it, perhaps getting it through the mail in nondescript envelopes. Most people had the sense to hide it, as Donnie's brothers did. Now everyone who turns on a computer has immediate access to graphic imagery in seconds, and it is not just provocative underwear anymore. Anyone can have long leisurely looks at any imaginable sex act or any bodily part, all merely by clicking a few keyboard buttons. And no one close to us ever needs to know. Neutral technology indeed.

Many recent devices attenuate, even eliminate, community standards and mores at an astonishing rate. Television and the internet continually break down taboos in order to catch and keep our interest and even encourage addictive behavior. Television grows increasingly and outrageously voyeuristic. This tearing down of taboos is not an accidental by-product; it is intrinsic to the kinds of technology that we develop, promote, and employ. Furthermore, in spite of the important issues at stake, very little corporate or community discernment about what is appropriate happens. Seldom do we encourage one another to be accountable about technology use. Finally, we need to take more seriously the relationship of technology to addictions, both how it exploits addictions and how technology itself can be addictive.

Revising Shock Levels

As a child, I was perplexed by comedies such as *The Dick Van Dyke Show* or *I Love Lucy* because married couples always had separate beds. My parents slept together, and when I visited friends or relatives there was only one bed in master bedrooms there too. The issue then—although I did not know this as a child—had to do with the kinds of standards and morality being upheld. It was considered improperly suggestive to show husbands and wives climb under the covers together. This strikes us as naive today.

When *Friends* and *Seinfeld* aired their final broadcasts after years of success, their characters had been in numerous amorous liaisons along the way, sometimes with each other, at times with serious (but temporary) partners, other times in casual relationships, and occasionally with strangers. Characters exchanged sexual partners more casually than computers, televisions, or stereo systems. (Jerry had the same Macintosh for a long time.) This is as unrealistic as seeing married couples in separate beds. David Myers notes:

> In 1896, a film called *The Kiss* outraged moral guardians by showing a couple stealing a quick kiss. "Absolutely disgusting," said one critic. "Such things call for police action." By the 1990s, prime-time network entertainment offered sexual remarks or behavior every four minutes. From their monitoring of network programs for Planned Parenthood, Louis Harris and Associates estimated that the average viewer witnesses 14,000 sexual events annually. Nearly all involve unmarried people. An analysis of one week of network prime-time TV found that intercourse was mentioned or intimated by unmarried couples 90 times and by married couples once. Rarely are there any consequences. No one gets herpes or AIDS. No one gets pregnant. No one has to change diapers, get up in the middle of the night, or heroically struggle to socialize a fatherless child. In fact, more than two-thirds of the time (in another analysis of 220 scenes of unmarried sex) the activity is portrayed as desirable, less than 10 percent of the time as undesirable.[4]

Violence grows more graphic. Crime shows—a major staple of prime-time television—depict increasingly horrific and brutal murders and graphically display wounds and bodies in various states of decay and dismemberment. "Reality television" specializes in voyeuristically observing the intrigues and antics of people who live in contrived circumstances staged to provoke conflicts, rivalries, deception, and—oh, yes—promiscuity too. The internet, as Harlan Coben notes, is profligate in what it offers everyone, including children: opportunities for "chatting with pedophiles or watching beheadings or gambling away their entire life savings."[5] Thomas de Zengotita writes of "our unseemly access to everything."[6]

> You've watched how many total strangers in what kinds of circumstances? Thousands of them, in their most extreme and intimate moments. People dying, people being born, being tortured, being saved, being operated on; you've been up their colons, in their wombs, you've navigated their blood vessels, you've entered their skulls to monitor their brain activity, you've watched them in their kitchens and bathrooms and bedrooms, you've watched them f**cking and sucking, engaging in every sexual act imaginable, you've watched them as they hear of the death of loved ones, you've watched them marry and divorce and cheat and lie and forgive and forget.[7]

Voyeurism was once considered a vice; now it is everyday reality. One could make a case that many things ought not to be broadcast at all, especially not in ways easily accessible by anyone (including children) at any time. We could also debate at some length what kinds of restrictions—if any—are appropriate for consenting adults. But my spiritual tradition is more cautious.

> Finally, beloved, whatever is true, whatever is honorable, whatever is just, whatever is pure, whatever is pleasing, whatever is commendable, if there is any excellence and if there is anything worthy of praise, think about these things.
>
> Philippians 4:8

The psalmist promises: "I will set no worthless thing before my eyes" and elsewhere prays, "Turn my eyes from watching what is worthless"

(101:3; 119:37 *Book of Common Prayer*). If one accepts such verses as instructive, it is increasingly difficult to justify casual and routine television watching.

Some years ago, I heard David Kline speak at a farmers' market event in Goshen, Indiana. Kline is an eloquent and elegant writer who gives crucial insights into Amish ways of farming. He told a story about a busload of Protestant tourists sightseeing in an Amish area. An Amishman is brought on the bus and asked how his folks differ from other Christians. First, he explained their similarities: all had DNA, wear clothes (even if in different styles), and like to eat good food.

> Then the Amish man asks: "How many of you have a television?"
>
> All passengers raise their hands.
>
> "How many of you believe your children would be better off without TV?"
>
> Most, if not all, passengers raise their hands.
>
> "How many of you, knowing this, will get rid of your television when you go home?"
>
> No hands are raised.
>
> "That's the difference between the Amish and others," he concluded.

It grows harder and harder to find people who argue seriously about getting rid of television, let alone more advanced technologies. The old John Prine song "Spanish Pipedream" recommended that you "blow up your TV." Whether or not to own one used to be a live and contentious issue in some Christian contexts, but it is mostly a done deal now. So I marvel at the clarity that Old Orders show in uniformly rejecting this medium. At the Elkhart Consultation, Donald Kraybill told us, "An Old Order person said, 'Well, why would we hook up . . . a sewer pipe directly to Hollywood, and have all this moral sewage right into our home?'"[8] Albert Borgmann says something similar: "Television is just like making a hole in the wall. . . . All kinds of stuff comes in, on the screen, that we would never allow to come in through the door."[9]

Does television viewing encourage greed and consumption, make people more immune to violence, and promote promiscuity? Some argue that television only reflects the standards that we already hold. Jacques Ellul bluntly states his opinion that television shatters the taboos, and creates the public need for shows of this kind. When people argue that the television industry is simply responding to the public taste and demand, they forget to add that this demand is the creation of television. Television is responsible for the kind of general mental climate of which violence and eroticism are a part.[10]

Many media developments—videos, internet, DVDs, interactive games—made pornography more accessible and available—that is, offering sexual relationships with images that impose no demands. Pornography is one of the primary accomplishments (and driving forces) of television and the internet. This deserves discussion and discernment. It is not just that these technologies promote pornography; but often pornography is also a major factor in their financial success. Other major forces propelling the success of the internet are advertising, gambling, and easy shopping—none of which can boast of building character.

Not only is pornography more *available*, but the materials also get more *provocative*. The stakes keep increasing. What once titillated now hardly startles. Entertainment violates social, moral, and sexual limits. Standards keep sliding, loosening, and changing: "As these moral sensibilities fade, the 'immoral' first becomes bizarre, then ridiculous, and finally boring."[11] Albert Borgmann makes an intriguing observation about taboo erosion. Television "has to mine ever new taboos. . . . To keep our interest it has to mine nonrenewable resources, things that were to be held as taboo or sacred."[12] He suggests that television would otherwise be boring, unable to keep our interest without becoming increasingly outrageous. You may recall that Jerry Mander argued that "technical events" kept us paying attention. Now technical events are not enough; we need to be shocked and unsettled as well.

It Didn't Mean Anything?

Technology often defines choices, sets priorities, and determines values. At one school where I taught, faculty had lengthy and vigorous discussions about whether the highest grade we would award should be an A+ or a simple A. As a teaching novice, I never knew that the pedagogical stakes could be so high over one issue and was relieved when we finally came to a decision. I was happy to support the policy of giving out the highest possible accolade, an A+. Within a few years, however, the registrar's office bought a new database. The program could not accommodate A+ and would only honor an A entry. Thus a new decision was made. The technology chose for us. There was nothing to discuss. Technology often has a certain and particular momentum, and unless we are conscious about it we risk being swept along.

There are rare examples of people of faith being discerning about technology. Donald Kraybill told our Elkhart Consultation that an Amish grandmother spoke about her community's decades-long discussion on telephones and said that they're "still on probation." Kraybill noted that they "haven't quite sorted that out yet."[13] In other words, more discernment was needed. Other than Old Order groups, are there many recent examples of churches or Christian groups discerning, let alone ever renouncing, specific forms of technology? Yet there are numerous examples of churches embracing technological options, treating them as essentially neutral.

Some Christians use explicitly violent video games as a recruiting tool to draw and attract youth, especially young males. Thus "leaders of churches and youth centers across Protestant denominations, including evangelical churches that cautioned against violent entertainment," nevertheless proceed with "holding heavily attended *Halo* nights and stocking their centers with multiple game consoles so dozens of teenagers can flock around big-screen televisions and shoot it out." Though *Halo's* name conjures theological themes, the game focuses on violence and mayhem. Church leaders say such games are "crucial . . . to reach their most elusive audience, boys and young men on their home turf." Gun bursts and bloodbaths become the agenda for youth gatherings. One leader compared such events to the fellowship one finds on a camping trip and that the shooting is only a matter of "pixels on a screen." But effective recruiting does not justify everything. Employing electronic pornography would also prove attractive to the "most elusive audience, boys and young men." For those who worry about pornography, it is "only pixels."[14]

Wooing kids to church via popular technology is an example of technology being judged strictly by standards of what appears effective and will attract people. Means are unimportant, as these are "only pixels" after all and thus essentially neutral. Yet computer games remove us from reality and morality. They teach us the attractions of causing pain without recognizing responsibility or consequences. After all, "The punctured flesh will heal at the touch of a button, the scream disappear into cyberspace. You'll be able to resurrect the digital dead and kill them again."[15] Yet studies show that violent video games "short-circuit compassionate tendencies and . . . amplify aggression."[16] In Jesus's Sermon on the Mount, he deepened the commandment about murder to include a rebuke against anger and insult. Similarly, he said "that everyone who looks at a woman with lust has already committed adultery with her in his heart." Both passages convey a strong conviction that virtual fantasy is not innocuous, let alone a "neutral" tool.

It is not enough to consider what effectively attracts. Jacques Ellul warns, "Since the Revelation of God in Jesus Christ took a certain orientation, a certain form, it cannot be spread by just any method. There is a need to discern and evaluate the means."[17]

Technology's Addictions and Addictiveness

New technologies enable various addictions—pornography, gambling, shopping—and its various media themselves can be addictive. The internet makes us all potential gamblers, voyeurs, and pornographers. We can pursue dark pleasures in privacy by accessing the web. "These impulses are age-old, of course, but they are now fantastically easy to satisfy."[18] One no longer needs to go to "adult" backrooms, travel to a casino, phone a bookie, or find an open store to indulge in deeply destructive behaviors. The barriers to such choices are low.

Addiction involves repetitive, compulsive, and obsessive behavior. It is commonly understood to be harmful and destructive to one's own health or mental well-being, or to relationships and responsibilities. Psychologist Chellis Glendinning explores "techno-addiction" and sees classic markers of denial, dishonesty, control, thinking disorders, grandiosity, and disconnection from feelings.[19] It is not just that technologies grant easy portals to vices, allow people to indulge addictions, or lead to addictions, but also that the technologies themselves become problematically habitual. People find it hard to get through the day—or night—without constant digital access and connection. We often hear of people who take their mobiles and Blackberries to bed with them. One friend regularly wakes at 3 a.m. and automatically checks email. When he told me this a couple years ago, I felt alarmed for him. Now when I am sleepless in the wee hours, I also find it all too easy to go first to my email. Camping and wilderness programs that work with youth frequently encounter outrage when teens learn that electronics are to be shut off for a day or more. Go to a fine restaurant, sit in a worship service, or visit friends, and marvel at how often people find the need to look at their screens.

Technologies are addictive, Palfrey and Gasser note, because their "fast pace of change and instant sensory stimulation effectively condition the brain toward external stimulation, rather than internal self-regulation and focus." Children are particularly vulnerable:

> A 2007 poll found that 8.5 percent of youth gamers in the United States could be classified as pathologically addicted to playing video games. In an online British study that same year, 12 percent of gamers demonstrated addictive behavior. In summer 2006, the first inpatient clinic for computer game addicts in Europe opened its doors; Korea . . . already has more than forty game-addiction counseling agencies registering thousands of cases per year. According to government estimates . . . , 2.4 percent of South Koreans aged nine to thirty-nine are addicts, and another 10.2 percent are borderline cases.[20]

This is not just a by-product or unintended consequence. "Addiction to video games and to online multiplayer games is not only growing, but is an implicit goal of game manufacturers."[21] David Shenk observes that both the "electrifying speed and strobe effect of the computer display monitor can be mildly hypnotic and addictive in the same way that television can, capturing people's attention for long, unhealthy periods of time."[22] We come more and more to count on the rush of a new email or fresh messages.

> Connectivity becomes a craving; when we receive a text or an e-mail, our nervous system responds by giving us a shot of dopamine. We are stimulated by the connectivity itself. We learn to require it, even as it depletes us.[23]

Even Stephen Spyker, a self-admitted technophile, has concerns. He sees three characteristics of addiction that are frequently true of people involved with technology:[24]

- *Mind- or mood-altering.* Addictions are often employed to alter, improve, or control moods. Many need technological devices to feel secure. Naomi Baron cites the "CrackBerry" crisis when millions were inadvertently disconnected in April 2007. An executive said it was easier to give up smoking than to be cut off from his Blackberry.[25]
- *Tolerance.* Addictions work by creating a desire for more. One dose no longer suffices; it must be increased. If we are stepping up the amount of time checking messages or surfing online, then we ought to consider whether our behavior is that of an addict.
- *Dependence.* Addictions create dependence. "How easy would it be for you to give up your PC, your telephone, your automobile, or your television?" Spyker asks. One sociological study suggested that it takes five years to withdraw from television use.[26]

As we ponder the challenges of eliminating limits, it is useful to consider warning signs suggested in a *New York Times* piece:

Sign 1: Do you always check your email before doing other things?

Sign 2: Do you frequently find yourself anticipating the next time you'll be online?

Sign 3: When you're online and someone needs you, do you usually say "just a few more minutes" before stopping?

Sign 4: Have you ever lied about or tried to hide how long you've been online?

Sign 5: Have you ever chosen to spend time online rather than going out with others?

Sign 6: Does going online lift you from a depressed or nervous mood?

Sign 7: Do others in your life often complain about the amount of time you spend using technology?[27]

Karissa Thacker, a management psychologist, suggests that reliance on electronic devices and communications needs to prompt several questions: "Can you manage your need for control? Can you manage your need to be important? Can you manage your need to feel in the know?"[28]

The Blessings of Limits

While we celebrate lack of constraint (in an era ironically obsessed with "boundaries"), limits have their place. Artists, poets, writers, sculptors, woodworkers, gardeners, letter writers, and cooks all make do with what they have, resources available, the time at hand. The erosion of limits is a frightening prospect, not an offer of freedom.

I love this set of lines from the Psalms:

> The boundary lines have fallen for me in pleasant places;
> I have a goodly heritage.
>
> Psalm 16:6

The psalmist's words remind me to cherish the fact that opportunities are not unbounded.

Bill McKibben shows that the ability to honor and act creatively within limits is an essential part of being human, not to mention a crucial aspect of religious heritage and even the ability to be artistic. "In the Western tradition, the idea of limits goes right back to the start, to a God who made heaven and earth, beast and man, and then decided that it was all enough and *stopped*."[29]

Counterbalancing Eliminated Limits

Can we reclaim good limits? What practices could help in such an endeavor? Ironically, one solution is technological. The other comes from classic spiritual disciplines.

Accountability Software

Particular technologies may constrain the damage of other technologies. Various accountability software seems to have been inspired by twelve-step programs that involve mentors or sponsors to whom one reports struggles and lapses. "Accountability" is a term used in Christian circles, and such software often has church or parachurch connections and was developed to help people struggling with online pornography behaviors or other addictive tendencies. The idea is simple. Online activity is automatically reported to a designated partner, mentor, or sponsor. Thus if you are tempted to look at a site that might contravene your values, your accountability partner will know. This option increases the barrier against viewing a pornography website. It slows you down, makes you consider your actions a little more carefully. You cannot even disconnect from the reporting software without your accountability partner's knowledge.[30]

Consciousness Examen

An important spiritual discipline is the *consciousness examen*, identified with the Jesuits. Some people perform it once a year (perhaps at New Year's Eve) or more frequently (on retreat or when seeing a spiritual director). But many folks do it on a daily basis every evening before retiring. After praying for the Spirit's guidance and discernment, one reviews a set period of time and pays attention to how God was moving there, where one was drawn toward God, where one was tempted or tugged from God, where one needs to make confession to God, and what one might resolve about how to live in the future. I consistently experience three realizations when I practice the *examen*.

First, it reorients my interpretation of life. My father used to speak about the "Boers curse." By this he meant "bad luck." He contended that our family was unluckier than most. If we were at an airport awaiting baggage, ours often seemed to come out of the chute last . . . or, worse, be lost! "That's the Boers curse," he'd say.

Pessimism is a sandy foundation for the spiritual life. God does not let me rest easy with that perspective. Sometimes I come to my examen before retiring, convinced that I have endured a terrible day. I feel discouraged. Then I prayerfully and carefully consider the ways and places I experienced God, felt connected to God, and was drawn to God. The list is often long, surprisingly so. I write down all those graces. I also enumerate places where I felt cut off or distant from God. On almost every day that I undertake this discipline, moments of grace far outweigh and outnumber those of dislocation and disorientation. "I guess it was not such a bad day after all," I invariably conclude.

Second, this discipline reminds me—forcefully so sometimes—of how I most powerfully connect with God. Spectacular epiphanies are unusual. Most days, I am in tune with God when I take time for a long walk, for saying prayers, for reading, for conversing with my wife. Such normal, ordinary matters are easily achieved. Reminding myself of their importance daily reinforces my commitment to keep observing them and giving them a place of honor and priority.

Third, the examen also helps me discover patterns that are harmful, distracting, and destructive and then reinforces my resolve to do something about them. I am embarrassed to admit that for a period in my life I noted every day my frustration with how much time I was spending on web-based computer games. When this came up regularly in my examen, I knew that I had to act. So I shamefacedly invited a trusty IT-savvy friend to block this site on my computer. I watched him do it. I could unblock what he did. But I have not done so. I'd be ashamed to after having him arrange things for me.

A fine and worthy resource about consciousness examen is the improbably titled *Sleeping with Bread: Holding What Gives You Life*. The authors write, "The examen makes us aware of moments that at first we might easily pass by as insignificant, moments that ultimately can give direction for our lives."[31] The examen is an act of deliberation and discipline that encourages and empowers one to live more freely and faithfully. This simple and straightforward spiritual practice can be surprisingly fruitful, enriching one's life.

8

ERODING ENGAGEMENT

My parents were traveling in a rented car in an unfamiliar city in another country. My mom had a map awkwardly unfolded, sprawled over lap and dashboard. My father was having trouble driving in the strange landscape and different traffic patterns while trying to follow her directions. Realizing that they were in a wrong lane, he glanced in the rearview mirror and, as all seemed clear, abruptly pulled to the right. When this move was met by a blaring horn, they realized that this unexpected shift had caused difficulties for someone in the car's blind spot. My father waved apologetically into the mirror.

Neither the map nor their written directions gave assurance about where they were heading. As uncertainty deepened, anxiety rose. Waiting at a stoplight, my parents conferred some more about where to go but were still unsure whether they were heading in the right direction or not. Then they saw a man standing outside my father's door. My parents were relieved. Obviously, this stranger had seen their struggle and was going to help them find their way.

As my father began rolling down his window, the stranger—my father's "victim" it turns out—yanked the door open. He grabbed my dad by his shirt and pulled him from the car. My mother comments at this point, "I saw his buttons pop through the air!" The man threw my father up against the automobile and began yelling at him, his flushed face only inches away from my dad's. The tirade was a combination of expletive-riddled cursing and complaints regarding my father's ignorance. In the meantime, the signal changed and traffic was moving again, flowing around the altercation. But my father was hemmed in. No one stopped, honked, or helped.

My parents were shaken. They expected the man to produce a weapon and do further damage. But once his verbal ire was expressed he let go of my father, walked back to his car, and sped around my parents' stopped vehicle, squealing tires as he went. My father breathed in and out, slowly and deeply for some minutes, slumped against the car, before he shakily climbed back into the driver's seat. My mother often recalls that first exposure to road rage. This was twenty-some years ago, and—as far as I know—we had not heard that particular term yet. By now most of us have experienced some versions of it ourselves, either at the giving or receiving end.

Road rage may not be listed in the *Diagnostic and Statistical Manual of Mental Disorders*. Nevertheless, it is cause for concern and in significant ways a technologically abetted—if not technologically induced—problem. This disorder is facilitated by how we interact on roads and by expectations that our devices raise. Brian Ladd is cautious about overreacting to the dangers and hazards of cars, but he acknowledges that "the freedom offered by the automobile encourages aggression."[1]

It is too easy to rant or gripe about modern life. Aggravations—traffic jams, computer crashes, email spam, internet viruses—are unfortunate by-products of daily realities. They are not, however, what most deeply concerns me. I do not want to devolve into mere crankiness about inevitable daily challenges.

There are deeper issues at stake. Technology use can promote impatience and undermine engagement with others in at least three ways. First of all, it raises expectations of ourselves and those around us about how much we can accomplish and how quickly we can do it. Second, it speeds encounters and makes conflicts and misunderstandings more likely. And, finally, our growing impatience erodes commitment to essential relationships. I fear a technologically facilitated loss of civility.

The Stress of It All

The speed, tempo, and pace of life are increasing. (See also chap. 10, "Taxed Time.") Think "fast food." Bennigan's restaurants offer a "Time Crunch Lunch." Workplaces, homes, families, leisure, television ads and programs, and films move faster and faster. Jacques Ellul argues that our increasingly harried pace of life contributes to and causes insomnia, nervous fatigue, exhaustion, and other adverse health consequences.[2] Yet we are encouraged to be impatient and to hurry. Consider a Turbochef stove ad: "Actually, the best things come to those who can't wait."

We once thought that email meant easier communication and a lightened workload. Instead it increases expectations. One day our school had no classes and thus fewer institutional demands than usual. Yet my email included two requests to mail books, one explanation from the academic dean about a student in serious crisis for whom I'm to provide counsel, registrar information about grades submitted, a refund because a book that I ordered cannot be sent, a query as to whether I would meet a pastor on sabbatical, information about an upcoming consultation, a request for materials on conflict resolution to be sent immediately, several exchanges about setting dates for upcoming meetings, inquiries about whether I would support someone I do not know who is facing cancer in another country, an invitation wondering whether I am available to converse with a person struggling with post-traumatic stress disorder issues, two missives from friends addressing me on personal matters (his vocational discernment, her conflict with me), announcements about new books to consider purchasing and reading, a report of a funeral for someone that I do not know, a surprise announcement of a colleague's elopement, and questions about an upcoming workshop that I was to lead. All of these took time and most (even those I neither expected nor initiated) required follow-up. Many of the emails were worthwhile and important. But their quantity and unrelenting arrivals overwhelmed me.

Busy lives, long work hours, and the desire to accomplish so much leave little time for deepening relationships or meeting new people. No wonder many are interested in online romance and "speed dating." In touch with growing numbers, our contacts grow shallower even as they multiply. Time gets divided into smaller and smaller increments as we share it with more and more people. When our daughter and son were small, self-help parenting articles advocated "quality time" with children. The implication was that quantity was not so important. The insidious suggestion was that it was okay to spend short speedy periods with them, as long as that was densely packed "quality time." The conclusion that quality and not quantity might be most important seems a little too convenient to be true for a society trying to do many things quickly.

While technology often promises to solve problems, at the same time it creates new needs and demands. GPS devices supposedly simplify lives—no more asking for directions!—but some users feel obliged to achieve arrival estimation times predicted by their gadget. Now we take speedy showers rather than leisurely baths. But, ironically, we shower more than we used to bathe and so may spend more time cleaning ourselves than before. I subscribe to various radio podcasts but end up aware of the building weight of those I have not yet heard.

Pressures mount from all the duties that we feel obliged to honor and accomplish and the standards we feel compelled and urged to meet. This is the real reason for many gripes mentioned above: traffic jams, computer crashes, email spam, internet viruses. They are not merely annoyances but also true obstacles to fulfilling steadily mounting obligations. Hence our frustration when we encounter hassles that stand in our way.

Technological exposure affects perception of time, and we learn to be impatient and less civil and hospitable; in such a context road rage makes a certain sense. Philo of Alexandria used to counsel—a line I've often found important as a pastor, teacher, counselor, spiritual director—"Everyone you meet is fighting a great battle." Impatience does not just affect human relationships. We also grow intolerant with anything that takes time, is difficult, or is not easily accessible because of complexity or "depth of meaning."[3] The spiritual life and our deepest, most important relationships are at risk. Quality time usually requires substantial quantity time, no matter what those parenting articles tried to tell me a few decades ago.

Reliably Accelerating Conflict

There are other reasons to worry about speeded up engagement. Technological formation reinforces hasty impatience, which can make us less civil and hospitable toward others. An iPhone ad reminds us, "Waiting is so last week."

Previously as a pastor and now as a professor who teaches, among other things, about good ways to handle conflict, I cannot begin to count the number of times that I've seen email exacerbate problems. It is one of the poorest possible ways of addressing communication breakdowns, and yet people resort to it quickly.

People fire off messages in the heat of the moment, sometimes writing things that they don't really mean, not giving sufficient time to calm down and sort out feelings, certainly not nuancing words or worrying about how easily language or ideas might be misconstrued. There is little space to ponder, reflect, plan, or sort out.

Once ill-advised or rash sentiments are emailed—and possibly forwarded to many others—they then become more difficult to retract and undo. Anxious people and systems like to move in haste. But this is the worst possible mode for resolution. A priority in conflict transformation is remaining calm. At such times, it is crucial for people to be reflective and find ways of opening themselves to creative and imaginative possibilities. Email, however, encourages and abets impulsivity.

Furthermore, it is easy to copy email to others and drag them into controversy. Both family systems theory and Christian traditions warn about the hazards of "triangling" others into conflicts instead of prioritizing one-to-one, face-to-face communication wherever possible. At one school where I worked, an administrator sent off an inflamed and complaining email about a sensitive subject; she forwarded the message to all the email addresses—faculty, administrators, staff, students, alumni, and donors—in the seminary system. Our president corrected her imprudence, noting that with email anything we say might immediately get to "the other side of the world." In fact, when a recent graduate took his life on campus, students were spreading this news across the country even before administrators were able to make sure that relatives of the victim could hear first.

A primary difficulty with advanced technologies is the "disinhibition effect," people showing a "tendency to act more aggressively toward other people online than face to face." A sense of anonymity is one reason for this. Another factor is that "many people . . . experience greater difficulty curbing their impulses online than . . . in real-space social situations."[4] Furthermore, there are no cyberspace authority figures that help check unruly impulses. (The flip side of "disinhibition effect" is that some people disclose too much and too freely, entering quickly into revelations that are not prudent or advisable.)

The problem with email is not just the tendency to say too much too quickly. There is also an issue of perception. Daniel Goleman, proponent of "emotional intelligence," shows that interpretation of email is usually skewed. Positive messages are seen as being impartial, and impartial ones are often read negatively because we are unable to communicate or accurately read "emotional overtones" through text onscreen. This is very different from phone calls or face-to-face conversations, where we read emotional nuance in nonverbal signals, facial expressions, voice tone, or intensity.[5] In fact, "studies show that email increases the likelihood of conflict and miscommunication." In other words, technology directly contributes to making problems worse. According to Shane Hipps, a Stanford Business School study "focused on business negotiations made face to face, over the telephone, and via email. They found that negotiations performed exclusively over email broke down far more often than face-to-face or even telephone negotiations."[6] Furthermore, while communication technologies are celebrated for convenient asynchronicity—not needing to be in the same place at the same time—this feature also intensifies email conflicts. Delays aggravate situations as people fret about what the lack of response might mean.

Clay Shirky shows several reasons why cybercommunications have a built-in propensity for misunderstanding. When people do not know each other, etiquette guidelines do not have persuasive power. "There is a kind of enforced politeness among people gathered in a dining room or a board room that does not always exist on the net; withdrawing from social situations takes some time in the real world, even if only to gather your coat and slam the door." In cyberspace, it is simple to leave a conversation. Because of easy access and relatively few etiquette guidelines, some people are quicker to enter into controversy and to be more outspoken with opinions, inflaming disagreements. Our emerging vocabulary shows how technology gets misused—not just in relationships but also in hostile or aggressive interactions with people we don't know. "Flaming" refers to heated and insulting exchanges. Shirky believes that internet controversies work in destructive cycles. "The net favors a ping-pong kind of arguing in which only continual disagreement keeps things moving." In fact, contributing to a discussion by merely agreeing is regarded as bad form. Furthermore, in "real life" getting along with others is valued but there are no reasons for doing so in a net community without "physical limits."[7] Various media organizations now revisit policies of allowing people to comment anonymously online about news.

Misunderstandings are less likely to occur when people know each other. But online we are frequently in contact with people we have little context for—and therefore little ability to understand.

> Consider, too, the "e-mail the guy down the hall" effect: as the use of e-mail increases in an organization, the overall volume of other kinds of communication drops—particularly routine friendly greetings. But lacking these seemingly innocuous interactions, people feel more disconnected from co-workers. . . . Saying "Hi," it turns out, really does matter; it's social glue.[8]

So, first email and other contemporary communication forms displace and hollow out collegial relationships and informal interactions, and then they leave us less prepared to deal with each other when problems arise.

We are all well advised to avoid handling conflicts by email. Issues requiring more than two paragraphs of explanation most likely should be dealt with in person. If annoyed or angry, do not respond for at least twenty-four hours. You might draft a written rejoinder, but do not finalize or deliver it. Once you write something, wait another twenty-four hours. (Since your "delayed" response may increase anxiety, consider sending a short acknowledgment that promises to respond when you have time to do so appropriately.) Extra time gives opportunity to gain perspective, perhaps even see how your response might be heard or read by someone else. It will also encourage you to pay attention to important matters that you may have missed in the sender's email, to let go of aspects of the problem that you do not need to put on the record, and perhaps to make room to be more gracious in how you deal with the provocation. You might also want a trusted friend or colleague to read what you write before you send it.

There are other technologically abetted problems. Parents deal with cyberbullying issues. This form of harassment might include insults, accusations, rumor spreading, or posting of embarrassing photographs. Jodee Blanco, a specialist on bullying, says that bullying has always been present: "The impulse for cruelty is the same impulse. The only difference is that the tools to achieve that have become more sophisticated."[9] Now taunts and smears can be broadcast near and far instantly, and bullies can hide behind technological blinds.

Planned Relational Obsolescence

Not just the practical and technical aspects of email but also the very spirit of how we deal with technology can encourage incivility, rudeness, and waning commitments. Patterns of device usage habituate us to treat others like devices. We want quick, predictable, consistent, reliable responses from family and friends, neighbors and coworkers—and when expectations are not met we may react by flaming with rage or rejection. "We unwittingly believe humans should perform like microchips: fast, efficient, consistent, multitalented, and available twenty-four hours a day, seven days a week."[10]

We are less tolerant of any kind of waiting. The internet, for example, promises the option of buying whatever we want whenever we want it. We can watch TV programs or films immediately. We expect instant communication. Fast food outlets promptly deliver food, and if there is to be waiting, we can do so in the comfort of our cars.

We know of "planned obsolescence" when it comes to consumer commodities and technological gadgets. Many devices—including expensive automobiles and appliances—are designed to be desirable only for a short period. Manufacturers seek to lure us into coveting their most recent design. Devices continue to work past their destined expiration date but are no longer in fashion or "cool." In late 2007, I began noticing Toyota commercials that said, "It's the time of year when people look for reasons to buy a new Toyota." Onscreen, Toyota drivers were destroying healthy-looking, recent-model vehicles—dropping one off a parking garage roof, allowing another to be dragged off a boat—so that they could purchase the newest version. It was an odd message from Toyota: only our most recent model is good enough for you.

It is harder and harder to find repair people willing to fix tape recorders, stereo systems, computers, answering machines, and microwaves. The few remaining repair people often give a predictable response that it would cost just as much to buy a new device as it would to try to fix the broken one. Our technically sophisticated inventions create insurmountable waste issues. Old computers and "e-waste" are sent overseas, where they are manually dismantled, exposing workers and local ecosystems to dangerous substances, deadly chemicals, and heavy metals.

I wonder whether our attitude toward obsolescence also frames the way we experience relationships. I remember my shock when a thirtysomething seminarian decided that her career's best interests meant moving far across the country when her husband was unable to go. So they divorced. It seemed casual and matter-of-fact. In our conversations, I never heard any sense of tragedy or loss. When I expressed sorrow and sympathy, she seemed uncomprehending of my concern.

One colleague early in his ministry received a hostile letter. "I don't need this," he exclaimed, crumpling the note and tossing it into the wastebasket. The following Sunday he announced his resignation effective immediately, and went looking for different work, preferably with better pay. I do not underestimate what he suffered; I know that pastoring is not easy. Still I wonder. I have learned that whenever I'm tempted to say, "I don't need this," I must pause and pay close attention because that may in fact be the very thing or person that I most need. It is when I engage criticism or unpleasantness within my relationships that I have the greatest potential for growth.

Not long ago, homes had a clunky, unappealing-looking black phone strategically placed, often in a front hall. It was heavy and solidly wired into the wall. The phone had to be patiently dialed or one relied on an operator to place calls. I grew up in a rural area and many friends had party lines shared with area households. It was important not to stay too long on the phone, as that would prevent neighbors from making or taking calls. With all these limitations, the phone was inconvenient.

Now we have multiple phones, in all kinds of sleek designs and a range of pleasing colors. They are easy to use; not only do they have push buttons, but many are also programmable. You can take a cal anywhere in the house to facilitate privacy. Or you can bring your por table phone or mobile to the kitchen, laundry room, or bathroom an

"multitask." Why waste time giving a caller your full attention when you can accomplish something else that is urgent or useful or more pleasurable too? Phones are equipped with call-waiting, answering machines, voice mail, and caller ID.

Levels of commitment to relationships are now so low that we even forgo the inconvenience of coordinating the timing of conversations in favor of "asynchronous communication." Convenience and ease lure us away from the challenges of maintaining human contact. My son was once informed by email that his part-time job was discontinued. Other friends have had romantic relationships cybersevered by Facebook or text messaging.

Counterbalancing Eroded Engagement

The current pace of life is too much for many of us. Several disciplines and approaches have helped me slow down and make room in my life for rich relationships and meaningful projects.

Slow Down Email

The more emails I respond to the more I get, and those also need a response, making life busier. So I usually do not answer email correspondence the same day. By putting off replies, I stem the incoming tide. If I write quickly I often realize later in the day that there was a better way to respond or that I needed to include additional information or that I did not want to say what I wrote in the first email. Then I have to send yet another.

I also humanize emails. Using my recipient's name alone is not enough. I usually start, "*Dear* So-and-so." I add friendly words of greeting and chat. It's important to retain a human touch and keep emails from being abrupt, demanding, curt, or uncivil.

Write Letters

My friend Evelyn Kreider is in her nineties and still writes letters every day. As a result, she also gets personal correspondence daily. Her mail carrier is astonished. Most of the mail he delivers to others now is composed of bills, ads, and flyers.

How quickly the art of letter writing disappeared, a consequence of ease of immediate communication. I am as guilty as anyone. A decade or so ago I carried on lively correspondence by post (now snidely called "snail mail") with friends far and near who had touched my life at one point or another. I now write fewer letters a year than I used to pen in a month or sometimes even in a week. Almost overnight, our culture eliminated letter writing.

Our young-adult son and daughter went overseas for extended periods of time as part of their college programs. They did not carry phones, but their school posted internet blogs and photos that we could follow, and there was sporadic email. Yet a significant aspect of going to another country is detachment from one's culture and location. Friends in missions, development, and service agencies express concerns about overseas workers who keep close contacts with home via email and internet. They worry that people with feet in two worlds are less able to commit to and settle into placements. Only by detaching from the familiar can one engage deeply with the new and unfamiliar.

I understand parents' longing to stay connected to offspring; but maturity for parent and child alike demands that sooner or later those ties change. The Bible says an adult "leaves . . . father and mother" (Gen. 3:24). If both parties stay in close contact, even during extended overseas travel, the maturation both need may be postponed.

As hard as longing might be, it is good to miss those we love, ponder their absence and what they mean to us, and look forward to their return. Naomi Baron worries about "the end of anticipation" and notes that now "absence may or may not make the heart grow fonder."[11] Should there not be a qualitative difference between how we experience near-and-dear relatives when they live at home attending high school, when they go to college some distance away, and when they spend months abroad? I wondered how following my children too closely day by day might detract from giving sufficient attention to the joy of their return. If I looked at all the photos online, would I have a special celebration when they come back and show me their slides and tell their stories?

I read their brief emails and sent an occasional one, but in order to preserve the opportunity for my children to grow and explore during their time away, I resolved to do the bulk of our communicating by letter. Each Sunday afternoon I reviewed the events and reflections of my week, sharing with my son or daughter what I would like them to know or what might be of particular interest and responding to whatever developments that I heard from them. Information ranged from small news about pets to big news about vocational challenges or changes. I found it refreshing to ponder my week and summarize what was most significant for me. I was writing not only for Paul and Erin but also for my own benefit. And when their sojourn was over, they had a tangible record of our exchanges and my love for them.

Letter writing is a form of communication that involves pauses and slow progress. It is labor intensive and an invitation to be thoughtful and reflective.

Blogs, emails, and on and on offer options for connecting promptly but also have limitations. A young mother, Melissa Seligman, wrote about how she and her husband—serving as a soldier first in Afghanistan and later in Iraq—tried to maintain contact by instant messaging, long-distance phone calls, and other technological means. She concluded that webcams provided only the illusion that "a two-dimensional image could transmit and sustain a three-dimensional marriage." They saw each other's faces and heard words, but there was not the time nor was this the medium for talking about deeper and more troubling things they felt and experienced. Their toddler begged to see her father on the screen but then did not engage him when he appeared.

They turned to letters. Ironically, they could read each other's moods in handwriting better than in pixilated screen images. Ms. Seligman paid attention to the pens and stationery she used. Letters gave leisure and luxury to carefully explain thoughts and perceptions, worries and concerns, and were less likely to be misunderstood or misinterpreted. With hard-copy mail, they could smell each other's fragrance and even hear each other's voice. Instead of an ephemeral experience that is gone as soon as power is cut or satellite disconnected, the toddler "would stuff her daddy's letters into her pockets and take them with her to the playground. At night, she would beg [her mother] to read the letters again. Over and over until she felt content enough to sleep." Seligman sees the irony. For those separated, "the burden to overcome was communicating without technology—waiting months for letters to arrive. For me and those still to come, it's learning to communicate despite technology."[12]

9

REMOTE RELATIONSHIPS

It was the kind of summer day that I like best. I had gotten up early and was taking the dog for our daily four-mile jaunt. Although it was July, the humidity was not yet thick. The sun shone in a brightly blue sky. A gentle breeze ruffled Abbey's fur. Bulky white clouds inspired the imagination as they trailed slowly above. Few people were up yet, and all that I heard were birds singing in the trees. The world was still and inviting. The dog and I were glad to be out and about, breathing fresh, clear air deeply into our lungs.

A white four-door car pulled to the curb. In it was a young man in an olive green service uniform and cap. It was a few minutes before the hour. I assumed that he had an appointment in a house nearby and was waiting until the proper time. In the meantime, he left his car running. His windows rolled up tightly, air-conditioning already going in his vehicle. As I walked by, I could hear a popular radio station playing loudly.

An identical white four-door sedan pulled to the curb. In it was a young man in a uniform and hat matching the other fellow, obviously a coworker. He also elected to wait in his car. Once again, I could hear his engine purring. His windows were closed; he also preferred mechanically cooled air. As I passed his vehicle I could hear that he was listening to the radio . . . to the very same station as his coworker!

Each sat in his vehicle, windows closed, idling the engine, and consuming gas to supply AC. Twenty feet apart and having comparable musical tastes, they preferred staying in car cocoons and listening alone to the same broadcast. They had no idea what a lovely day—fresh air, cool breeze, sounds of nature—they were missing; perhaps they did not care. They were oblivious to each other and their surroundings. They preferred the manufactured consolations of machinery.

There is much enthusiastic commentary these days about how technology helps form new kinds of communities and relationships. In this instance, two young men had a lot in common—clothes, occupation, aversion to morning air, appreciation for a particular radio station. They relied on identical technology—white automobiles, air-conditioning, radios. But they used those devices in such a way that they were cut off from each other. A Blackberry commercial urged, "Connect to everything you love in life in a bold new way." But there are reasons to question that promise. Stephen Talbott writes, "There is . . . one absolutely unavoidable fact: technologies for 'bringing people together' do not necessarily *bring people together*."[1]

My friend Arnold was bicycling through an unfamiliar neighborhood with two preteen daughters. One bike developed a flat, and he did not have tools and supplies to repair it. Much to his dismay, he was unable to find a pay phone to call his wife and ask for rescue. He was also surprised that no one stopped to offer help, even though he and the girls were obviously in a predicament. He concluded that folks now generally assume that everyone has a cell phone and can take care of himself or herself. No one assisted the family in distress. Now he too owns a cell phone, even though he never wanted one.

A Sprint TV ad showed three skiers trapped on a chair lift. They look at each other for an uncomfortable nanosecond and then with great relief pull out their phones. Carl searches for new apps (and plays a virtual skiing game), Candace "mixes business with pleasure" by texting, and Rose gets "updated on her sleek and slim Palm Pixi." Imagine the torture of having to make conversation with someone beside you. Christine Rosen writes, "Public trust among strangers in social settings is eroding."[2]

Evidence shows that we are growing more isolated. Yes, there are certainly ways that people connect via technologies, but such connections tend to be tenuous, issue- or hobby-specific, and limited. Less and less are our relationships complex, ongoing, face-to-face, year-after-year. One airport's wireless service, Lily Pad Free Wi-Fi, boasted that its access would "foster a vibrant community and enhance the quality of life in the region." Yet I felt as isolated and disconnected as I do in any airport, even if I was able to check my email and surf the web.

Relationship alerts that bear closer attention include the fact that technology is increasingly isolating us. Our engagements with others are indirect, mediated through technologies. And along the way we rely more and more on virtual communities.

(Not) Getting to Know You, (Not) Getting to Know All About You

Even as families shrank during the last few decades, garages expanded: "The number of homes with multicar garages . . . almost doubled— one in five new homes has a three-car garage."[3] An Infiniti ad claimed, "Your garage is sacred." Garage development reflects other significant changes in house design. Norman Wirzba spells out the implications:

> The . . . physical shape and arrangement of our homes communicate anonymity, separation, and movement away from each other. The garage is given copious pride of place, large and in front, demonstrating that cars and the mobility they afford are high priorities. Noticeably absent . . . is a welcoming front porch, a place that looks out into the wider community and that encourages time spent relaxing and conversing with each other. Backyards are small and are surrounded by privacy fences. We don't spend much time out and about; we prefer the solitude and protection of interior rooms and the control and comfort of home entertainment centers. Kitchens and dining rooms, which used to be focal points of gathering, places where people could interact face to face (rather than around a television or computer screen), have been significantly reduced in size and use because we can presume that people . . . eat less and less together. And so our architecture, even the way we arrange our furniture, rather than fostering and communicating our life together, in fact encourages separation from each other.[4]

Suburbs reinforce privacy, disconnection, isolation. In the morning, many go to the garage directly from inside the house, get in a car, press a button to open the door, and drive away, without encountering anyone. In the evening, one reverses the process and never has to deal with neighbors. But there is significant loss. Jane Jacobs established that it is in the abundance of casual, informal, and impromptu street encounters that trust and security are built.[5]

David Myers writes, "Since the 1950s, supportive social connections and informal networks have weakened. Eye-to-eye interactions are waning, thanks partly to drive-through food pickups, ATM machines, and e-mail. In the era of what Robert Wuthnow calls 'loose connections,' people visit with one another less, belong to fewer groups, and more often live alone."[6]

We are actively discouraged from personal contacts. Banks often charge a "teller rationing" fee for human encounters.[7] It is easier to deal with a machine, get frustrated if so inclined, and not worry about etiquette and congeniality than to do the hard work of engaging another live human being in conversation. I pump gas with my credit card; it speeds things up. But there are losses in choosing technological transactions over human encounters. As communication technologies evolve, quality of life declines.

> Psychologists Robert Kraut and Vicki Lundmark studied the effects of Internet use on ninety-six families over two years. . . . The more time individuals spent online, the greater the degree of depression and loneliness they experienced. This is . . . because increased Internet usage resulted in some loss of close friendships.[8]

As reported in the *American Sociological Review*, a cross section of Americans in 1984 had around three confidants. Less than twenty years later, in 2004, those numbers dropped to the point where as many as one-fourth of Americans said they had no confidants, "no one at all with whom to talk openly and intimately."[9] Statistics Canada discovered that "the proportion of Canadians reporting they have at least two friends has dropped across almost all demographics in recent years."[10] Time spent web surfing, television watching, or driving displaces social opportunities with family or friends. According to John Freeman, two-thirds of North Americans spend more hours in front of computers than they do with their spouses.[11] Norman Nie of Stanford says, "The

Internet could be the ultimate isolating technology that further reduces our participation in communities even more than did automobiles and television before it."[12]

Several years ago in Winnipeg, Manitoba, a fifty-three-year-old man went to bed, died during the night at his condo, and was not found for over a year and a half. No one pursued what happened to him because all his bills were paid regularly. Lianne George notes that the "primary factor in the delay" of discovering him "was technology—or more specifically, automated banking." His disability pension went directly into his bank accounts and "condo fees, utilities and other expenses were then deducted automatically." George notes that this "tale illuminates a chilling fact: . . . new technologies like electronic banking have created a system in which it's possible to become so physically disengaged from the day-to-day administration of your own affairs that your life can effectively go on without you, perhaps indefinitely."[13]

We could dismiss this bizarre story as an unlikely exception. But then recall the 1995 Chicago heat wave where hundreds perished. Many victims were elderly and impoverished. "Those who died had run out of water, had no air-conditioning, did not leave their rooms to find cool refuge, and were not successfully checked up on." Senior citizens were so frightened of their dangerous neighborhoods that they kept windows closed and doors locked rather than circulate air with fans.[14] Sociologist Eric Klinenberg noticed that adjoining communities had strikingly different results: "The heat-wave death rate in North Lawndale was 40 fatalities per 100,000 population, while right next door in South Lawndale, the death rate was fewer than 4 per 100,000." In North Lawndale, people stayed in apartments and never walked around because their area had no parks, stores, or places to meet and visit with others. People were not used to getting out, and thus they had not built connections and relationships that might have saved their lives and were

> unacquainted with storekeepers who could welcome them into air-conditioned space. They were afraid . . . to leave their apartments, for fear these would be burglarized while they were out. For the same reason, they feared strangers who came to check on them.

In South Lawndale, more people survived.

There the elderly were accustomed to walking outside. There were plenty of places . . . to go on the district's bustling, crowded streets. They knew storekeepers and had no hesitation about hanging around in their air-conditioned spaces, where they also had access to water. They felt secure about leaving their apartments, and they trusted those who came to check on them, some of whom they knew as acquaintances.

The contrasting experiences show that how we structure communities and employ technologies are crucially important. North Lawndale was disastrously shaped by the fact that the only way to survive was to have access to automobiles. The same dilemma was a problem when Hurricane Katrina struck New Orleans; those without cars were left behind without resources.

In *Outliers*, Malcolm Gladwell writes about Roseto, a mining town in Pennsylvania inhabited by Italian immigrants. In the 1950s, while cholesterol and heart disease were high in the United States and most of Pennsylvania, such ailments were rare in Roseto.

> Virtually no one under fifty-five had died of a heart attack or showed any signs of heart disease. For men over sixty-five, the death rate from heart disease in Roseto was roughly half that of the United States as a whole. The death rate from all causes in Roseto, in fact, was 30 to 35 percent lower than expected.

Also notable was the absence of suicide, alcoholism, drug addiction, crime, and ulcers. No one was on welfare. Old age was pretty much the only cause of death.

Stewart Wolf, a physician studying this, wondered whether the old-world Italian diet made the difference. But Rosetan menus were un-healthy, and residents did not get much exercise. Genetics was not the factor. Relatives who lived elsewhere were not living as long as Rosetans. Neither was location the issue; people in nearby towns had three times the heart disease death rates. Wolf and his colleagues concluded that how Rosetans related to each other was the key.

> Rosetans visited one another, stopping to chat in Italian on the street, say, or cooking for one another in their backyards. [Wolf and his researchers] learned about the extended family clans that underlay the town's social

structure. They saw how many homes had three generations living under one roof, and how much respect grandparents commanded. [Doctor Wolf and a colleague] went to mass at Our Lady of Mount Carmel and saw the unifying and calming effect of the church. They counted twenty-two separate civic organizations in a town of just under two thousand people.

Gladwell concludes: "Rosetans had created a powerful, protective social structure capable of insulating them from the pressures of the modern world. The Rosetans were healthy because of where they were *from*, because of the world they had created for themselves in their tiny little town in the hills."[15]

Our lives are increasingly shaped in ways that disconnect us. It is common for face-to-face conversations to be interrupted by cell phones. Such devices have a dominating and intrusive presence. One school where I taught restricted cell phone use to certain areas because people employing such devices—whether in halls, classrooms, or lounges—tend to speak with more volume than usual and thus dominate and even inhibit work, study, or conversations around them. Calls interrupt meals, hospitality, and meetings. We no longer see this as rude; gadgets are our default priority.

MP3 players mean that we can ignore others on the street, in the subway, next to us on the couch in our living room, or around the table. Lianne George describes the same "dysfunctional family dynamic" in the car: "You can have one kid in the back watching a movie, one listening to an iPod, and mom and dad up front—each in their own custom climate-controlled environment."[16]

A friend, partial to weight machines, has been faithfully going to the YMCA for many years, and he's observed a few changes along the way. When he started, he noted the camaraderie of fellow exercisers. They would laugh and chat, much as I did with pilgrims at water fountains in Spanish villages. Over time, he got to know some of them a little and they would pick up the line of conversation from when they had last seen each other. Then one year, televisions were installed. Conversation diminished, as people uniformly focused on the screens. There were occasional comments on or laughter about what was shown, but there was a lot less visiting than previously. Some years after that, people began exercising with their own MP3 players and now everyone was cut off from each other. The frightening aspect of this story is that many of us prefer this situation.

Do we know what we've lost?

Technologically Mediated and Altered Relationships

More and more relationships and conversations go through technology. We speak by phone, email, fax, instant messaging, text, Tweet, or what have you. Less and less do we have opportunity to converse directly, face-to-face. Even in offices with desks a few feet apart, many prefer to communicate by email or texting. Email displaced face-to-face talking and telephone conversations. Edward Tenner observes, "In the last thirty years, the office may have grown more quiet but it has also become more tense and lonely."[17] Ursula Franklin speaks of "non-communication technologies," the many devices that discourage face-to-face interaction.[18]

Nina Lanctot is an experienced pastor who models excellence in ministry. At the Elkhart Consultation she told a story of pastoring a church that shared news items, announcements, joys, and concerns in worship. Yet there were often people absent who might not hear pressing news. Why not, thought Nina, send out the sharing by email after the service? "Isn't that a good idea? So people who weren't there could hear the prayer requests and pray," she noted. But she made an unhappy discovery. Before when someone missed church, they might make a point of being in touch with another member from the congregation to find out what is new or important. Or members might take the initiative to fill in someone who was missing that day. This was a chance to connect personally. Now those ways of relating atrophy and disappear. Nina's not suggesting that we dispose of technology.

> I am glad I can send an email saying, "When can we meet?" and we can sort that out. That makes sense. But a prayer request? I'm not sure it does. Poor judgment about technology destroyed the fabric of Christian community.

I long to hear more folks work at such distinctions. I have been employed for years by fine Christian institutions with compassionate, caring colleagues. Every day my email inbox has one, several, or even many items with a subject heading of "prayer request" or "prayer concern" circulated to dozens, sometimes hundreds of names. Recipients are told of someone who died or is dying, is ill or awaiting a diagnosis, was in an accident or is traveling, or is facing a challenging test or surgery. In other words, matters that affect people's lives, situations that merit being commended to God. Even so, as I often have no idea who these people are, such communiqués feel inappropriate. The ease with which one is able to email encourages careless discernment of what to send to whom.

What does it mean for prayer requests to be distributed to all and sundry? Such emails may include hundreds of people in several different countries. I have no issue when friends, acquaintances, students, or colleagues email me or even a select list with a concern. I am uncomfortable, however, with blanket prayer petitions circulated routinely and casually. My email inbox already has far more submissions than I can reasonably deal with in a day. When intrusions mount, no matter how important each might be, they all decrease in value.

Often emailed requests reveal personal details, making me feel more like a voyeur than an intercessor. Even prayer, one of the spiritual life's most intimate acts, is now mediated through a screen and no longer requires gathering believers, bowing heads, folding hands, bending knees, let alone calling a meeting "where two or three are gathered." We tap out petitions on a keyboard, alone at our desk, another assignment in the day's clutter. When such notices pop into my box, what is being asked? Am I invited to set aside work, close my eyes, and focus on the petition? Does my employer approve? Do I wing or whisper a quick prayer heavenward, along with all my other multitasking before moving on with my pressing agenda? I'll be honest: I sometimes have trouble keeping up with requests already on my prayer list, those from people I know directly who personally requested my intercession.[19]

Prayer should have flesh on it. If you want me to pray, ask personally, don't spam me. There is a simple solution for Christian institutions. Invite people to the chapel at a set time to come together. Or declare an email-free day every week and set aside a quarter hour that day for corporate intercession. Prayer requests need to be invitations to substantial and true communion. They ought to have more integrity and a different format than the daily solicitations that invite us to experiment with Viagra.

Technology alters relationships. Our lives, friendships, and society are being changed. We saw in the last chapter that the relative anonymity of technologically mediated interactions—whether by email or driving in cars and hence cut off from other drivers—encourages aggression. There are several other dynamics that we need to note.

First of all, relationships grow easy to enter and exit. Every week, complete strangers email me and invite correspondence. Or acquaintances want me to join their Facebook community or what have you. Such connections have a low threshold of entry, and it is easy to disappear quietly without explanation. This contributes to intrinsically unstable and ambiguous networks. That is one reason why it is so easy to misinterpret—or be misled by—what happens online. Such conditions do not foster deep ties.

In early 2009, Burger King launched a program awarding a free burger to anyone who unfriended at least ten Facebook "friends." Over 200,000 folks were dropped! Burger King delivered the news, informing "castoffs . . . they'd been dropped for a sandwich (or, more accurately, a tenth of a sandwich)."[20] Given the tenuous connections, technology makes it easier to risk losing relationships. After all, what is the cost of giving up a so-called friendship that was easily acquired and can just as easily be replaced? Such relational ambiguities explain why cybersex threatens human interactions. Promiscuity has not traditionally been condemned merely because it is distasteful or icky but because it undermines trust.

Second, we divert time to virtual relationships. "For better or for worse" wedding vows or Ruth's promise to her mother-in-law that "where you go, I will go" (a text often used in weddings) reassure partners that they are in this together for the long haul. "Relationships that are not based on shared responsibilities, shared difficulties, and shared experience . . . are superficial and unsatisfactory."[21] Strange inversions occur: "Frequent e-mail makes a distant and unknown person seem closer and more responsive than your friend next door, or . . . a colleague on the same floor remains cool and distant until he or she begins to open up and confide in you through e-mail."[22]

Third, online relationships make it easier to disguise motivations, identity, reputation, and history. Attention is devoted to "impression management." Yet ironically, as Christine Rosen observes, technologies that grant increased access to others may engender mistrust. Online pseudonyms are common and lead to other forms of disguise.[23] Richard Stivers shows that ambiguity of information also contributes to widespread loneliness. This erodes reason and ability to trust what other people present about themselves. While actual relationships become less substantial, we may come to count on celebrities and TV's "pseudo-intimacy" and relate to onscreen personalities to alleviate loneliness.[24] We get wrapped up in reality-television melodrama or talk-show confessions. In the meantime we do not realize that our neighbors are trapped in the heat or that the fellow in the condo upstairs is slowly mummifying. Intimacy is inverted: we have too much information about distant screen characters who may or may not be real and too little knowledge about actual people nearby.

Virtually Unreal Communities

None of this means that technology cannot help with communication or even build community. We all know of promising possibilities. I reconnected, for example, with high school acquaintances through the internet, and this contributed to a rewarding reunion some months later.

My colleague Kaarina Hsieh needed to be quarantined during the 2003 SARS epidemic in Toronto. She was not allowed outside her house, and people were not permitted to visit either. So they showed up at the street by her window, waved at her, and called her on their cell phones. Their friendly faces encouraged her. Their solidarity was appreciated.

At the Elkhart Consultation, my former colleague Gayle Gerber Koontz recalled how missionaries in a previous era did not hear the news of a parent's death in North America for over three months. Her uncle, however, had died that week in another state and Gayle was able to phone and offer consolation right away to those who were grieving. Gayle and her husband, Ted, have always been committed to maintaining relationships with overseas students and use technology to build on friendships that began when those students studied at their school.

These justifiably heartwarming stories are powerful examples of technology supporting and reinforcing community. I do not underestimate or dismiss their significance. But notice what they have in common. In each instance—high school reunion, Kaarina's care from friends during a quarantine, Gayle's connecting with grieving families and alumni—technology is used to build on relationships that were already in place.

There are other positive possibilities. Social and literary critic William Deresiewicz writes about what the internet offers people who are alone: "Under those circumstances, the Internet arrived as an incalculable blessing. We should never forget that. It has allowed isolated people to communicate with one another and marginalized people to find one another."[25] David Shenk cites examples of meaningful online connections around common interests and "opportunities afforded to linguists, Latinos, teenagers, environmentalists, ethicists, folklorists, engineers, documentarians, therapists, movie buffs, studio musicians, plumbers, and freelance writers. Being able to share one's personal thoughts, ambitions, accomplishments, trials, and tribulations with other like-minded people is part of the joy of being human."[26] When my uncle was diagnosed with Lou Gehrig's disease (a.k.a. ALS), he and my aunt lived in a remote area. Internet access helped them relate to others struggling with that ailment, and they received vital support and information. Nothing they learned, of course, ultimately saved his life, but they moved forward with a sense of solidarity with other sufferers and made more informed decisions because of such connectivity.

Yet we must question how rich relationships can be when they are entirely dependent on devices. Clay Shirky says that "technology won't ever change the number of people to whom you will donate a kidney."[27] Hal Niedzviecki ruefully observes about his own Facebook reality: "Seven hundred friends, and I was drinking alone."[28]

"Community" is an amorphous word that suggests groups connected by practices, priorities, experiences, or interests. But watching the same television program or enjoying YouTube videos or playing games online are not true *communities*. Those networks are what Kenneth Gergen calls "symbolic communities." Such networks "are linked primarily by the capacity of their members for symbolic exchange—of words, images, information—mostly through electronic means. Physical immediacy and geographic closeness disappear as criteria of community." Gergen lists sports-fan networks and electronic churches as "symbolic communities," whose level of interaction and mutual commitment is found wanting.[29] Many so-called communities—online or virtual—are thin replacements for rich local relationships.

Another issue is that virtual communities tend to be self-selecting. One can deliberately choose to engage with certain people but not others. They give, in other words, too much control. The way we use technologies often contributes to "group polarization." We interact with people who agree with us or view materials that fit our worldview.[30] In theory the internet could expose us to great varieties of opinions and points of view; in practice, not so much.

Ursula Franklin calls these new realities "pseudocommunities."[31] Many technologically engaged activities are often merely a *shared experience carried out in private.*[32] Like those young service repairmen who listened to the same radio show in different cars, people are separated from one another, in spite of the appearance of having something in common. Vartan Gregorian of the Carnegie Foundation argues that using information technologies contributes to decreasing involvement with musical concerts and art museums. He observes, "It's ironic . . . that while the Internet has made it possible for us to have more contact with more people in more places than ever before, this 'contact' is not face-to-face but virtual, made by individuals acting in isolation, staring at lonely computer screens."[33]

Is this community? Maggie Jackson, citing Barry Wellman, a researcher of social networks, calls this "networked individualism." Connections are thin, based on little information and not much history. Jackson says, quoting Wellman again, "Connectivity is up, cohesion is down."[34] David Lyon laments, "Whereas face-to-face contacts have characterized all previous human history, today they no longer predominate."[35]

Years ago, a Lotus (IBM) ad read: "You've solved the problem of being in 50 places at once quite simply. By being in 50 places at once." Kenneth G. Gergen's *The Saturated Self* shows that mobility and flexibility have a debilitating effect on relationships, encouraging a lack of intimacy and commitment. With easier "connectivity," our communications also become "more incidental, more shallow."[36] Bodies are ignored, overlooked, and dismissed in the ways that we live today. If all that we have are virtual relationships—if even most of what we have are virtual relationships—then we live in an era of depleted relational realities. Devices displace and thin out the kinds of connections that we all deeply need.

Lutheran pastor Heidi B. Neumark recounts a remarkable experience when she took a year off from university to live on an island off South Carolina. She volunteered in a community torn between the interests of the Gullah descendants of plantation slaves and real estate developers. She grew close to Miss Ellie, an elderly woman who lived in a one-room wooden house. Somewhere between ninety and one hundred years of age, she had a lifelong friend Netta. Miss Ellie had to walk several miles to visit that friend. Their houses were not far apart, but were separated by a stream, and one could only cross the water safely by going far out of the way.

Neumark, a young do-gooder, recruited men to build a simple bridge over the stream as a way of facilitating easier visits between two friends. The project took only a day, and Neumark was understandably eager to surprise Miss Ellie. But her

> face did not register the grateful, happy look I expected. There was no smile. . . . Instead for a long time, she looked puzzled, then . . . shook her head and looked at me as though I were the one who needed pity: "Child, I don't need a shortcut." And she told about all the friends she kept up with on her way to visit Netta. A shortcut would cut her off from Mr. Jenkins with whom she always swapped gossip, from Miss Hunter who so looked forward to the quilt scraps she'd bring by, from the raisin wine she'd taste at one place, in exchange for her biscuits, and the chance to look in on the "old folks" who were sick.
>
> "Child," she said again, "can't take shortcuts if you want friends in this world. Shortcuts don't mix with love."[37]

Counterbalancing Remote Relationships

Growing isolation, machine mediation of connections, and depletion of relationships call for comprehensive responses. Even seemingly small steps can affect us in good ways.

Turn Off the Telephone (and Other Gadgets)

I attended university in far-gone days when telephones were solidly attached to the wall, mounted or tethered by a cord that could not be disconnected. The only way to avoid phone calls was by taking the receiver off the hook.

During those years, however, we did know a telephone pioneer. Faye Males was the spouse of our InterVarsity chaplain. We attended the same church and often visited for meals, tea, or whenever personal crises struck. On our first visit, as we sat at a table in the small kitchen, Faye got up and walked over to the wall-mounted telephone. She yanked at it and it came right out. She had figured out how to disconnect her phone. We had never seen anything like it. This was before telephone jacks were introduced. Faye explained that she always did this when she had company: "I want to pay attention to my visitors. That's simple hospitality. I don't want our visit to be interrupted by the phone."

Technology for turning devices off exists. Our willingness to use it is the issue. Rather than being perpetually available to others far away, let us choose to be present and attentive to the person nearby. While we're at it, let's turn off televisions and MP3 players and other digital devices when we're at table. As Swedish physicist Bodil Jönsson says, "Conversations should take place in disturbance-free zones."[38]

Eat Meals Together

As we have seen, it is hard to overestimate the importance of eating together. Some decades ago, Robert Farrar Capon penned *The Supper of the Lamb*, a book that made clear the deep connections between daily meals and religious realities. The whole volume is devoted to exploring the preparation of one celebratory meal. Albert Borgmann told me that this book was key to his early ideas about focal practices. Borgmann argues that what we do at our home tables is vitally connected to what Christians do during the Eucharist; both are examples of what he calls the "culture of the table." Borgmann sees meals as one of the most important issues for family life today. He said, "Yes, fornication is bad, adultery is bad, but not sitting down to dinner is worse."[39]

10

TAXED TIME

As an adolescent I almost succeeded in killing off my whole family one Sunday.

I had all the usual reasons for wanting to drive. I dreamed and fantasized about greater mobility, impressing friends, and taking young women on dates. I was not much for macho, but this was one rite of passage that I did not want to miss.

In my case there was an added motivation. We lived out in the country, far from public transit. Wherever I might go—school, library, church, youth meetings, recreation, visiting friends—involved motorized transport. So not only did I require my parents' permission, but I also usually needed them to give me a ride as well. As more and more friends acquired their drivers' permits, my longing to be mobile grew urgent. I prepared by practicing hour after hour in a large parking lot behind our house. Once I had a beginner's permit, my next goal was in sight: I wanted to drive the family vehicle on our regular excursions while under the supervision of my parents. I began proposing this every time that we stepped into the car.

Then one day I got my wish. We were returning from church. About three miles from home, my father pulled over to the shoulder of a secondary highway. It was a straight drive back to the house with a steady speed limit, fifty miles per hour, and no lights, curves, or turns.

I took charge. This felt like one of the most important moments of my life. I was exhilarated and a little surprised that the rest of the family wasn't noticing the monumental significance of this opportunity. They just kept discussing the usual postchurch fare: opinions of the sermon, parking lot gossip after worship, what we would eat for lunch, plans for the rest of the day. But when I jutted my elbow out the window I found out that my father was watching; he sternly corrected me and I assumed the "ten and two" position with my hands on the wheel.

As our house came into sight, a third of a mile away, I took my foot off the gas to slow down. The conversation ceased, and now people did pay attention to my driving and the significance of the moment.

"You have to slow down," my father told me, with urgency in his tightened voice.

"I am," I responded, annoyed to get such obvious advice so soon after taking the wheel. "I've taken my foot off the gas."

"But that's not enough," he protested.

He was too late, however, as I had already started turning the wheel to get into our driveway. Gravel crunched under our wheels, and I was surprised that fifty-miles-per-hour momentum did not dissipate easily. The inertia first made us skid and slide to the left and then took us airborne. Beside our driveway was a marshy field, a four foot drop. We sailed twenty or thirty feet through the air and then landed with an ominous thump on all four wheels.

Luckily, the car did not tip and no one was injured. It could have been worse, far worse. But I can assure you that this was one mortifying experience for an adolescent. In that moment, I thought that my driving days were over and I might never live down my shame.

The auto was not damaged but was impossible to extract from the field by ourselves. My father called the local service station to bring a tow truck. My parents did not want too many neighbors or passersby to see the car's unlikely position—and I agreed. We knew the truck driver; John was in a service organization with my father and ribbed my dad about what kind of party he was at the night before and how much he must have imbibed. My father took it all gallantly, never saying a word of correction, never explaining who had put the car there.

That auto accident reminds me of Donald Nicholl, who wrote in a book (on holiness of all things), "The first thing one needs to know about a car, or any machine for that matter, is how to stop it. The same applies to the traffic of our daily lives."[1]

Busy, Busy, Busy

Somewhere along the way, I began noticing more and more people complain of being too busy. It may have been when I was in grad school and someone gave me a planner, and I for the first time began carefully plotting how I spent each and every day. (I ruefully admit that I now always have my calendar nearby but don't always have a Bible at hand.) It may have been when our children were in grade school and were already expected to use a planner.

I suspected busyness was an issue more when I became a pastor. It did not matter where or with whom the conversation was—congregants, colleagues, friends—everyone talked about being pressed for time. The common question "How are you?" was often answered with "Busy," usually said with a small sigh. Yet many of us were secretly pleased; busyness is a mark of status and importance. We would be uneasy about the professional abilities of a doctor, attorney, or specialist if his or her calendar were wide open.

There is a prevailing sense of having too much to do, getting tugged in too many directions at once, and not having enough time for priorities. In the 1980s, we started hearing about "the hurried child," and these days many retirees tell me about not having a sense of calm and control. So we're now hurried from cradle to grave.

This was not the future projected for us. Not long ago, we were told that machines and "labor-saving" devices would make life so easy that a major challenge would be too much time and leisure. My high school sociology course, Man in Society, misled me. In a homework assignment, we were urged to start planning for hobbies and leisure possibilities because in two or three decades, when middle-aged, we would work half-time or less. The concern was that if we did not prepare, we would encounter the serious stress of not knowing how to cope with so much free time. Of course, that prediction now seems absurd. As one newspaper headline, coauthored by a former provincial premier, declared,

"Modern time crunch hijacked 'leisure society.'"[2] Too much leisure has not been a problem for most of us; rather, finding space in our days has.

How we function within time has everything to do with living the good life. Time is a matter of spiritual and religious importance. As a family of Dutch Calvinist immigrants, we spent Sundays more strictly than other churchgoers. In high school, a friend of mine was Jewish, and his week—and indeed his year—was ordered otherwise than mine. Muslim schoolmates also lived their lives differently. Marking time is a matter of religious distinction. The Essenes were a unique group of Jews living during the days of Jesus. They were the only ones who operated by a solar calendar. The Western and Eastern Orthodox churches diverge on how to calculate when Easter is. This dispute was also at play in early controversies between Celtic and Roman-influenced Christians in the British Isles. Time is a crucial aspect of how culture is ordered, and those who control schedules have significant power and authority.

Where Have All the Hours Gone?

Concerns about being too busy are not merely imaginary or empty nostalgia for good old days. Several years ago, a national study in Canada revealed that

> more than money, their health or their children, Canadians . . . worried about time. Thanks to a multitude of stressors, they didn't have enough hours in the day to spend with their families, never mind their friends or colleagues or their own interests. On a list of 19 personal concerns, the No. 1 worry of people from 18 to 55 was never having enough time. Slightly more than half thought they were busier than their parents. Sixty-four percent reported they almost never had extra time.[3]

Much of our language shows a competitive and even hostile experience with time. Long-standing clichés—killing time, racing against time, saving time, and even the clock is ticking—grow only more potent in our day.

We are obsessed. A Mitsubishi ad says, "Life's busy. Fit more into it." I see the advertisement's idea symbolized in my own life by the omnipresence of clocks. There are two in my study at home, two in my office at work, two in our living room, and two more in the kitchen. There are clocks on our phones, microwave, and stove. Jim Forest comments:

> It is a pity we have stripped so many walls of their crucifixes and put up so many clocks in their place. We are surely more punctual than our ancestors, but we are spiritually poorer. Contemplating a crucifix, many of our forebears had a different idea of how to make use of time. A crucifix may not tell the hour, but it offers crucial advice about what to do with the moment we are living in.[4]

Once, most people had no clocks. Phil Cousineau writes about medieval pilgrims going "to the Temple of Time in Rome where the first public clock was displayed. Crowds waited for hours to file past the elaborate clockworks, torn between admiration for the wondrous precision, and suspicion, for they knew that *their* time was no longer theirs."[5] Clocks became so important that philosophers and scientists came to regard God as a clockmaker. The great sociologist Lewis Mumford contended that with the invention of clocks we settled for lesser measures of time—rather than ordering our lives by eternity and God's priorities.[6]

Monks invented clocks to call themselves regularly to prayer. Slowly nearby communities and villages also began to have clocks or bell towers in central places. Their original purpose was to announce worship; later they gave notice of the commencement of work, commerce, or industry. Neil Postman comments on the irony:

> The clock was invented by . . . [monks] who wanted to devote themselves more rigorously to God; it ended as the technology of greatest use to men who wished to devote themselves to the accumulation of money. In the eternal struggle between God and Mammon, the clock . . . favored the latter.[7]

Eventually the wealthy possessed watches that they could wear (at first in pockets and later on wrists). In *Gulliver's Travels*, the Lilliputians are convinced that Gulliver's watch was his god because he looks at it so often. As timepieces progressed, their finer and finer measurements also reflected an increasingly detailed preoccupation with keeping track of time.

While earliest clocks had only an hour hand, the minute hand was added as time became more precious—and then a sweeping second hand, which moved in endless circles. . . . Seconds were divided by the "stopwatch," first into tenths and then into hundreds. Ultimately, the computer provided a further division of time beyond human perception—the nanosecond, one billionth of a second.[8]

Not so long ago all time was still local, determined by the sun's movement across the sky. This meant that towns just a short distance from each other might operate by different clocks. With the introduction of railroads, there was growing interest in regularizing time and eventually developing a standardized system of time zones. When I lived in Indiana I was on the western edge of the eastern time zone, and my friend in Maine was at the eastern edge, a thousand miles or so apart. Even though we were supposedly in the same zone, we experienced sunsets and sunrises at notably different times. Rebecca Solnit observes that by imposing time zones, railroads overrode the importance of honoring locality and, in fact, "eclipsed the sun" as they became the prevailing way to set the time.[9]

Numerous studies and statistics show that North Americans are working longer hours than ever. Others argue that North Americans in fact have more free time but admit that people live increasingly stressed and pressured lives now. They contend that the problem is how we use discretionary time. Some studies suggest that on average North American youths spend about twelve hours per day focusing on screens.[10]

Large forces contribute to increased work, including the power and demand of corporations and the diminishing influence of unions.[11] Many people are burdened by health-care costs and college debts, meaning that either they or their immediate families have to work harder and harder. Other factors are also beyond our control. Various life circumstances—small children, single parenthood, launching a business, caring for elderly or aging relatives—make busyness inevitable. But I am a middle-aged academic, my children are grown, none of my close family is ill, and I have a schedule that is flexible. I still, even now, feel the pressure of busyness. While particular life circumstances might seem conducive to a more relaxed way of life, they do not necessarily help.

Yet the truth is that busyness itself can be a rush. It can be compulsive, resemble an addiction. We may choose it. Many of us like it.

Why should we be concerned?

Malcolm Gladwell reports a startling study at Princeton University. Two psychologists tested a group of seminarians. Each student was given an assignment to prepare a short, extemporaneous presentation. Some were asked specifically to speak on the good Samaritan. Others were assigned the subject of vocation. Each seminarian had to go to a building elsewhere on campus. What they did not know is that on their way they would encounter "a man slumped in an alley, head down, eyes closed, coughing, and groaning." In some instances, the down-and-outer was positioned in such a way that students had to step right over him. As the seminarians went off to give their speech, some were told that they were late but others were assured that they had plenty of time. The results were discouraging. Those who thought they had ample time were more compassionate. Only one of ten of those who thought that they were late stopped. Even being assigned to speak about the good Samaritan did not mean that the seminarians would act like a good Samaritan. All that made a difference was whether or not they understood themselves to be late. Gladwell concludes

> that convictions of your heart and the actual contents of your thoughts are less important, in the end, in guiding your actions than the immediate context of your behavior. The words "Oh, you're late" had the effect of making someone who was ordinarily compassionate into someone who was indifferent to suffering.[12]

Well-meaning seminarians acted in ways contradicting their professed, deeply held values.

Do you remember the famous Stanley Milgram "obedience studies" in the 1960s? "In a series of about twenty experiments, hundreds of decent, well-intentioned people agree to deliver what appeared to be increasingly painful electric shocks to another person as part of what they thought was a learning experiment." Various factors affected why subjects did or did not comply. One dynamic was "time pressure." People who "had to make decisions quickly" were often matter-of-factly cruel. "Rushed and disoriented, they were likely more compliant than they would otherwise have been."[13] This is not surprising. After all, "empathy and compassion" both need "a calm, attentive mind."[14] The authors of the Princeton study, according to Judith Shulevitz, realized that "ethics becomes a luxury as the speed of our daily lives increases."[15]

What happens to us and our character, compassion, and communities when we hear over and again from the surrounding culture that we're late and there's more to do and more important things to be about? We might consider how our hectic pace erodes capacities for compassion. And we might begin to question our way of life.

When it comes to how technology affects our experience of time, three places in particular demand attention. Technology consumes our time, eliminates breaks and pauses, and ramps up our expectations.

Technology as a Time Thief

Owning and paying for technology takes up much time and alters our experience of time too. A great deal of our earning and work is devoted to acquiring goods. A big part of our problem with time is our desire for an affluent lifestyle. The connection between consumerism and busyness is not accidental or coincidental. Early in the twentieth century, business leaders and industrialists were alarmed by predictions of a future "golden age of leisure" and by movements advocating shortened work hours. Henry Ford and others concluded that "people must be taught not to want leisure but to desire possessions." They wrote books with titles such as *The Threat of Leisure*.[16] There was a concerted effort by industrialists, business people, and even government officials to promote consumerism. Their concern was that if people's needs were satisfied and saturated, then they would no longer purchase additional goods. Emphases moved to encouraging people to buy more and more.

This chain of events was not inevitable. There was once a movement toward shorter shifts. In 1933, Congress almost passed a bill supporting a thirty-hour workweek. In the 1930s, W. W. Kellogg changed the working day in his cereal plant from eight hours to six. Workers were given only two extra hours in a day, but the change made a substantial impact.[17] People used extra time in caring for family members (young, old, ailing), cooking, home repair, crafts, hunting, and fishing.

In the last half of the twentieth century in North America, however, production has more than doubled. In other words, we could now produce our 1948 standard of living (measured in terms of marketed goods and services) in less than half the time it took in that year. We actually could have chosen the four-hour day. Or a working year of six months. Or, *every worker in the United States could now be taking every other year off from work—with pay.*[18]

Busyness, then, is partly our own doing and choice. Technology is expensive: "Once you add up the monthly service charges and amortize the cost of comparatively modest televisions and computers, you'll find that the annual total for a well-wired home actually rivals the average Canadian household's yearly food expenses."[19] Ownership takes a lot of time and effort.

Some years ago, I started paying attention to issues of busyness and noticed that certain authors (Juliet Schor, John de Graaf, Catherine Wallace) helped me come to grips with this disturbing way we fill our days. More recently, I began researching the development of consumerism and discovered that many of the writers who were most helpful in thinking through the attendant issues were already familiar to me. They had also been wrestling with busyness and time usage. They saw the connection.

Canadians now average thirty-two working days per year commuting.[20] This does not include additional time spent on or in cars—other trips, searching for parking spots, earning money to pay for cars (and their permits, our license, taxes, tolls, upkeep, gas, oil, insurance). In the 1970s, Ivan Illich noted that cars are also responsible for "time spent in hospitals, traffic courts and garages; time spent watching automobile commercials or attending consumer education meetings to improve the quality of the next buy." He calculated that given all the hours we devote to cars, we actually are only moving about five miles per hour; in other words, about the speed that many people walk.[21] Do we really want to allocate this much time on and in motorized vehicles? Or would we rather devote it to other possibilities? A Comcast ad shows a woman asleep with her head on a table and says, "Hundreds of channels. Thousands of choices. So little time for anything else."

My friend Rosie has for two decades been an effective and congenial administrative support person. When her job was being reconfigured, she needed to do a work audit to measure how she used her time. She anticipated that she spent twenty to thirty minutes a day on email but was astonished to discover that the total was three hours. Email requires more time than we expect. And added to the time it takes to compose an email is momentum lost to interruptions. An attorney told me that in law school they learned to charge at least ten minutes for each phone call, even if the conversation lasted only a minute, because when the momentum of work and thought are interrupted it takes at least ten minutes to get back into a productive state.

Email adds work in other ways too. People may not only email about a meeting but add attachments, an agenda, documents, and other information that they expect recipients to print. Administrators sometimes claim that email "saves time," but what it actually does is offload tasks from some people onto others. As institutions cut support staff, others are expected to do the work. Where once a secretary might duplicate agendas for a meeting, now each participant personally does it and so the task takes additional time. It is quicker and more efficient to have one person run ten copies than to have ten people each run their own copies.

A deeper problem is that the same devices that cost time also change how we perceive time. We may view TV—or play video games—for hours with no sense of the passing of time and can later hardly remember what we did. Design and technology writer Tom Vanderbilt notes that studies have shown, "The longer we drive at high speeds, the harder it is for us to slow down."[22]

My watch certainly appears to move more slowly when I am on foot. In an essay titled "Time by Design," Linda Breen Pierce explains why. She argues that driving exposes one "to both faster speeds and greater stimulation" than walking. Consequently, the brain must "work harder as you focus on safety and process all that you see." It pressures us with "a rush of sensory perceptions."[23] Walking, then, is not just physically slower, but mentally slower as well.

The story is told of a corporation that comes to a "primitive" region and hires a number of locals to work long hours seven days a week to make steady and quick progress on an urgent project. Eventually, the locals just take a day off and refuse to work, even with the promise of hefty overtime pay. When the manager inquires about what is going on, they explain, "We have to let our souls catch up with our bodies."

Speed Traps

A second major issue of time and busyness is our expectations.

Ironically, so-called labor-saving devices, rather than sparing us effort as their label coyly promises, often make us busier. Able to do more, we feel pressure for greater accomplishments. When I first acquired a computer I was delighted to realize that it cut in half the time needed for many tasks. Instead of enjoying newfound leisure and spending more time with our preschool children, however, I tried to double my writing output. Time saved meant working more.

Conveniences paradoxically take time. TiVo was promoted because people could program what they wanted to watch on television and avoid commercials. But people with TiVo in fact increase TV watching, viewing more programs! The technology "encourages them to watch greater amounts of television by making it a thoroughly personalized experience."[24] Furthermore, the variety of choices—whether on television or the web or via other technologies—takes a toll: "All the new options in life may increase our flexibility. They are also major time sponges."[25]

Dutch historian Geert Mak wrote a book about his father and commented on the sepia and black-and-white pictures that he studied for research. These were accurate "color" photos in a sense. People mostly wore brown or gray, as these colors hide dirt and stains. Lighter or brighter tones require careful upkeep and more frequent laundering.[26] For many families, gone are specific "laundry days" each week. Washing machines run frequently, if not every day. Brighter lights and better vacuum cleaners raised our expectations of what cleanliness needs to look like. Furthermore, letters now need to be perfect and immaculate. Using technology increased expectations not only of how much we should accomplish but also how impressive it needs to appear.

Technology design affects behavior and expectations. As I've already noted, friends with a GPS that tells them how long a trip will take report to me that they feel pressure to meet that time expectation. I am embarrassed to admit that I drive with a lead foot. When I try to slow down, my speedometer shows ridiculously higher potential rates. Even when I am speeding, the gauge suggests that I am only driving at half of what is possible. What if the gauge only showed a maximum possible speed of eighty miles per hour?

Design could move in other directions. Our latest car gives immediate feedback on how many miles per gallon I use at any given moment. I am startled to see my rate drop dramatically when I accelerate or indeed whenever I drive over sixty miles per hour. Since I aim to be environmentally responsible—and, let's face it, save money—dashboard feedback now encourages me to drive slower and steadier. I choose to pay attention to those goals rather than the fact that my car can apparently (according to the speedometer) drive another one hundred miles per hour faster. When other cars race by, I smugly console myself, "But they're not getting fifty plus miles per gallon."

Impatience is exacerbated by gadgets that promote multitasking, implicitly discouraging us from waiting or focusing on one thing at a time. Anthropologist and author Thomas de Zengotita believes that multitasking moves us into regarding little as important. It "means missing most of what goes on around you but learning not to regret it because nothing is that much more valuable than anything else."[27] Ironically, multitasking is not necessarily productive or effective. Numerous studies conclude that one cannot multitask important challenges and do them well. Albert Einstein once famously joked, "Any man who can drive safely while kissing a pretty girl is simply not giving the kiss the attention it deserves."

Multitasking can be dangerous, even fatal. Two major studies "concluded that when drivers were talking on phones, they were four times as likely to get into serious crashes."[28] Jennifer Steinhauer and Laura Holson note that it is not only problematic for drivers: "Fatal accidents stemming from texting while . . . crossing the street or engaging in other activities is on the rise."[29]

Multitasking not only slows productivity, but it also increases the likelihood of making mistakes. While it is popularly believed that the young are better at multitasking, this too is proving to be a delusion.[30] Human brains are not wired to pay attention to more than one thing at once.

There are times when multitasking is needed, appropriate, even inevitable. In the days when our children were small and my wife and I juggled part-time jobs and took turns staying at home, we had to learn how to do several things at once—watch the children, begin supper, do laundry, and attend to whatever crises or needs they had.

There are simple, nondemanding tasks that we can do simultaneously. Author Winifred Gallagher points out that most people can in fact chew gum while they walk. Nevertheless, as she also goes on to note, it is extremely difficult to focus on more than one demanding situation at the same time. You cannot do everything equally well; performance declines. You actually get less accomplished than if you do demanding tasks sequentially, one step at a time.[31]

Religious traditions have long counseled us to be careful about how many things we do at once. I remember hearing of a monk's two-handled mug. When he drank, he used both hands to make sure that he wasn't multitasking. Thich Nhat Hanh makes a case for paying attention to what one is doing and doing only one thing. He likes to use the example of cleaning dishes.

> If while washing dishes, we think only of the cup of tea that awaits us, thus hurrying to get the dishes out of the way as if they were a nuisance, then we are not "washing the dishes to wash the dishes." What's more, we are not alive during the time we are washing the dishes. . . . If we can't wash the dishes, the chances are we won't be able to drink our tea either. While drinking the cup of tea, we will only be thinking of other things, barely aware of the cup in our hands. Thus we are sucked away into the future—and we are incapable of actually living one minute of life.[32]

Give Us a Break

Finally, technology eliminates breaks, pauses, and respites.

Once, we understood that physicians needed to be "on call," and we felt sympathy for them and their families. When I lived in inner-city Chicago in the 1980s, drug pushers on our streets had pagers. They too were perpetually available to clients. But now it is a common expectation that most or all people be reachable at any time. The remaining few without cell phones are regarded as odd exceptions, and sometimes people even demand to know why they do not own such devices. We are now expected to work anywhere at any time. Arlie Hochschild calls this "the long arm of the workplace."[33] The opportunity for "relentless access to others—and them to us— . . . leaves many of us exhausted."[34] Being permanently accessible—always tethered to tasks and responsibilities—is now an expectation. A Microsoft Office campaign said "The I'm out of the office and out of the loop era is over." Ads featured people wearing dinosaur masks. They went on to say: "Microsoft Office has evolved. Have you?" In other words, if you are not keeping up with the latest technology, you are an outdated, prehistoric creature risking extinction.[35]

Experiencing our homes as workplace extensions affects how we live in them. Journalist Maggie Jackson notes that while farmers, crafts-people, and tradespeople used to work at home, there were boundaries—"natural rhythms of sun and season" and rooms set aside for work.[36] Not anymore. Not only have we brought work home, we can do it in any room of the house. Even time on the toilet can be "productive." Many telecommuters report that while working at home increases pro-ductivity, it often happens "at the expense of leisure time" and can also "lead to stress and burnout, because [telecommuters] tend to work much longer hours at home than at the office." The promised freedom of choice results in work-extending gadgets that put us under increased pressure.[37] A Dell laptop ad bears the line, "I want to work anywhere I

ARE WE SLAVES OF TIME … ?

choose." The slogan more accurately means, "I must always be available to my job."

Looking back, I see an unexpectedly positive function of my father's smoking. His habit of four and a half decades undoubtedly caused his several heart attacks and also the cancer that first appeared in his throat, then in his lungs, spreading from there. But as I remember him working in his office or on a construction site, I can still see him pausing and ritualistically taking a cigarette from its package, lighting it slowly, drawing hard on it, and looking off into space for a few minutes. His habit did more than feed an addiction. It was a pause for reflection; it was time for thoughtful consideration of his next moves and solutions to his quandaries.

We have all seen smokers huddled outside the doors of institutions, even in the coldest weather. A health consultant tells me that now in many businesses and corporations the only people who take adequate breaks are smokers. Others often stay at their desk and computer all day, sometimes even working through lunches. I mentioned this at a retreat once, and a young woman told me that she long ago noticed that only smokers were not begrudged breaks. She began bringing candy cigarettes to work so that she could also have a little needed time off.

In *Timelock*, Ralph Keyes observes that a troubling aspect of our culture is the disappearance of pauses, noting transitions from buttons to zippers to Velcro; stove to pressure cooker to microwave; tellers to drive-up banking to ATM machines; and diner to drive-in to drive-through. Each "advance" reduces waiting. But losing moments to pause and catch our breath, we forgo the chance to ponder actions, goals, and priorities. Keyes quotes Jacques Ellul: "Man or woman in the technological society has suppressed the natural respites in their rhythm. . . . The time for choosing, adapting and collecting oneself no longer exists."[38]

Not only the small breaks that once punctuated our days suffer; but larger pauses do as well. People cope with busyness by cutting back on sleep. In the last one hundred years, Americans have adapted to fewer than seven hours of sleep a night when the average in 1900 was eight and a half hours.[39] Of course, sleep was first eroded by the technology of electric lighting, which extended the time available for work and activities. 7-Eleven stores were once considered innovative for being open from 7 a.m. to 11 p.m. Now stores are routinely open 24/7. The web also means we can work or shop any time and any place.

Blue laws once protected, among other things, a day a week from shopping. Now the idea of "Sabbath" seems a lost cause. When I speak to seminary students—of all people!—about the importance of taking off one of every seven days, many stare at me in disbelief. Some react with anger. The notion that one day out of seven could be free from work and worry, productiveness and accomplishment, is inconceivable. If well-motivated, theologically informed folks find it hard to honor the Sabbath, how can we expect to persuade others or lead by example?

Counterbalancing Taxed Time

Putting Timekeepers in Their Place

Some years ago I realized how odd it was that, given my concerns about busyness, I always wore a wristwatch. It was my first piece of jewelry. Now I see it as a symbol of our bondage to time.

When I was one of his students, Robert Webber used to tell of a pastor who found a bulletin in the church building on Monday morning. On it, someone had noted in pencil the exact times and durations—to the second!—of every element of the service: call to worship, announcements, confession, hymns, Scripture reading, sermon, et cetera. Webber rightly concluded that someone was missing the point. When trained as an Anglican acolyte, I was instructed that no one who was vested should wear a wristwatch; its presence would distract servers and congregation alike. God's *kairos* time always supersedes clock preoccupations.

The most passionate worship I encounter—Eastern Orthodox, Pentecostal—all has at least one thing in common: worshipers are there for as long as it takes. Clocks are set aside, and one must be prepared for hours-long services—much of which will take place standing up. I once attended an African American service in Detroit, and the guest Pentecostal preacher (the third of many guest preachers that day) admonished us:

And we will not look at our watches this evening! When a Tigers game goes into overtime, we are happy and excited. So if our worship goes into overtime today, then we will give God the glory!

Some years ago, I sat in a dark bar with a wise, retired pastor on the other side of a thickly scarred wooden table. I was asking for help in a difficult vocational dilemma. He began telling me how important it was for him as a pastor to give up his watch. He led worship differently and did pastoral visitation more attentively. He told me, "So just throw the damn thing away."

I still need to pay attention to time; I have responsibilities, after all. And I value punctuality. So I could not quite bring myself to dispose of a watch completely. But certainly I could take it from its place of prominence on my arm. I purchased a pocket watch. I can keep track of time, but now I look at it less frequently. And when I'm in a conversation that takes all my energy, I am not tempted to look surreptitiously—or not so surreptitiously—at my wrist. I explained all this at a church workshop once. A retired professor who was raised Amish told me that the Amish may keep watches in their pockets but not on their wrists.

I also put a prayer rope on my watch. It reminds me of my priorities; there are eternal matters more important than preoccupation with the sweep of the second hand.

I have not found a way to live without my watch. Nor can I get rid of my planner. But I can put them in their proper place. I have a small picture of an icon in my planner. It is a representation of St. Moses the Ethiopian, a Desert Father who inspires me. Whenever I open my calendar, I see him and am reminded of the priority of my faith. As I write things on my to-do list or clip in notes, I also ask myself—under Abba Moses's watchful eyes—whether the to-do items fit with my faith priorities.

Reclaim Sabbath

Several religions set aside a day a week for worship and freedom from demands of work, worry, productivity, and consumption. Judeo-Christian traditions speak of the importance of Sabbath. Jews have many different ways of observing Sabbath, as do Christians. The finest book ever written on these matters is by the late Jewish theologian Abraham Joshua Heschel. It is not only deeply insightful but also eloquently written. "There is a realm of time where the goal is not to have but to be, not to own but to give, not to control but to share, not to subdue but to be in accord." Heschel sees that realm as having everything to do with keeping technology in its proper sphere. "On the Sabbath we live . . . *independent of technical civilization*; we abstain primarily from an activity that aims at remaking or reshaping the things of space."[40]

Intriguingly, many secular and nonreligious folks are interested in Sabbath. William Powers, in *Hamlet's Blackberry*, describes his family's technology Sabbath.[41] Lauren Winner, herself an author of a book on Sabbath, says that in spite of a bumper crop of books on Sabbath observances in the last ten years or so, "it's unclear . . . that many people are implementing them."[42]

A Jewish young-adult organization called Reboot launched a "Sabbath manifesto" that has the following ten recommendations:

1. Avoid technology.
2. Connect with loved ones.
3. Nurture your health.
4. Get outside.
5. Avoid commerce.
6. Light candles.
7. Drink wine.
8. Eat bread.
9. Find silence.
10. Give back.[43]

Heschel writes:

He who wants to enter the holiness of the day must first lay down the profanity of clattering commerce, of being yoked to toil. He must go away from the screech of dissonant days, from the nervousness and fury of acquisitiveness and the betrayal in embezzling his own life. He must say farewell to manual work and learn to understand that the world has already been created and will survive without the help of man. Six days a week we wrestle with the world, wringing profit from the earth; on the Sabbath we especially care for the seed of eternity planted in the soul.[44]

I am not interested in legalistic lists of dos or don'ts. Rather, I want to help people rediscover life-giving rhythms so we can all live richer, more satisfying lives, enjoying one another and the many graces that God offers.

11

SUNDERING SPACE

Some months after a memorable week spent canoeing in the Boundary Waters of Minnesota, a companion gave me photos from our trip. One picture of a campsite was aesthetically poor, badly composed, and improperly exposed. Taken with a disposable camera, I believe. I had to strain my eyes to make out details and even to recognize some people. But it was one of my favorite shots. In a week of exemplary camping spots, this one excelled. It was on a lovely rocky peninsula that jutted into crystal clear water and afforded long views to the north, south, and west (so we could enjoy a spectacular sunset). The place was blessed by a breeze that made for fewer insects. The forest provided firewood. The pebbled beach was a good place to dry the day's laundry in the sun. And the shallow bay made for sun-warmed water, perfect for swimming, floating, drifting, and soothing muscles after a long and taxing canoe ride to get there.

A quick glance at that photo helped me realize that I did not in fact need pictures. Even now, years later, I can easily recall and describe in great detail what each campsite that week looked and felt like. I can smell the smoke and taste the gritty coffee. I hear waves lapping on nearby rocks. The chilly water on my skin refreshes weary muscles. I feel the slope and dip of the ground beneath my sleeping bag. I can still see exactly where every tent is placed.

And I remember more. I reminisce about jokes first told in each place and can bring to mind particular stories and disclosures. I think back to confessions made and encouragements offered. We did not know one another that well at the beginning of the week, but bonds developed over meals, in working together, and around campfires.

All campsites were different, and yet each had its noteworthy compensations. On one, we had to squeeze our tents between bushes, but the cool water offered a respite after the first day of canoeing. Another was so well treed that it provided shelter from intermittent rains. A third, after a harrowing and furious paddle over storm-swept waters, greeted us with abundant and ripe blueberry patches that were just the thing for our pancakes, cheesecake, and cobbler. We counted the unique blessings of each place.

When the photos arrived, I had just stayed a night in a luxury hotel. After a frustrating day of delayed flights, I found myself around midnight stuck in a large city, being evicted from the airport terminal, and needing to find lodging quickly. My only reasonable option was the nearby hotel. Both my income and my thriftiness usually nudge me away from luxury accommodation expenditures. Here I had no choice. But if I hoped to enjoy the anomalous event, I was soon disappointed.

Most hotels are alike. They combine a bed or two, a sink, a bathroom, and a television. The one mystery—oh, the suspense!—is whether the bathroom will be at the front or far end of the room and whether the beds will be on the right or left. Even televisions all over North America are now hooked into the same entertainment network so that announcements are in the identical voice, no matter where one stays. Sure, some are cleaner and more nicely appointed. Other than that, a notable difference between economy and luxury lodgings is the quantity and quality of soap, shampoo, and other personal care products. A hotel room obviously costs more than camping. It is reliable. It is easy to find and access. It is quick. It is safe. It is convenient.

And not memorable in the slightest. Hotel rooms are a backdrop for other activities, rest, or anonymity, but most are not in themselves of any worth. They are not a proper end, nor are they intended to be. They are a means. Usually hotel rooms are deeply forgettable. Mass-produced "art" on the walls is supposed to soothe but be ignored, not stimulate, teach, or inspire. Rooms are designed for anonymity: if one finds reminders of a previous tenant (hair or skin flakes or possessions), that would be cause for offense and a stern complaint to the management. One enters anonymous rooms, bides a while, and moves on, knowing that one's own traces will soon be eliminated. Such rooms have their place, but do we want them to define our lives?

Chain hotels are another sorry manifestation of the spreading "geography of nowhere"[1] and "non-places," which are "devoid of the symbolic expressions of identity, relations and history: examples include airports, motorways, anonymous hotel rooms, public transport."[2] Rising interest in recent years in bed-and-breakfasts is in part rebellion against the geography of nowhere and specifically the nonplace lodgings of hotels. I far more easily recall the configuration and personalities at bed-and-breakfasts I stayed at a decade ago than the shape of the room or even the faces of hotel clerks where I stayed a few months ago. Not every bed-and-breakfast venture was a raging success, but they were all uniquely memorable. Rather than monotonous sameness, even exasperation at quirky hosts and conditions is preferable.

Campsites are even better. It is only in middle age that I am being won over to their pleasures. Camping always seemed like too much hard work. Now I know the joy of discovering just the right stump or rock to perch myself on. Feeling appreciation for invisible predecessors who figured out the best spot for a campfire. Gratitude for hard work well rewarded. Appetite and appreciation for meals that inevitably is stirred outside; food never tastes as good anywhere else.

As *focal places*, campsites demand discipline and hard work: setting up, finding wood, lighting fires, cooking, preparing food. They connect us with others: companions and previous guests who appreciated and tended the site before we arrived. They put us in touch with realities greater than ourselves: trees, rocks, soil, animals, water, and weather. Costs—physical not financial—are high, but rewards and internal goods and benefits are great and clear.

The remarkable attraction of such locations brings us to the final alert: how does engagement with technology affect relationship to the actual physical places and spaces where we are located?

Erasing Distance

Beginning in the nineteenth century, technologies such as trains and telegraphs began altering our experience of space and place, geography and locale. Now it became imaginable to travel or communicate great distances, hundreds of miles, in a short period of time, or to cross North America in a matter of days. This was accelerated, of course, with later forms of transportation. Cars create the casual option of going previously unheard-of distances. As a pastor I was surprised, for example, that some people drove up to an hour to visit our congregation (and bypassed many churches in the process).

When my parents and maternal grandparents emigrated from the Netherlands in the mid-twentieth century, shortly after the Second World War, everyone assumed that they would not visit their homeland again. A ship journey was too expensive and time consuming. In fact, my grandfather and grandmother never returned, not even for a visit. As transportation over great distances became easier, traveling to Europe became more possible. In the last decade of my father's life, he went back at least twice a year to visit his mother and other relatives and to conduct business.

When I was a child, contacts with overseas relatives were maintained by letter. My mother and her mother-in-law wrote each other every week on a special one-page airmail form, squeezing as much as they could in the allotted space because it was too costly to mail more than a page or to put in enclosures.

Similarly, phone practices have altered. Forty and fifty years ago, my parents called overseas relatives only for Christmas and birthdays (unless there was a death in the family). It was too expensive and unwieldy to call more often. First we contacted the long-distance operator, who would place the call. Then we waited twenty minutes for the operator to phone us back. The ensuing conversation was like hollering down an echoing tunnel. Our words took so long to get to their destination that often relatives would start talking before they heard us. We could hear the other person, but not clearly and distinctly. Conversations were stilted. But long distance has changed now. When I walked the Camino pilgrimage, I phoned my wife across the ocean almost every day and the sound quality was as good as being in the next room.

Technology erases distance. With the telegraph it became possible to communicate quickly and efficiently with people far away. Prior to that invention, "a message could be transmitted at most just one hundred miles by horseman in a day."[3] Horse-delivered messages were only for the privileged. Folks might not know for years whether a war was over. In the Battle of New Orleans, two thousand lives were lost even though a peace treaty had been signed two weeks earlier.[4] This kind of disconnection is unimaginable when we are accustomed to instant news—watching live as police chase O. J. Simpson or the Twin Towers smolder and collapse on September 11. And with landlines, cell phones, faxes, instant messaging, email, Twitter, and who knows what will be invented next, we take for granted continual and instant access to anyone, anywhere, at anytime.

Some authors speak of technology as *conquering* or even *annihilating* space.[5] I was glad to keep in close contact with my wife while on my pilgrimage. She shared my joy immediately on the Sunday when I arrived at the end of my long journey. There are obvious benefits and advantages in staying connected with those who are important to us. But are there downsides?

When I first transitioned from pastoring a church to teaching at a seminary, my wife and I chose a house near the school. This made sense on several counts. We liked the idea of my being able to walk to work; doing so was better for the environment and better for me, physically and spiritually. We remembered that when I was a student many professors lived within easy walking or biking distance.

A lot can change in twenty-some years. Now few professors lived nearby. Newcomers mostly bought houses some distance from campus. None of the school's key administrators lived in the city. People reported that travel to and from school helped them disconnect and detach from work, perhaps even pray. Several warned me against purchasing a place too close. Boundaries and all that. They wondered whether I would be tempted or lured into overwork if my job was only a stroll away. There was another change as well. Even though my colleagues' homes were at a greater distance from work, now they were tethered to seminary business in more complicated ways. With wireless access they could work at all hours, and many did just that. A number of them sent emails late in the evening, early in the morning, and even in the middle of the night!

Our final alert has to do with space and place. We see in this chapter and the previous one that our relationships both to time *and* to space are affected by technology. Technology alters how we relate to people nearby and far away. Recall the young servicemen who both listened to the same radio programs in air-conditioned cars on a lovely summer morning. Or, remember the local school principal, teachers, and staff who went for a bike ride one summer Sunday afternoon and encountered almost no children, as pupils were inside, presumably watching television, surfing the net, or playing video games. We have seen that our busy culture and the organization of our suburbs disconnect us from neighbors.

There are several problems inherent in how technology may conquer and annihilate space. One is that it is easy to get distracted by and focus on the distant and different rather than valuing and appreciating what is here before us. We consequently allow our own locales to grow uglier. And, finally, we disconnect meaningful presence from the location of our bodies.

Anywhere but Here

A disturbing aspect of technology's impact on our relationship to space and place is how it diminishes the importance of where one is while accentuating the priority of distant locations. Gradually, we find ourselves compelled and convicted that important, vivid, and robust realities and priorities are elsewhere. I am still amazed that the Bruce Trail, filled with such beauty, was so near during my adolescence—but I was too mesmerized by TV.

As a young teenager, I attended a middle school that was within walking distance of my house and next to a half-acre woods with a small stream. In eighth-grade science we went out to study that neighboring stream and its creatures. We took water samples to our classroom lab to learn what we could of the biology next door. I remember feeling bored by it all. It was not just that science was not my favorite subject. Rather, I could not be convinced that anything noteworthy would be found so close to home. I was only living out the implications of so much of what the media communicate. E. B. White wrote, already in the 1930s, "Television will enormously enlarge the eye's range, and, like radio, will advertise the Elsewhere." Such technologies, he asserted, "will insist that we forget the primary and the near in favor of the secondary and the remote."[6] We are being convinced that not only is the grass always greener elsewhere but also that only elsewhere truly counts.

At the same time, we learn to disregard our surroundings. If we do not cherish them, seeing their worth and beauty, it is easy to pollute. If we find everything around us ugly or unremarkable, what does it matter if we toss trash out of speeding cars, pour chemicals down drains, or overload landfills? Earlier we noted how many screens preoccupy us. They also cut us off from what surrounds us. No wonder environmentalists are so frustrated over the inability to get people concerned about global climate change.

Even daily news prioritizes what happens at a distance. Ursula Franklin comments on how the media often focuses on faraway events and does not pay attention to local things that most influence us: "Danger lurks when the far so outperforms the near."[7] Ironically, when we are distracted by international happenings we cannot affect, we are less inclined to get involved locally where there is a greater possibility of making a difference. As Guy Davenport noted: "Distance negates responsibility."[8]

When I was a young adult, my father and I often disagreed about politics, sometimes heatedly. We both kept trying to find ways to connect on issues we might hold in common. He was excited one year in the late 1980s when the news was preoccupied with a multinational effort—involving traditional enemies on American and Soviet ships—that worked in tandem to free whales stuck in the ice between Alaska and Russia. But I was living in inner-city Chicago and was offended that news agencies (even in Chicago) were preoccupied with one unusual crisis thousands of miles away when I knew that youths in my neighborhood contended with ongoing hazards of gangs, drugs, violence, poverty, and illiteracy. There is something distressingly easy about focusing on those far away.

Greater appreciation for the nearby prompts people to emphasize the importance of purchasing locally—such as the "one-hundred-mile diet" that limits adherents to consuming food grown and raised nearby. Ideas like this were developed in the spirit of such prophets as Wendell Berry (who champions the priority of one's immediate surroundings) and Indiana essayist Scott Russell Sanders (who testifies against North

American ease of mobility in *Staying Put: Making a Home in a Restless World*). Writer and activist Jane Jacobs long ago taught us the power and priority of being committed to local neighborhoods.

Christian spiritual traditions also counsel that if we do not learn how to detect God standing still, we'll not find God when we're moving around either. In response to people's tendency to seek stimulation in new environments, a central Benedictine vow is stability—the promise to remain committed to a single place and its community for the rest of one's life, trusting that God will speak and convert even, and perhaps especially, when that spot no longer easily entertains. Thomas Michael Power notes that much in our culture encourages rootlessness and mobility: "Those seeking to maintain a commitment to place and people are forced to pay a high price."[9]

The Scriptures counsel us to attend to God's meeting us here in this place at this time, in the person before us. We confess incarnation—God encountering us in the flesh and on the ground. Think of Jacob's surprise: "Surely the LORD is in this place—and I did not know it!" (Gen. 28:16). Later he ran into God in that very spot again, and they wrestled for a blessing.

Brother Lawrence learned how to "practice the presence of God" in the kitchen where he prayerfully conducted chores that at first he resented. In fact many spiritual disciplines—*lectio divina*, meditation, contemplation, centering prayer, to name only a few—could all be summarized as teaching us how to be aware and attentive here and now. Christian spiritual tradition at its best reminds us to take seriously our daily life and daily realities in the place that we are located. It is here that we meet God and experience God's grace.

A son of immigrants, I also became an immigrant in middle age. My experience was less successful than that of my parents. I expected that immigrating would be easy. But I was wrong. Being an expatriate, I discovered, does not agree with me.

My immigration was not the all-or-nothing enterprise of my parents and grandparents. I phoned my mother every week, usually just to chat. We drove back to visit relatives several times a year. So there were good connections. Still, I missed the accents, cultural assumptions and references, politics, reliable coffee and tea. The longer I was away, the more Canadian I felt, and the more I longed to be home. Each year my mother gave us a subscription to Canada's weekly news magazine. I disagreed with its politics and disdained its sensationalism, but I was grateful to be in touch with at least some headlines from north of the border. I was delighted to find that I could listen to Canadian radio, especially the Canadian Broadcasting Corporation (CBC), over the internet. What a pleasure to hear again the voices of newscasters and radio hosts that I formerly listened to every day back in Canada; to be offered news that was not deemed a priority south of the border—not just Canadian developments but international ones as well; to be informed about what was preoccupying fellow Canadians. Suddenly I did not feel so homesick anymore.

But I wondered whether steeping myself in Canadian news was such a good idea. Did such listening distract me from paying attention to real issues in the community where I was living? Did indulging in the CBC reinforce my cultural snobbery? Did technological connections to Canada, cyber-umbilical cords, prevent me from committing myself to the country where God placed me? Simone Weil said:

> Let us love the country of here below. It is real; it offers resistance to love. It is this country that God has given us to love. [God] has willed that it should be difficult yet possible to love it.[10]

For a time I thought that the internet helped me maintain a vital and life-giving connection. Slowly I began to wonder whether it was in fact debilitating my capacity to listen to God's providence where I lived. While I fed my longing for Canadian news and accents, I suspect that my choices adversely affected my ability to commit myself to my new home. No surprise, then, that I only lasted seven years before returning to Canada.

But I did not get everything wrong during my Indiana sojourn. Remember when I was a middle schooler and could not be bothered exploring the woods and stream nearby? Hiking got me to connect closely with the geography of my adolescence. And from there, I began canoeing and kayaking in northern Indiana where I lived. I was growing increasingly curious about everything: soil, trees, animals, and how water moved. How much do great blue herons weigh? Are there reptiles—besides snakes—that far north? Why was local soil sandy and why is dark dirt fertile? So I signed up for a "master naturalist" class and studied various aspects of the geography and biology of northern Indiana. I realized the wisdom of Annie Dillard, who once wrote that we need to "explore the neighborhood, view the landscape, to discover at least where it is that we have been so startlingly set down."[11]

My experience is not unusual. Ruth Mallory's interest in birding led to many other passions as well, including butterflies, wild flowers, trees, and perennial gardens. One small focal practice can lead to deeper investment in a wider ecology.

There's No There There

Perhaps it's not so surprising that many find it hard to pay attention close to home. A lot of local settings have become uniformly bland and, alas, even ugly.

When I was growing up in southern Ontario, we often visited relatives and acquaintances in various places. Different communities each had their own unique appearance. The small town of Niagara-on-the-Lake, where my grandparents resided, was dominated by cottages, affluent mansions, and—on the main street—nineteenth-century architecture and a clock tower. St. Catharines, where I was born, was working class. Blocks and blocks of the city were occupied by wartime housing, small two- and three-bedroom homes that were erected during the economic boom of the Second World War and its aftermath. At the age of nineteen, I moved to London, Ontario, to attend university and was charmed by two-story, yellow-brick, century-old houses. Other cities too—Niagara Falls, Toronto, Kitchener—all had distinctive architecture. If you blindfolded me and dropped me off in any of those places, I would know immediately where I was as soon as the blindfold was removed.

A recent radio gag about an Ontario city went like this: "Meet me at the Tim Horton's coffee shop at the corner of Main and Maple. Not the one at the southwest corner. Not the one at the southeast corner. Not the one at the northwest corner. But the one on the northeast corner." Canada's coffee chain is ubiquitous. The gag points out that what we once knew as "a particular sense of place . . . has given way to a kind of numbing sameness."[12] The developing outskirts of cities are full of crowded subdivisions focused on the realities of commuting by car. Everything looks the same.

Did we grow preoccupied with the distant because our own localities are so off-putting? Or did our own settings deteriorate as we focused increasingly on what was far away? Either way, the result is the same: there may be no place like home, but it's often not a place that we're particularly fond of anymore.

When I first lived in Elkhart in the 1980s, the downtown was bustling and there were three movie theaters on Main Street. My friends and I regularly patronized them all. Business suffered a little from the new Pierre Moran Mall erected a couple of miles away from the core; it was in the city, but barely. Shortly before we got to Elkhart, a larger, fancier complex, Concord Mall, with a flowing fountain at its heart, had been built several miles even farther away; it was starting to draw commerce from Pierre Moran. A regional mall, it attracted shoppers from up to twenty miles or so. When I moved back to Elkhart years later I was surprised that both Pierre Moran and Concord were faltering. In another city fifteen miles to the west, a power center of national chain and box stores attracted shoppers from as far as forty-five miles; it was beset by traffic jams, especially around Thanksgiving and Christmas. By now, downtown Elkhart was in intensive care. There were no cinemas, many businesses were shuttered, plenty of storefronts vacant. Cars were a major driving force—no pun intended—behind all these changes. As people could casually travel to various stores, local merchants suffered. Now, of course, online shopping and the high cost of gas may obliterate box stores as well. Then we can expect mega-merchandising locations to become abandoned, vacant, massive eyesores. With each step, the ugliness around us grows and beauty is diminished.

Many people sense that something is missing. Erik Reece writes about how folks in New York City so keenly felt the disappearance of green space that some started "rolling out Astroturf in curb-side parking spaces, plopping down lawn chairs, and feeding quarters into the meter all day in exchange for this makeshift pastorale." That strategy is desperate. We need true greenery. "Decades of research have shown that in urban areas, PPI—people-plant interaction—results in reduced stress and anger, lower blood pressure and a higher sense of self-worth for individuals, as well as higher property values, reduced crime and increased neighborliness." Reece's headline reads: "Happiness Grows Out of Tiny Parks, Not Huge Televisions."[13]

Richard Louv convincingly shows that "a growing body of research links our mental, physical, and spiritual health directly to our association with nature—in positive ways."[14] He makes the case that becoming disconnected from natural surroundings harms emotional, physical, and intellectual well-being. That is why gardening, tending plants, and being in contact with animals such as pets is beneficial. Interaction with nature can reduce stress, anxiety, and depression, and can increase a sense of self-worth. Jonah Lehrer notes, "Studies have demonstrated . . . that hospital patients recover more quickly when they can see trees from their windows, and that women living in public housing are better able to focus when their apartment overlooks a grassy courtyard."[15] Even domestic violence rates decrease if one's lodging has a view of greenery. And absence of greenery is correlated with depression. Yet, Louv laments, "You'll likely never see a slick commercial for nature therapy as you do for the latest antidepressant pharmaceuticals."[16]

Our deep need for the natural is not satisfied by virtual or technological substitutes. Louv is leery of synthetic and artificial depictions of the wild, whether online representations, "nature-oriented retailing," stores that imitate natural surroundings, or "mood tapes" employing recorded or manufactured sounds of animals, wind, and water.[17]

The most convincing analysis I know of the crucial importance of natural reality is in Albert Borgmann's *Crossing the Postmodern Divide*.[18] He invents a scenario. An executive who lives in Missoula is offered an attractive position in a large city. As she adds up the pros and cons of the possible move, she realizes how much she will miss her daily runs in a nearby wilderness park. "The employer counters with an offer of a paid membership in a health club where they have treadmills positioned in front of video screens so that the person who is running feels herself moving through the landscape that unfolds on the screen. The employer . . . offers to have videos shot in the candidate's favorite running trails." Of course, this is a "poor substitute," as the reality will include a room crowded with other exercisers and noisy mechanical devices. But let's imagine, suggests Borgmann, that technology could more clearly emulate the reality of a wilderness jog: "a panoramic, fine-grained, and vividly colorful screen, a running surface that rises and banks in coordination with the view that is being displayed, scented and temperature controlled blowers that simulate the air movement and fragrance according to the changes of shade, sunlight and season; speakers that produce sounds of rushing water, chirping birds, and whispering pines; monitors that adjust the velocity of sights, sounds, wind, and running surface according to the effort the runner expends." What then? Would this be a worthy replacement?

Some argue that technological substitutes are better than the real thing. Paul Wells raves about the advantages of a virtual digital concert hall over attending a live event. From the comfort of his Ottawa location he watched a "live" concert broadcast from Berlin. He loved the "surprisingly rich sound and visuals." Digital viewers can see more and from more angles than concert goers, do not "have to dress up for the night out," do not spend as much money on tickets, and can choose part of a concert rather than listen to the whole thing.[19] Long-distance telephoning used to be promoted with the promise that it was "the next best thing to being there." Now, some believe that technology delivers something better than being there!

Borgmann raises questions. The executive's virtually enhanced gym may resemble the trail, but there are crucial differences. If she saw a mountain lion during her run—something that she longed to observe for years—she would count that a rare blessing. Viewing a mountain lion on a programmed video does not compare with the serendipity of seeing one in nature. In the wild it would be an encounter that is totally beyond one's control, completely gift. After her gym exercise is finished, "[s]he goes to the locker room, showers, changes, and steps into a muggy, hazy afternoon in the high-rise canyon of a big city." Her virtual run cheapened and hollowed out both worlds: her imaginary encounter revealed nothing deeply important; it only provided a brief distraction from her actual location.

A crucial difference between reality and virtual experience is that the latter is at the consumer's control and disposal. The runner can start the program wherever she wants and end it just as casually. She could also load in other preferred scenery. Wells celebrates the virtual concert because one can choose to focus on individual portions and would not even have to get up from a couch and dress nicely to engage music. But I believe that there is merit in not always being in control. I was mesmerized by nature programs on color television when I was a teen; yet I spent little time outside. Thirty years later I discovered that walking in nature reoriented my appreciation for what surrounded me, recalibrated how I understood distance and time, gave me new faith in what my body could do, and converted me to the meaningfulness of nature.

I have marveled at the rapidly growing popularity of a pilgrimage route in northern Spain. One reason that its popularity is so surprising is because practicing the Christian discipline of pilgrimage has not been emphasized in church teaching in the past few centuries. Protestants have been particularly leery, seeming to prefer a metaphorical, not geographical, journey. We may not be encouraged from the pulpit to take part in a pilgrimage, but Christian hymns are filled with pilgrimage imagery. And two classic Christian texts, John Bunyan's *Pilgrim's Progress* and C. S. Lewis's *Pilgrim's Regress*, use pilgrimage as an allegorical way of describing the Christian life itself.

Presently, there is still one pilgrimage tradition that even many Reformation-minded Protestants honor: going to Israel. Christians travel to the "Holy Land," experiencing firsthand places where Bible events happened and Jesus walked, enlivening scriptural imagination and understanding. Some tours even offer a baptism-renewal service in the waters of the Jordan. Invariably, people return speaking of how they understand Bible texts better because they encountered places directly and firsthand. No amount of book learning substitutes for being there, walking those paths, touching those stones, dipping into Jordan's waters.

Self-Multiplication and Antigeography

Earlier we noted considerable evidence to suggest that people are experiencing thinner, more virtual versions of friendship. Folks have fewer and fewer confidants. It shouldn't be a surprise that our loss of intimate friends coincides with unprecedented mobility, celebration of asynchronous communication, and use of devices that keep drawing our focus and attention to the distant and far away.

Joel Kotkin describes the effect of many communications devices as "antigeography." He notes, "Executives at major multinationals increasingly work in one country while essentially living in another, using the new technologies, air routes, and time-share arrangements in local hotels."[20] We are invited to think that where we are does not matter and that being in the same place as loved ones is not necessarily a priority. I am disturbed by a sentimental Oreo commercial. It begins by showing a father and son eating the treats. We see first one and then the other as they twist open their cookies, lick off icing, dip pieces in milk, and then finally consume the entire thing. It is a charming vignette of a father-and-son ritual. But then the camera pulls back and we realize that they are communicating online through a computer screen. The two are on different sides of the globe, the boy (in pajamas) is about to go to bed and the father (putting on a suit) is about to go to work. During the 2008 presidential election campaign, it was regularly reported that Barack Obama kept in touch with his daughters by video chats. He was portrayed as a caring, responsible, and involved father. I do not question his parental qualities. But is cyberconnecting with one's children sufficient?

Clearly, there are times when online communication is the best that we can do. A close friend lived in Canada while his son had major surgery overseas, a series of procedures that took him away for months. Every week they connected by video chat. It was important. But both knew something was missing. Their video conversation was never fully satisfying, even if they could "see" each other weekly. They eagerly anticipated when the dad could visit Japan and even more longed for the time when the family could be reunited in Canada once more.

Even while in the same place we do not necessarily take advantage of opportunities to connect. When we bring work home—via cell phones and the internet—or spend time cultivating online relationships or gaming with people elsewhere, we lose opportunities of paying attention to those who are nearby. Indulging in such practices, we are neither fully here nor there! Shane Hipps believes that one way technology undermines close and vital relationships is that technological mediation—online social networking, for example—often "inoculates people against the desire to be *physically present* with others."[21] We may settle for digital communication when what we most need is to have face-to-face, eye-to-eye, in-the-flesh contacts and encounters.

Psychologist Kenneth Gergen observed that a century ago important relationships were confined to walking distance, but now we experience self-multiplication, "the capacity to be significantly present in more than one place at a time." He writes that mobility and flexibility have debilitating effects on relationships, including lack of intimacy and commitment. He warns that we are implicitly expected to be in touch and have meaningful contact with increasing numbers of people. He shows that such developments contribute directly to our culture's crisis of eroding "intimacy and commitment."[22]

Counterbalancing Sundered Space

While there are many ways to reconnect to locales, two simple practices can help—walking and gardening.

Walking

I recently volunteered to be endangered. I became a Toronto pedestrian when the media was preoccupied with the number of walkers killed on our streets.

On and off over the decades, I've exercised on foot. One year, I walked seven kilometers every day at 5 a.m. I wondered if I could do something similar again when I moved to Toronto. I explored the area around my home, looking for a pleasant early morning route. I was unable to find a good walking path because although we are within city limits, it's a solidly suburban area, reflecting the "geography of nowhere." Many of the houses are designed identically, large garages jut out toward the street and dominate one's view, and there are chain stores in abundance.

Around then I read a book about urban walking, and the author made a throwaway observation that people once did not think twice about walking an hour to work. That struck a nerve. Many friends casually drive an hour or more each way everyday. Why not walk for sixty minutes?

I wondered what would happen if I strolled an hour toward the school and then grabbed a bus the rest of the way. I was delighted to find that sixty minutes got me into East Don River Park. Then not much distance remained. So now on most days, I walk to work. It takes between sixty-five and seventy-five minutes, depending on sidewalk conditions and how I feel that day.

When I begin my walk I'm often preoccupied by what lies ahead in the day and all the tasks that need completing. As I proceed, I gradually release my preoccupations. When I reach the park, I'm no longer anxious but in a good space to enjoy the scenery of stream, trees, and fields. As I descend from the street into the greenbelt, traffic noises recede and I am embraced by growing silence. Even better, I see wildlife right in the city. One morning I studied a clump that looked like a deer. I realized that it was only a bush but then heard a noise, turned around, and saw a fox trotting nearby. The following week I saw another bush that resembled a deer. This time it was two deer!

What would happen if you resolved to walk regularly to at least one major commitment in your life—school, work, church, library, shopping?

Gardening

Leroy and Winifred Saner were neighbors down the road in Elkhart. They not only have a large backyard garden, but for ten years they organized a major community garden for the seminary where Leroy, Winifred, and I worked. They gave guidance to students who wanted to learn how to cultivate plants. Leroy also occasionally came to our house and lent my wife a hand with her garden.

Winifred recalls: "I was in the garden as soon as I could walk because my mother was a devout gardener. Just playing around in the dirt, pulling weeds, eating some things right out of the garden." Winifred's mother had learned gardening from both her mother and grandmother who had come from Russia in the late nineteenth century. I visited in midwinter, and their pantry was lined with jars containing jams, jellies, beets, peaches, tomatoes, and pickles. In the freezer were packages of corn and blueberries. When I visited, they'd just eaten their last onion from the summer before, but they still had many potatoes in the garage.

Leroy also learned gardening at home. While he did not necessarily have the same appreciation for it, Winifred's passion was contagious. "Growing up on the farm, I appreciate the outdoors and it's good exercise, and it's something we can do together. And I like to eat," he smiles.

Gardening obviously connects Leroy and Winifred to the soil. But gardening also networks them with many people—with parents and grandparents who taught them, with friends and in-laws who compare notes with them, with seminarians they taught to garden and the foreign students from Japan, Taiwan, and Laos who taught the Saners a thing or two as well. In fact, they now grow bigger tomatoes because of what they learned from Korean students.

The Saners enjoy the company of international students at church and often have them over for home-cooked meals, offering produce from their own garden of course. Winifred noted: "We like to do a lot of entertaining because we can use our own food products, the jellies and the fruit that we preserved. So we share, we share from the garden, we share around the table."

Winifred and Leroy see numerous benefits of their focal practice. They like knowing "where your food comes from," and "that it's organic, natural, clean." They enjoy saving money and being self-sufficient—not to mention delicious food. Winifred added, "For me it's a release of stress and tension. I can go out there and pull weeds, meditate, pray. Probably more prayers have been said there than in the house. Because you're alone out there, you're with nature, you realize what God is doing with these little tiny seeds that you plant. There's a certain faith that comes with that."

Our conversation was filled with grace and gratitude. Winifred and Leroy are especially mindful of the meaning of Thanksgiving because of their experience growing food over the course of their lifetimes. Reflecting on her childhood, Winifred said, "You could come rejoicing because the harvest was in. Thanksgiving was a real celebration." They never took produce for granted. They knew its source and the hard work that went into it and how much depended on things beyond their control—rain, frost, hail, and sunshine.

Part 3

FINDING OUR FOCUS

12

FINDING AND FUNDING FOCAL FUNDAMENTALS

Many friends and acquaintances seek balance but are not always sure how to find it and are sometimes surprised when they do. Take Harold for instance. Every year, he goes hunting with a group of macho buddies, but never brings home a single kill. He does not even load his rifle. Harold is deeply reserved. When in a group, he goes along with the agenda. Or, if he cannot do that, he just disappears and does not participate at all. He never suggests alternatives, argues, expresses opinions, or tries to get anyone to honor his preferences. He's either fully involved or completely absent and—either way—one never is completely sure what Harold is thinking. So, year after year, Harold goes along with the gang, heading north to hunt. He has a rifle, camouflage outfit, camping stool, and various other paraphernalia crucial to stalking deer. But he never brings along bullets.

As it turns out, Harold does not just go hunting for the camaraderie or because his friends are doing it. He has an ulterior motive. He loves the woods and its stillness. All year long he looks forward to spending a week just sitting in the bush, breathing the air, and waiting for nothing in particular. It is not clear to me that his comrades ever know his true agenda. Do they wonder—or tease him—about his pitiful hunting record? I have no idea. But the rewards of being in the woods, whatever the price, are worth it to Harold.

I also think of Walter. He lost his driving license after one legal infraction too many. He was not allowed to drive for a couple years. Because of this, he had to walk two miles to work. Commuting on foot is not something he would have normally chosen, but it beat breaking the law or covering the cumulative expense of a taxi.

He found that he liked the walking. Going to work in the morning, he prepared himself for the shift ahead. He could anticipate the day's challenges and psyche himself up to face whatever he might have to do. Rather than arrive at the last possible minute, barely having woken up, rushing his breakfast, and driving at top speed, he got there collected and composed. The job went better for him. At the end of the day, he reversed the process on the way home. This was an opportunity to re-view what he had seen and experienced: to debrief about any intense interactions or emotions of the day; to let go and set aside unfinished business that troubled him. And when he got home, he was fully there, completely available to his family. Walking helped him to be present to his work and to his family, each in its own sphere. It was a good phase in his life.

Harold's and Walter's discoveries surprised them. What did they find? The wonders of being still and waiting in the woods with no particular place to go, nothing to do but enjoy the pure giftedness of the moment, the simple pleasure of walking to and from work and discovering a richer rhythm of life.

I am often caught off guard by overlooked blessings, many truly simple epiphanies. I find myself over and again forgetting the most basic lessons of life. I keep falling for the same distracting traps and patterns that lure me from what matters most and gives me the great-est rewards.

One springtime I was doing a little review of my life and realized that in the midst of a lot of maddening busyness—which included some accomplishments with which I was justifiably happy—my greatest joy came from two simple facts. I was glad that the dogwood, my favorite tree, was blooming in the backyard that year; it's old and I never take it for granted. And I was deeply pleased that bluebirds were nesting in our yard for the first time ever. Every day, I spent time gazing at the tree and its flowers and looking out for the nesting bluebirds.

Often, things that are most satisfying are very simple. They may take little effort. While I water and nourish the tree and put up the bluebird box in a propitious place, there is little to nothing I can do to guarantee that the tree blooms or the birds nest. All that is in my power is to make room for these blessed events and to pay attention to them if they occur. As Harold and Walter remind me, it takes very little effort to encounter wonder again. All you need to do is sit still, listen, go to the woods, pay attention, walk, slow down.

Yet we find it difficult to make space in our lives for encountering wonder. The most stunning thing about the August 2003 blackout that affected huge parts of eastern Canada and the northeastern United States was that in all the analyses of "what went wrong" and "how can we prevent this from happening again" no one suggested that updating infrastructure was not enough. I cannot recall a single soul saying

that perhaps the blackout—precipitated in part because of extensive air-conditioning that especially hot month—ought to call our lifestyles into question. Perhaps we need to find different ways of living, ones that do not use so much energy.

Dorothy Day and Peter Maurin, founders of the Catholic Worker Movement, used to argue that one reason to work for social change is to make our society into a place where it is easier to be and do good. I believe we have moved in the opposite direction. We live in a time where it is easier to avoid the good. And, truth be told, sometimes it is easier to do bad.

Yet that does not have to be the end of our story. In one course, I required students to fast for three days from the technologies that most enamored them. Many resisted my suggestion. But all were surprised by what they discovered: how much time they spent with wired options, how much fun conversations could be by candlelight, how suddenly there was more time for prayer, reading, and sleep. After that experience, several made resolutions about limiting computer use, for example, or having a monthly twenty-four hour technology fast or an annual three-day fast. A small experiment had big payoffs.

Unless we figure out why we're selecting our lifestyle choices, it will be hard to make discerning decisions and careful choices about living differently. Dietrich Bonhoeffer famously warned, "If you board the wrong train, it is no use running along the corridor in the opposite direction."[1]

Default Positions

The groundwork for our patterns of technology use have been established for us already. It is increasingly difficult to live without computers, television, cars, cell phones. New technology brings additional obligations. Just because people can reach us at all times, we feel that it is our duty to respond to the latest call—whether we are in a crowded room, on a bus or jet, or at an intimate dinner party.

Using technology becomes our default mode. We can hardly imagine alternatives. Stan and Carolyn Smith raised three fine children without television. The focus of their living room was a homemade bookshelf filled with books, and they played lots of music together too. One day a neighbor commented that the Smith children seemed clever and then added, "Just think how smart they'd be if they could watch Sesame Street."

Karen and John resolved when they married over three decades ago that they would not have television. Their first place, a rental unit, unfortunately included an installed television. They turned it to the wall, left it unplugged, and covered it with a blanket. When they moved, they were glad to be free of the thing. But then when their children were small, the parents discovered that they were unable to recruit babysitters without a television. And not just any set: it had to be color, include cable, and have an attractive array of subscribed stations.

We get swept along by the agenda of others. Think how hard it is to abide by the speed limit on a highway when most other vehicles pass you going twenty miles an hour faster. A Purdue University psychology professor noticed that individuals quickly learn in groups to keep pace with others. "The larger the group, the more the members felt compelled to maintain the speed. . . . Those who tried to deviate from it were treated like outcasts."[2] One of my Ethiopian students felt stunned by the North American pace of life. Many Americans and Canadians had little time for visiting, socializing, or hospitality. But within a year he found himself telling family members back home about his busyness. He started to wake up when those relatives teased him about how North American he had become.

Why Do We Settle for This?

On the Camino de Santiago we celebrated what used to be common experiences: enjoying nature, exerting oneself physically, long uninterrupted conversations, enough time to rest and think, convivial meals and hospitality, surprisingly rich encounters with strangers. Most of those experiences are still within reach.

During the major power grid failure of 2003, many people reflected on what life was like without electricity. In Toronto, folks spoke about the joys of eating by candlelight, visiting neighbors on the porch, playing games, having leisurely conversations with loved ones, and seeing stars at night. But when the electricity was turned back on, there was no evidence that Toronto residents had changed their daily habits to more easily incorporate the kinds of simple pleasures they'd enjoyed during the blackout. So the questions need to be asked: If we do not enjoy our way of living, why do we choose it? Why not opt for other habits? Why not find how to move toward true joy and fulfillment?

It is easy to get cranky about uncritical use of technology. So it's helpful to remember the wisdom of the ancient Jewish philosopher Philo of Alexandria: "Be compassionate, for everyone you meet is fighting a great battle." I recalled this when Lorna and I went out for lunch recently at one of our favorite Middle Eastern restaurants. A couple was dining nearby, and the man was talking on his cell phone. I was about to rant, but Lorna slowed me down: "People are just desperately looking for connections." I need to remember this, even if I question the ways others try to meet their needs.

Many factors lend themselves to uncritical acceptance of technology. Our advertising-cultivated desires goad us to purchase the latest gadgets. In 2007, a United States Consumer Electronics Association survey found that the hope people most fervently cherished was for a new computer, even more than they longed for "peace and happiness."[3] Expectations are continually inflated by technology. What once seemed a glamorous luxury soon turns into a common necessity. When we moved in the early 1990s, I noticed where the phone jack was in our new house and felt that it was in an inappropriate and inconvenient place. Someone suggested that I purchase a portable phone. I scoffed; I hardly knew anyone with such a device. Now, however, portable phones are common and cell phones ubiquitous. Gradually what seems new and innovative comes to be seen as a vital need. Luxuries become essentials.

Technology's allure involves a second factor. Our culture's most impressive achievements usually have to do with technology: the space shuttle, advances in digital communications, instant availability of information via the internet. Albert Borgmann speculates that one "reason for embracing technology might be the understandable desire to embrace what's distinctive about our culture. It's difficult to accept the notion that the things that are most characteristic of our lives should not be most central."[4] In Aleksandr Solzhenitsyn's novels, such as *The First Circle*, it is striking how many Soviet citizens were unable to critique the downsides of Stalinism—and not only because of the threat of punishment. Even people imprisoned on false and trumped-up political charges were likely to defend their own country's political system. When Christian churches dominated medieval culture and their cathedrals commanded city skylines, it was hard to challenge abuses of faith. If technology is at the center of our lives, how frightening it must be to suggest that perhaps there is something wrong at the core of what our civilization regards as most worthwhile.

A third barrier to raising question is that this seems ungracious. We are aware of many benefits: lives saved by vaccines, well-being enhanced by central heating, amazing surgeries and medical technology that improve the efficiency of diagnosing and treating major diseases. Many technological advances benefit us. Borgmann argues that "roughly from the middle of the 19th century to the middle of the 20th, technology was very beneficial. It remedied the miseries of hunger, confinement and illness." But technology "imperceptibly moved to colonize the center of life."[5]

Borgmann notes that "the great defensive devices that protect us from hunger, cold, disease, darkness, confinement and exertion" have been in place for a long while. We really do not need much new or much more. "Technology now mimics the great breakthroughs of the past, assuring us that it is an imposition to have to open a garage door, walk behind a lawnmower, or wait twenty minutes for a frozen dinner to be ready."[6] The truth is that our understandings and expectations about what we require are deeply shaped by available devices that come to dominate our lives. "Technology is . . . a principled and skillful enterprise of defining and satisfying human needs."[7] And, we might add, of creating false but no less compelling needs as well. We can go too far, even with new technologies, no matter how useful they might seem. Bill McKibben argues that "up to a certain point something is good, and past that point there's trouble," noting the difference between one beer or eight and driving 55 miles per hour or 155.[8]

A fourth reason we settle for devices and practices that are ultimately unsatisfying is because so often we are just too tired to do otherwise. When we feel a lack of energy, we may be more likely to drive, even though the exercise of walking or bicycling might give an invigorating shot of adrenalin. When I go to work in the morning and there is a car in the driveway and my legs are sore from the previous day's walk, it is easy to take the car. When too tired to read or converse, we turn on the television, even though that is generally not satisfying, as many studies show. At the end of a hard day—encountering and dealing with all those "labor-saving" devices and their relentless demands—we resolve eating choices by opting for the quick and convenient. Cooking food, dreaming up meals, studying recipes, eating things that are unfamiliar all feel too taxing. People under pressure are lured by convenience.

A fifth reason for involvement with gadgets and technology is that technological innovations tend to be designed to increase our use of them. While I am grateful to have air-conditioning in my car, that comfort can lure me into driving more. Evidence indicates that people are driving longer on their commutes (a side effect of adding highways!) and that we use cars for more trips. I've noticed that when I acquire a new device—CD player or MP3 player or iPad—it's never enough just to get that one thing. Other gadgets are required: chargers, cords, software programs, headphones.

The question remains: if we want to live differently, how do we achieve that?

Focal Affirmations

When folks find Borgmann's portrait of focal living appealing, sooner or later someone asks, "Can you please help me understand what you mean by living *focally*?" They like the idea—in theory—but they're still not sure they get it.

At the Missoula Consultation, Borgmann told a personal story of a turning point in his life. As a young man, he moved from Germany to the United States for undergraduate work. He fell in love with many aspects of American culture and with Nancy, a German major from Illinois. He described himself as feeling "grim and bitter" about returning to his native Germany to do doctoral work. Around the time of his relocation, he was directed in a retreat by the renowned theologian Hans Urs von Balthasar. Von Balthasar tried to uncover whether there were moments of God's grace even in the midst of a challenging time. Borgmann developed four focal affirmations that he now uses with students, asking when they were last able to affirm the following:

> There is no place I would rather be.
> There is nothing I would rather do.
> There is no one I would rather be with.
> This I will remember well.

Folks around the table were sophisticated, well educated, articulate, and thoughtful. They grew hushed as Borgmann told this story; they recognized its truth. He called his retreat conversation an experience of "*kairos*, the moment of grace where things are properly centered in a way that we don't have to unsay them or surpass them at a later moment."[9] There are times in life when everything feels properly ordered, when all seems right with the world, where nothing more is needed.

But think about those affirmations. Even now, over a decade later, people who were present at the consultation tell me that this was the most important moment of the meeting.

No place one would rather be? Much technology (faxes, email, instant messaging, wireless communication, texting) seductively lures us into being significantly present elsewhere, but not here. Our culture promotes attention deficits.

Nothing one would rather do? Go to church and watch people toy with portable phones and MP3 players in worship. Commercials boast that we can play computer games, converse with others, or receive photos during tedious meetings and no one will be the wiser. A Blackberry ad says, "In a boring meeting, it's the perfect excuse to pretend you've just received a very urgent email."

No preferred company? I hear too many stories of spouses who prioritize email over family, children who do not converse at home but spend hours instant messaging, and adults who prefer deceptively anonymous cyberrelationships to messy, complicated, in-the-flesh versions.

William James proposed that the best way of learning a person's

> character would be to seek out the particular mental or moral attitude in which, when it came upon him, he felt himself most deeply and intensively active and alive. At such moments, there is a voice inside which speaks and says, "This is the real me."[10]

I want to live in a way that enables me to offer these focal affirmations often. I want to fully be where I am. I want to wholeheartedly do what I am doing. I want to intentionally spend time with the people around me. I want to spend my days in ways worth remembering. While complicated and challenging, living a life with focal affirmations in view is not impossible. That possibility energizes and informs this book. How can we all move toward lives that are less distracted and alienating, richer and more fulfilling?

Worse than You Think but More Power than You Realize

It is easy to be overwhelmed by how devices may distract us from the kinds of thoughtful and meaningful lives we would like to lead. When I first began teaching about ALERTS, I noticed that some folks grew despondent. So I began to say early in my presentations:

> There are three things that I hope you hear from me.
> There is a problem; this is not something we are only imagining.
> The situation is far worse than we often understand.
> But we have more power than we realize.

People may feel discouraged when I warn that matters are far worse than we imagine. But we cannot hope to engage such issues with the energy and creativity they require unless we realize how far gone our circumstances are. We will not know how to address what is amiss until we have a realistic grasp of what is truly wrong.

In spite of our situation, we do have power and agency. It is easy to give up and just turn responsibility over to other people, forces, or institutions. Numerous writers communicate important truths to us about the complications and diminishments of our lives—Wendell Berry, Neil Postman, Jacques Ellul, Ivan Illich, E. F. Schumacher, George Grant, Ursula Franklin. They are sometimes dismissed as pessimistic naysayers. Or they are considered hopelessly naive and misguided, perhaps a little too Amish. Being as judicious as the few Christians who take technology seriously isn't a bad thing. Amishman David Kline points out: "The Amish are not . . . against modern technology. We have simply chosen not to be controlled by it."[11] I appreciate authors and groups whose clear-eyed analysis points the way forward. They live faithfully. Our work is not done until we can see that we also have power to make life-giving choices.

Folks often talk about things they would do "if only I had more time": tend to children, work for charities, host meals, volunteer, play music, garden, exercise, take better care of themselves.[12] Professing a desire to live differently while denying the ability to do so is troubling. It could suggest that folks are enslaved by forces within or without, that they have no choice. Or it may mean that we live deeply divided lives, with loyalties torn in several directions, distracted by all the possibilities. Do we want to settle for that? We are not—to paraphrase the Eagles' song "Hotel California"—merely prisoners of our own devices.

Let's face it, even when we know something is awry and we want to do something about it, actually determining the best way forward can be difficult. People declare new priorities, but then those become another thing to squeeze in and tackle. We need robust strategies for alternatives ways of living.

There are choices to be made and most of us have the ability to choose well. We can embrace more fulfilling lifestyles—cooking, offering hospitality, engaging in conversation, exercising, learning arts and crafts. As Borgmann says, "The good life is within reach for most of us."[13]

In Praise of the Lonely Eccentric

For some months, my friend Gary (an alias) went outside every evening after supper to walk for a couple of hours in the city where he lived. He enjoyed the exercise. He grew fit and lost excess weight. He breathed in the cool evening air. And he had a chance to decompress from the challenges of his demanding work. But here's the thing: he hardly dared tell anyone that he did this. He knew that people would find it odd behavior, and he was right. Yet curiously many think nothing of driving two hours a day—or of spending that much time or more surfing the net or watching television. But 120 minutes moving on foot—enjoying scenery, pondering the day, praying about things that matter—marks one as peculiar. What makes Gary an oddball? Why should he explain himself?

There is no way around it. If we want to live more deliberately, then we need to make choices and take a stand. Reflecting on Ecclesiastes, Jacques Ellul wrote, "Once you have acquired a certain knowledge and experience, you must walk alone."[14]

Parker Palmer argues that significant social movements begin when individuals step forward and decide that they will live "divided no more." They act, even if they must do so in solitude. His shining example is Rosa Parks's refusal to go to the back of the bus. He writes that "to live divided no more is to find a new center for one's life, a center external to . . . demands" of others, culture, or institutions. We may face consequences, even harsh ones. Yet, Palmer contends, "No punishment anyone lays on you could possibly be worse than the punishment you lay on yourself by conspiring in your own diminishment."[15]

I am encouraged by an editorial composed by a monk I first met while walking the Camino. Curtis Almquist oversees the Society of St. John the Evangelist. He once wrote that monks are sometimes seen as *eccentric*, not merely in the sense that some may seem quirky or odd. He wrote, "Rather, I mean eccentric in an etymological sense, as in the Latin *eccentricus*, meaning 'having a different center.'"[16] I have been arguing that too much of our lives revolves around—or centers on—unhelpful ways of engaging technology. Yet the possibility remains that we can center our lives differently, putting other priorities in a place of prominence. Having choices about things that are most important and valuable to us is an intrinsic part of human dignity.

When I interviewed salt-of-the-earth folks devoted to focal practices, most were surprised that I was interested in quilting or gardening or bird-watching. Without exception they asked toward the end of our discussion *why* I was talking with them and *what* my project was attempting to accomplish. When I explained focal practices, they immediately understood. They got it. More importantly, however, this theory legitimized what they already knew at a gut level: there is something deeply significant about their commitments. Our discussion of their practices reinforced their devotion and commitment to their particular avocation. While I came away inspired by their insights, they went away reinforced in their convictions and priorities.

Mihaly Csikszentmihalyi and Eugene Rochberg-Halton argue that personhood depends on the ability to make choices about where we focus energies and passions. They contend that decisiveness is key to being a whole, integrated human. Most psychological pathologies— schizophrenia, paranoia, obsessive compulsive disorder—are "disorders of attention."[17] It is our ability to choose where, when, and how long to focus that separates our cognitive ability from a reptile's primitive brain stem or a mammal's limbic brain.

We each have options of deciding to live committed to our highest priorities.

Communities of Congruence

Middle-aged Richard and his two brothers, one older and one younger, decided to run the Chicago Marathon. They lived far apart, in three different states, but here was a project they could jointly take on. Every week they checked in with each other by employing technology—phone and email. They reviewed the week's goals and held one another accountable. They offered encouragement and support. Their successful completion was all the sweeter because they did so together. When Richard spoke to me a year later, he was preparing for his second marathon. This time neither of his brothers could run. He found it far more difficult to get ready for the challenge without their regular encouragement and solidarity. It was not at all clear whether he would make it to the big Chicago event, let alone whether or not he could succeed in the running.

Parker Palmer notes that the next stage of social movements happens when like-minded people rely on one another. They "discover . . . and form communities of congruence that offer mutual support and opportunities to develop a shared vision."[18] Few hold out for long when functioning as solitaries. The most dramatic lives of witness and countertestimony are usually intertwined with others, as Rosa Parks's was. The Amish live close together—within walking or horse-riding range—and share priorities. Even monastic hermits have a community connection. They are part of an order or tradition or group that supports them in what they are doing.

When my parents immigrated to Canada, gathering with other Dutch people was vital. But they worked long hours, usually on farms, six days a week. Sundays became all-day affairs of church and meetings, coffee and conversations. They supported each other through the hardships of their transition and in trying to make sense of the strange culture where they'd landed. I saw the same thing when I had a collegial relationship with a Coptic Orthodox priest, Father Athanasius Iskander. Sundays at his church were always well-attended events that began early in the morning and lasted until late afternoon. People ate and met and worshiped and talked together.

In my interviews with people about their focal practices, it was clear that a vital aspect that sustained them was being part of a wider circle of folks who did similar things, or taught them the practice, or supported the practice in significant ways. I cannot do well all the things that my friends do: birding, home construction, pottery, letter writing, quilting. Yet they are allies in trying to aim for a life that is more deliberate and focal. I want to celebrate what they do and encourage them in their practices because of the intrinsic value of such activities and because I know that all of us are richer for them.

It is not enough for individuals to be *eccentric*. Acting alone, it is too easy to be persuaded, diverted, or thrown off by larger forces, even invisible ones. Emerging "social contagion" literature suggests that both good behaviors (happiness, good diets, quitting smoking, conviviality, temperate drinking) and poor behaviors (unhappiness, obesity, smoking, loneliness, alcohol abuse) can be passed on through networks of friends, families, and acquaintances. "Staying healthy isn't just a matter of your genes and diet, it seems. Good health is also a product, in part, of your sheer proximity to other healthy people." The case was made most strongly by two social scientists, Nicholas Christakis and James Fowler. Their detailed study was published in *The New England Journal of Medicine* in July 2007. We get caught up by the directions and "subconscious signals" of those around us. Individuals are not as fully in control of choices as they might like to think. Christakis says: "You don't ask an individual buffalo, 'Why are you running to the left?' The answer is that the whole herd is running to the left."[19]

Those who wish to live differently and deliberately need circles of like-minded folks who reinforce in us the priorities we want to honor. They help us ask good questions about *why* we live as we do. And they encourage us to imagine creative alternatives. It is not that we tell each other what to do. But we learn how to think about discernment and ask one another careful questions about choices.

Perhaps we need new models of community, networking, and support. Traveling in the British Isles some years ago, I was struck by the "dispersed communities" model of Iona and Northumbria. Each group is made up of people who live at some distance from one another but make mutual pledges about lifestyles, priorities, social justice, ministry, and ways to be accountable to each other for their promises. People are sustained in eccentric faithfulness by being connected with each other.

As we look to others for help, support, and reinforcement on such crucial matters, there are a number of strategies that we might consider employing.

Let's Get Fundamental

Borgmann introduces useful vocabulary for talking about living with greater discipline, discernment, and intentionality. He speaks of fundamental decisions and daily decisions.[20]

A fundamental decision sets a priority for some time to come. I am a Benedictine oblate, obliging me to pray a version of the daily office, live out Benedictine values, and be accountable to the abbot of a particular monastery *for the rest of my life*. This is a fundamental commitment, as was becoming a husband and a father, choices that set priorities for the rest of my days. Certain goals are worthy of being fundamental decisions.

It is equally important, however, to understand *daily decisions*. A daily decision is made and needs to be in line with fundamental priorities. Borgmann's example is the fundamental decision to learn Shakespeare's works. This would mean making space in one's life to regularly interact with Shakespeare: attending performances of plays, reading his writing, taking a class, memorizing passages. A fundamental commitment cannot be haphazardly fulfilled. It will not work to consider afresh each day whether or not one will engage Shakespeare in some way. Commitments must be in place over a period of time.

Every day we are faced with options. I prefer a mode of transport that exposes me to fresh air, gives opportunity for exercise, and minimizes my ecological footprint. Daily decisions are shaped by bigger commitments, fundamental choices already made and set in place. Small choices facilitate my ability to be a responsible and committed individual who contributes to others' well-being and my own.

When unclear about fundamental priorities, urgency becomes the default position. Daily decisions develop their own momentum or are determined by the fundamental decisions of others. That's why Princeton seminarians ignored homeless people who required assistance; they felt pressured by the admonition that they were "late." And it's one reason why folks in the Milgram experiments were more likely to administer lethal electrical shocks. Our culture with its omnipresent clocks and ringing phones and nonstop emails can sweep us along with a cascade of small daily decisions that *distract* us from our professed fundamental priorities.

It is problematic, then, to make inadequate or hazardous fundamental decisions. Borgmann offers the example of a father who with the best of motives buys a television "to surprise and gladden his family." He saw it as a way to enrich family life: "They would be able to see a play by Shakespeare, watch the news, follow a ball game, and otherwise life would proceed as always, albeit more richly informed."[21] But what the father has overlooked is that his fundamental decision has unanticipated daily implications that TV will displace family time. When technology is a fundamental priority, focal practices are pushed aside.

Conversely, fundamental priorities mean setting limits. I try to spend time every day praying, walking or exercising, reading, and doing family chores. Because these important activities take time, other options are precluded. Acknowledging and then living within the limitations we have is hard for many of us. We prefer unlimited possibilities. But we can't leave focal practices to spontaneity and happenstance alone.

We need to build practices that help us move in the directions we most value. William James argued that character growth had everything to do with deliberately cultivated habits. He had four recommendations for habit formation.

> First, initiate new habits with determined commitment.
> Second, do not allow exceptions to habits until the habits are firmly established.
> Third, never hesitate to practice the habit that you have chosen.
> Fourth, do small things every day to remind you of this habit's priority.[22]

Fundamental choices and decisions help our entire life take on a certain direction, pattern, and consistency. Fundamental decisions, then, need to be strengthened; they require commitment, dedication, and even devotion. Otherwise they are not true priorities and are always subject to our whims, our feelings, whatever is going on at the moment.

Crossing Thresholds

Albert Borgmann points out that the *thresholds* for technology use are low. It is easiest to drive when communities are spread out, have inadequate public transit, and don't have sidewalks or bike paths. The driving threshold is low. In the evening when we tiredly sit in comfortable chairs, it does not take much to snag a remote control and snap on the TV or a video game.

Borgmann contends that focal practices—hiking in the woods, prayer, walking, socializing with family—have a higher threshold in our culture. They take effort, intentionality. In some respects, the threshold is imaginary. Is it really so hard to write a letter? Turn off email? Go for a walk? Sit in the woods? Play with one's children?

Activities with a low threshold, those requiring little effort, correspondingly have little payoff. In an extended reflection on his passion for running, Haruki Murakami quotes a Tokyo gym poster that echoes this interesting quality of thresholds: "Muscles are hard to get and easy to lose. Fat is easy to get and hard to lose."[23]

Conveniences casually consumed—microwaved meals, television at the push of a remote control button—never have the reward of practices that take effort and energy. Science writer Stefan Klein argues, "Activity . . . intensifies both the anticipation and . . . enjoyment itself."[24] Church-growth advocates promote "seeker-friendly" worship that lowers thresholds and barriers to prospective seekers, employing enticing forms of technology. Yet "rewarding experiences . . . almost invariably require concentrated involvement and interaction with complex information. The things that give people 'natural highs'—playing music, a close game of tennis, an intense and meaningful conversation with a friend, a job well done—all require that we pay attention, that we look, listen, and act with care and skill."[25]

A young adult acquaintance, Alex Taylor, has given careful thought to these matters and spoke to me of "the extraordinary non-addictiveness of spiritual disciplines." He observes how easy it is to get "addicted" to television, surfing the internet, or any number of traps, but not Scripture reading or praying. Low thresholds and high thresholds.

Raising Thresholds to Discourage Casual Technology Use

One strategy, then, for building a richer life filled with focal practices is to raise the thresholds for things that are not high priorities. This requires finding ways to put technology in its proper place. The essentially *negative* choice of limiting technology is the least important step. Borgmann admits that there are appropriate times to use devices and even to indulge in mass commodities. "There are always occasions where a Big Mac, an exercycle, or a television program are unobjectionable and truly helpful answers to human needs."[26] But a well-focused life, rooted in focal practices, will lead to "an intelligent and selective attitude toward technology."[27]

To be focal requires deliberate and intentional commitments, not just acting automatically. When we had two vehicles, I never had to give much thought to accomplishing certain tasks. If Lorna was driving the car, I could always take the minivan. No planning was needed and no negotiation either. This changed when big-city living with reliable public transit meant we could easily get rid of one vehicle. Now if I think about using the car, I first need to consider whether it's in use. I have to plan with Lorna. Sometimes we have to coordinate, and sometimes we have to negotiate. We've raised the threshold against automobility.

Sharing a car gives us reason to pause and ponder. How necessary is this drive? Are there other ways to accomplish this errand? Better ecological options? We try to resist the assumption that because we have a car and can afford fuel we should use it. As a result, we make more careful decisions about car use. And practicing the discipline of assessing the necessity and ecological implications of car usage makes us better able to think critically in other realms of daily life. We begin to see that every time we use a technological device we make a moral and theological decision. Raising thresholds for technology use allows us enough time to choose well.

Lowering Thresholds and Redeeming Our Lives

More important than raising thresholds is prioritizing what we value by lowering other thresholds—making priority choices easier and more pleasurable. We examine our lives and lower thresholds for activities that support fundamental decisions and focal practices.

Stan Smith resolved to bike to work all year round. It was challenging to figure out the appropriate clothing for each trip. So he created a chart that he put near the door, detailing what kinds of layers were needed for various temperatures. He also confirmed the truth that higher thresholds have greater payoffs. At first he started biking as a personal challenge. He noticed that it was a cheaper and healthier way to commute. But when he realized how much he was enjoying himself, he grew committed to cycling as his main form of transportation.

We can make it easier to do the things that are most worthwhile. Evelyn Kreider writes letters almost daily. She lowers the threshold by having a lovely wooden table for writing in her home's most important room, an area with plenty of natural light because of large picture windows. She keeps good pens and an assortment of note cards nearby. She stocks stamps and envelopes. She does everything possible to move easily into a practice that is life-giving for her and her many correspondents.

If walking, jogging, or running is a priority, find inspirational places to do so. Go at a time of day when you feel energized and motivated. Make sure that you have good footwear and clothes. In other words, get technology to *support* not *supplant* your practice. As one lowers the threshold of priorities and more frequently engages in these focal practices, the easier it becomes to keep doing them. They are their own reward and gradually perpetuate themselves, developing their own momentum.

Commitment to a focal practice is its own best motivator. When our children lived at home we emphasized having suppers together and spending them in conversation instead of watching television or listening to music. Afterward, we prayed and shared together. We all had different reasons for participating. As a teacher, I was glad for what we learned together; other family members appreciated the chance to visit and chat; one of us was in it only for the hugs we shared at the end of our time. But that focal practice formed us in good and vital ways. As a parent, I'm grateful that our adult children continue to prioritize eating with others, sharing meals and extending hospitality.

Abstinence Makes the Heart Grow Fonder?

Dealing with technology and all its choices does not offer simple or clear-cut solutions that apply equally at all times and in all circumstances.

One strategy is abstaining altogether from certain devices, temporarily or permanently. Old Order believers are famous for the technology that they *reject*. While guidelines vary, they might refuse to own automobiles, radios, televisions, or computers. The Amish have standards that they review together to decide whether or not certain devices fit their priorities. That is an impressive commitment. How curious, then, that we in affluent countries speak casually about "appropriate technology" for so-called developing nations but do not often raise questions about whether or not certain technologies are *appropriate* for us.

There can be good reasons for abstaining from particular devices, temporarily or permanently. I know several families who gave up television years ago. They found that they did not miss the machine and that in many respects life—especially family life—was better without it. I have yet to meet anyone who regretted that move. Many writers—often people who consider themselves neither spiritual nor religious—speak of the merits and benefits of technology sabbaths. Chris Balish authored a book titled *How to Live Well Without Owning a Car*. He lives in North America's premier car city, Los Angeles, and says:

> Once you start doing it, you figure it out. There are definitely pros and cons, but there are pros and cons to any choice you make in life. You gain some stuff and you lose some stuff when you get rid of a car. But your personal benefits, your financial benefits, your peace of mind benefits—all these things start to add up, and that alone tips the scale in favor, in my opinion, of not having a car. But then you add in all the bigger societal things—independence from foreign oil, less greenhouse gases, less pollution, on and on—and it's like a no-brainer.[28]

Wendell Berry is a notorious abstainer. For farming, he prefers horses over a tractor. A prolific writer, he does it all by hand and then his wife types up his work on a typewriter. Berry's essay "Why I Am Not Going to Buy a Computer" expresses his preference for a computer-free life without denouncing computers. Not only is such a machine expensive, he explains, but it also means losing the close working relationship that he and his wife cherish. When that essay was published in *Harper's*, it attracted a firestorm of controversy and outrage. Berry was caught off guard by the intense reaction and concluded that it reflected "technological fundamentalism"; the readers of *Harper's*, he observed, wouldn't abide the questioning of technology usage.[29]

It's easy for me to get self-righteous about forgoing certain kinds of technology. So I appreciate Anne Fadiman's self-mocking essay that confesses that she and her husband were proud of their "retrograde status" in not owning a modem, car, microwave, food processor, cell phone, CD player, or cable TV. While she finally got email, she admitted that it was "hard to give up that sort of backward image."[30] Like her, I don't want to take myself too seriously or cling too tightly to the importance of my own choices.

Discriminating Uses

Abstinence is related to another strategy: restraint and discrimination. We all are limited by how much we can do and have to make choices accordingly. Time and money restrictions mean we cannot have every new device that comes onto the market. We cannot have it all or do it all. Rather than make challenges of availability or funds our only means of deciding, why not base choices on significant values and priorities?

Sometimes technology itself can usefully restrict accessibility. In the chapter about limits, I noted accountability programs that help people avoid websites and online behaviors that are destructive and undesirable, whether gambling or pornography viewing. When I get too hooked on an online game, I find it helpful simply to block that website from my computer access.

AND ON THE 7.434.863.541.329.707ᵗʰ DAY ...

... GOD DISCONNECTED CABLE-TV

There are other possible restrictions. Just as society changed smoking practices by gradually expanding "no smoking" areas, we can do the same with technologies. At the beginning of concerts we are reminded to turn off phones, pagers, and other devices. When I traveled by train in Europe I was impressed that certain cars were out-of-bounds for mobile conversations. Meals with friends and other loved ones should offer such sanctuary as well.

When I interviewed Albert Borgmann in his university office, I was surprised not to see a computer. I kept looking and wondered how a professor could get on without one. I knew that my employer would not give me such an option. Finally, I spoke up, "You don't have a computer here in your office." He laughed and opened a desk drawer. "I have it here. I call this putting technology in its place."[31] Putting something in its place does not solve or resolve all concerns about how we engage technology. Nevertheless, it points us to being deliberate, discriminating, and discerning about what we use and how.

We might be acting paradoxically. Remember those tourists in Amish country who agreed television was bad for their children but did nothing about it? Like them, we know there's something awry, but we do not follow through.

Christine Pearson, coauthor of *The Cost of Bad Behavior*, saw this lack of follow-through in extensive studies of rising rudeness and increasing incivility in the workplace.

> When I ask audiences whether anyone considers sending email or texts during meetings uncivil, almost everyone raises their hand.
>
> Then, when I ask whether anyone in the audience sends texts or email during meetings, about two-thirds acknowledge the habit. (Presumably, there are still more who don't want to admit it.)[32]

Christine Rosen comments on our capacity to be "endlessly forgiving" for the rationalizations we use to justify our own misguided behavior.[33]

Only very recently North America changed its Sabbath observance. I grew up in a Dutch family that was moderately strict on Sundays. As a teenager I heatedly debated the most faithful way to honor Sabbath with other devout adolescents. We tried to agree on rules but had little success. Predictably someone always pointed out that nurses, doctors, ambulance drivers, and firefighters did not get the day off. But necessary exceptions against strict Sunday observance may have opened Pandora's box. Now it is increasingly common for people in all kinds of occupations to be expected to work on Sunday. Freeing ourselves from Sabbath constraints meant binding ourselves to less-than-life-giving priorities.

People used to argue against blue laws for the sake of freedom to do what one pleases and chooses. But the results have not been liberating. Judith Shulevitz, in her book on the disappearing Sabbath, notes a parallel development: that spending time with one's family and one's community is also on the decline.[34]

Ultimately, we cannot rein in technology use with rules, limits, or fences. As Albert Borgmann says, "Technology will be appropriated . . . not when it is enclosed in boundaries but when it is related to a center."[35] Elsewhere he notes, "The answer is not to find a line, but to remember and invigorate those centers in our lives that engage our place, our time, and the people around us."[36]

Centering and Counterbalancing

A proper center is ultimately more important than determining limits. Boundaries must be related to commitments and priorities. When we know what is most important, then we are less likely to get distracted by the allure of a technological gizmo. As I prioritize silence and the outdoors, it is not a sacrifice to turn off my iPod while walking in the woods. I get to listen to the stream and look out for wildlife. I enter my day refreshed and energized rather than overwhelmed and distracted.

Because I prioritize walking, I buy good shoes. The extra expense is worthwhile. Because I hike and bike, I acquire the equipment I need for doing these activities in all kinds of weather. I use the technology to bolster my priorities. "A focal practice engenders an intelligent and selective attitude toward technology," says Borgmann.[37]

When I visit Amish homes I notice sophisticated technology. One couple had an expensive propane refrigerator and freezer. They willingly pay for costly appliances that fulfilled the law of not having electricity but also allowed them to be hospitable to children, grandchildren, church members, and others who visit regularly.

In my interviews with people about their focal practices, they invariably spoke of machines and gadgets that helped them. The carpenter's workshop is full of electric saws. The baker has ovens, the gardener his rototiller, and on and on. Technology did not distract from but rather supported enjoying and savoring one's most important priorities.

Ruth Mallory took up bird-watching late in life, approaching her so-called golden years. When she had trouble hearing bird songs, she knew that it was time for hearing aids. These devices can be programmed for various frequencies. Ruth had hers tuned to high pitches. In fact, she brought a birdsong tape to the technicians, to make sure that they programmed her hearing aids correctly.

Being conscious of central priorities helps us make decisions in the face of the choices that bombard us constantly from all directions. "What is needed . . . is the recovery of a center and a standpoint from which one can tell what matters in the world and what merely clutters it up. A focal concern is that center of orientation."[38]

Focal priorities not only center our lives but also encourage us to make choices that reinforce those commitments. They are a counterweight, a counterforce, a counterbalance to all other options. I know that I am more content, more fruitful in my labor, and a better friend and family person when I observe a life that has sufficient prayer, reading, exercise, social engagement, and outdoor time.

CONCLUSION

Earlier I lamented a long day I spent in an airport. But I did not tell you the whole story of that trip. The missing details also bear on what we have been considering. As I described, that experience seemed a microcosm of my daily life. I spend so much time running, scurrying, and hasting to no apparent end or purpose. In the heat and pressure of the moment, I do not spare enough thought or attention for discerning choices. Nor do I have sufficient contact with others to help me with my priorities. In daily life's hurly-burly, I am frequently isolated and alone, cut off from the people and places and priorities that are most important to me. Too often, I feel stressed and lonely.

But I have not given up on flying. Nor have I relocated to some remote spot with splendid scenery. Even in our suburban "geography of nowhere," there are consolations and rewards. We enjoy suppers as a couple, we host guests in our home, we walk to church. I travel on foot to work and I find places not too far away for hiking, kayaking, and canoeing. Life is full and busy, and there is room and time for matters that count, including worship and prayer, reading and writing. And there is beauty, even wildness, to find hereabouts. Sparrows, juncos, chickadees, blue jays, and cardinals visit. A sharp-shinned hawk regularly haunts our small backyard as well, misinterpreting the "bird feeder" concept. On my walk to work, I have encountered foxes and deer, even in our busy and crowded metropolis.

After my purgatorial airport sojourn, as I tried to go to sleep that night in an overpriced hotel, I engaged in the ancient Christian discernment of *consciousness examen*. I looked back and pondered where I had met God, not just what drew me away from God's reality and presence. I realized that a day full of disappointments and frustrations also had telling moments of grace. There were many gifts; more than enough to help me through the day. And that list suggests, I think, strategies for spiritual thriving.

At the very first airport, as the gate waiting room grew increasingly crowded, I ended up sitting close to a couple in uniform. Our tight proximity gave us a choice: pretend to ignore each other or get acquainted. The lengthy delay sped by since we had so much to discuss. We even talked about controversial political and military policies that were then in the news. As a pacifist, I do not routinely run into people who dedicate their lives to military service. It was inspiring and encouraging to get acquainted with folks who at first glance seemed so different from me. By the time our flight was called, we were regretful that our conversation had to end. At first glance, we had little in common, but by the end of our visit we had a real connection.

There were other gifts of the day too.

I found quiet spots and was able to spend time praying, reading, and doing important work. I accomplished significant and satisfying things. One task was to read through a lengthy manuscript, a student's master's thesis, and provide feedback. I spent a fair bit of time on that. But when I was given the overly thorough search at a security post, the manuscript with all my notes was misplaced by one of the guards. I did not realize this until I got to my gate and was ready to board the plane. It was actually fortunate, then, that my second flight too was delayed. I had enough time to get back to the security station and, yes, retrieve that work.

When I finally did get onto a flight, I was for some reason put into first class. I did not mind so much, then, when the jet stayed on the runway for a couple hours. I was blissfully unconcerned about which airline would cover the cost. And I happily accepted the flight attendant's offer of a certain pricey Dutch beverage.

Once we were in the air, I read for a while. But then off to the east, an electrical storm put on a dazzling light show. I turned off my reading light and watched. The beauty moved me, and I was able to relinquish some frustrations of the day.

I was freed from usual obligations and demands. Turns out I missed a meeting at school that was not so crucial after all and managed quite fine without me. As Thomas Hylland Eriksen says, "Delays are blessings in disguise."[1] My experience that day reminded me that seldom is all lost. What I learned could apply to much of my life.

For one, look for surprises and serendipity. Spiritual masters teach that God is present not only in the euphoric but also in the mundane, even in the troubling and unsettling. One can listen for what God says, even in circumstances one would not choose.

For another, presence of mind requires discipline, even in settings that may not seem conducive. I was able to work in spite of obstacles. In airports I often look for relatively quiet corners where I can pray the daily office. Thich Nhat Hanh tells what he once did when his flight was delayed four hours.

> I enjoyed sitting cross-legged right in the waiting area. I just rolled up my sweater and used it as a cushion, and I sat. People looked at me curiously but after a while they ignored me, and I sat in peace. There was no place to rest, the airport was full of people, so I just made myself comfortable where I was.[2]

We have options and choices. In fact—get this—Nhat Hanh now likes to go to airports early.

> I always leave for the airport an extra hour early, so I can practice . . . meditation there. Friends want to keep me until the last minute, but I resist. I tell them that I need the time.[3]

While I do not share his fondness for airports, there are ways to care for myself when I travel. I can figure out how to read, write, pray, converse, and relax. I can make conscious decisions and choices in the midst of whatever circumstances I encounter.

Once when I was at O'Hare, I needed to take a tunnel between two terminals. The distance of the tunnel is ameliorated by moving sidewalks that transport people from one end to the other. Space-age music plays on an endless loop. And lights of various colors flicker all the way, reinforcing the science fiction feel. Most people look fairly subdued as they travel through. But I once watched a woman dancing on that moving sidewalk, interpreting for all around the soundtrack being played. And no sooner had I got out of the tunnel than I passed a Starbucks where a long line of passengers waited to purchase a drink. There a man was practicing his tap dancing while standing in the queue. We always have choices about how we use our time.

Nhat Hanh even regards the ringing of a phone as a call to prayer.[4] Why not? I am often annoyed by the random inappropriateness of phones. Perhaps I should accept the discipline of seeing them as a call to pause and pray—for the disrupted meeting, for the caller, for the distracted responder. Technology can serve such ends. The first clocks, as we recall, were developed by monks as an invitation to pause and worship. It is only later that they came to be used to drive commerce and industry and to pressure us into accomplishing more. We can still use technology to point us to our priorities.

As much of this book has detailed, there are reasons to be concerned by our patterns of technology usage. But we need not settle for sullenness, boredom, frustration, or hyperactive overextension. We have agency. Barriers may seem huge, but we can choose to exercise patient endurance even in the face of things that bother and threaten to overwhelm us.

Sometimes as I talk about focal practice, listeners wonder whether my suggestions are elitist, favoring those who have time or money to afford them. But most people have opportunities and options for gardening or cooking, do-it-yourself home repair or building, reading or writing, conversation or hospitality, quilting or singing, letter writing or birding. None of these activities requires a heavy financial outlay. Most of us, if we are willing to disconnect from devices that keep us entertained and in constant communication, can find room for things that give us the most energy and enrich our lives. Everyone—not just those with resources to spare—has time for visiting friends and inviting people over to share meals and conversation.

Years ago I read of a group of Westerners who were traveling overseas in a country well known for inefficiency and red tape. Finally, they were ready to go home. At the airport the Westerners learned that bad weather had shut down flights for twenty-four hours. In fact, the storm was so fierce that they could not even leave the terminal. The locals, used to delays and setbacks, took this in stride. They produced bottles of wine and sturdier beverages, pulled out decks of cards, and proceeded to laugh, carry on, play games, drink, and generally have a good time. The Westerners, however, could not settle down. They regularly stormed up to ticket counters, demanding to know when they could depart. The answer remained the same: "Not until mid-afternoon tomorrow at the earliest." In their anxiety, they did not even sleep that night, hoping that some sudden change would allow them to take off. As predicted, however, jets did not depart for twenty-four hours. After the long delay, the locals commenced their travel, relaxed and refreshed. The Westerners were wrung out and worn down by their disquiet and, of course, did not leave any sooner than the locals. Nothing was gained by their anxiety and stress and much was lost.

I was once stuck in a small airport, snowed in and uncertain about when we would depart. I was frustrated by loud cell phone conversations and a little anxious about the day. But nearby a dreadlocked individual pulled out his guitar and practiced for an hour, playing a soothing blend of gentle jazz.

Another time I was in an airport all night long, waiting for a dense fog to lift. As time went on, people grew friendlier and friendlier. We conversed with each other, laughed at our travails, watched out for each other's possessions. And gradually, we all nodded off, sleeping for hours on uncomfortable airport seats. It was an adventure, and we were not alone.

We have choices. Many of them. And there is always grace. Lots of it. All things considered, there are plenty of other places I'd rather be than airports, but even in the face of burdens and barriers, I need not be shaped, determined, or formed by them. When I pay attention and act with deliberation, when I stay alert and make careful choices, when I honor awe and reverence, then my life is meaningful and fulfilling. At such times I find myself engaged and satisfied. Not all is lost. Not by a long shot. It is still possible to live the good life.

This I want to remember well.

NOTES

Introduction

1. Albert Borgmann, *Real American Ethics: Taking Responsibility for Our Country* (Chicago: University of Chicago Press, 2006), 58.

2. Arthur Paul Boers, *The Way Is Made by Walking: A Pilgrimage along the Camino de Santiago* (Downers Grove, IL: InterVarsity, 2007). For the next pages, I adapt material from that book.

3. Eugene H. Peterson, *Christ Plays in Ten Thousand Places* (Grand Rapids: Eerdmans, 1989), 57.

4. William Greider, "The Future of the American Dream: Imagining an Economy That Puts People First," *The Nation*, May 25, 2009, 11.

5. Gregg Easterbrook, *The Progress Paradox: How Life Gets Better While People Feel Worse* (New York: Random House, 2004), xix.

6. Bill McKibben, *Enough: Staying Human in an Engineered Age* (New York: Henry Holt and Company, 2003), 44.

7. I have permission to tell all the stories of readily identifiable people that I mention. Where necessary (either I was unable to contact the subject or the story might seem embarrassing) identifying details were changed.

8. Borgmann, *Real American Ethics*, 150.

9. Three sources of Albert Borgmann quotes are not footnoted each time: the Missoula Consultation at the University of Montana (March 2001); interviews I conducted with him in his university office (September 2007); and the Elkhart Consultation at Associated Mennonite Biblical Seminary (March 2008).

Chapter 1 Stumbling into Focus

1. Ronald Rolheiser, *The Holy Longing: The Search for a Christian Spirituality* (New York: Doubleday, 1999), 33.

2. Marjorie Connelly, "More Americans Sense a Downside to an Always Plugged-In Existence," *New York Times*, June 6, 2010, www.nytimes.com/2010/06/07technology/07 brainpoll.html.

3. Albert Borgmann, *Technology and the Character of Contemporary Life: A Philosophical Inquiry* (Chicago: University of Chicago Press, 1987), 4.

4. Albert Borgmann, *Crossing the Postmodern Divide* (Chicago: University of Chicago Press, 1993), 108.

5. Borgmann, *Technology and the Character of Contemporary Life*, 196.

6. Ibid.

7. Richard E. Sclove, "Making Technology Democratic," in *Resisting the Virtual Life: The Culture and Politics of Information*, ed. James Brook and Iain A. Boal (San Francisco: City Lights, 1995), 86. There were other consequences: "Introducing water pipes added incentive for also replacing donkeys with tractors in field work. (The fewer tasks a donkey is asked to perform, the less economical it is to maintain it.) This eliminated any remaining practical use for donkeys, while increasing villagers' dependence on outside jobs for the cash needed to finance and operate their new tractors and washing machines." Ibid., 90.

8. Borgmann, *Technology and the Character of Contemporary Life*, 119.

9. Maggie Jackson, *What's Happening to Home? Balancing Work, Life, and Refuge in the Information Age* (Notre Dame, IN: Sorin Books, 2002), 71, 77.

10. Robert D. Putnam, *Bowling Alone: The Collapse and Revival of American Community* (New York: Simon & Schuster, 2000).

11. Borgmann, *Technology and the Character of Contemporary Life*, 157.

12. David Wood, "Prime Time: Albert Borgmann on Taming Technology," *Christian Century*, August 23, 2003, 22.

13. Borgmann, *Crossing the Postmodern Divide*, 112.

14. On the correlation between television viewing and civic disengagement see Putnam, *Bowling Alone*, 228–46.

15. On the loneliness spiral see Robert Kubey and Mihaly Csikszentmihalyi, *Television and the Quality of Life: How Viewing Shapes Everyday Experience* (Hillsdale, NJ: Lawrence Ehrlbaum Associates, 1990), 133.

16. On the irony of isolation see Daniel J. Lohrmann, *Virtual Integrity: Faithfully Navigating the Brave New Web* (Grand Rapids: Brazos, 2008), 152.

17. The University of Washington study is cited in Eric Nagourney, "Childhood: TV Reduces Adult-Child Conversations," *New York Times*, June 15, 2009, www.nytimescom/2009/06/16 /health/research/16chil.html.

18. Christine Rosen, "Virtual Friendship and the New Narcissism," *New Atlantis* 17 (Summer 2007): 30.

19. Sherry Turkle, *Alone Together: Why We Expect More from Technology and Less from Each Other* (New York: Basic Books, 2011), 243.

20. Todd Friesen, Elkhart Consultation, Associated Mennonite Biblical Seminary, 2008.

21. The characteristics are explained in Borgmann, *Crossing the Postmodern Divide*, 119–20.

Chapter 2 Awe and Inspiration

1. Bill Mason, *Path of the Paddle: An Illustrated Guide to the Art of Canoeing* (Scarborough, ON: Van Nostrand Reinhold, 1983), 3.

2. John P. Robinson and Geoffrey Godbey, *Time for Life: The Surprising Ways Americans Use Their Time* (University Park, PA: Pennsylvania State University Press, 1997), 47–48.

3. Haruki Murakami, *What I Talk About When I Talk About Running: A Memoir*, trans. Philip Gabriel (New York: Knopf, 2008).

4. Edward Abbey, *Desert Solitaire: A Season in the Wilderness* (New York: Ballantine, 1971), 241–42.

5. Thomas de Zengotita, *Mediated: How the Media Shapes Your World and the Way You Live in It* (New York: Bloomsbury, 2005), 213–14.

6. Abbey, *Desert Solitaire*, 258.

7. Dacher Keltner, *Born to Be Good: The Science of a Meaningful Life* (New York: W. W. Norton & Company, 2009), 258.

8. Margaret Visser, *The Rituals of Dinner: The Origins, Evolution, Eccentricities, and Meaning of Table Manners* (New York: Grove Weidenfeld, 1991), 17.

9. Margaret Visser, *Much Depends on Dinner: The Extraordinary History and Mythology, Allure and Obsessions, Perils and Taboos of an Ordinary Meal* (New York: Collier, 1988), 15.

Chapter 3 Focal Connectedness

1. Gary and Joanie McGuffin, *Wilderness Ontario* (Erin, ON: Boston Mills, 2007), 8.

2. Robert Kubey and Mihaly Csikszentmihalyi, *Television and the Quality of Life: How Viewing Shapes Everyday Experience* (Hillsdale, NJ: Lawrence Ehrlbaum Associates, 1990), 141.

3. Gordon S. Mikoski, "Bringing the Body to the Table," *Theology Today* 67 (2010): 24–25.

4. Reprinted with permission from the *Psalter Hymnal*, 1987, Faith Alive Christian Resources, 1987, text by William Kuipers, 1933; based on Revelation 4–5.

5. Margaret Visser, *Much Depends on Dinner: The Extraordinary History and Mythology, Allure and Obsessions, Perils and Taboos of an Ordinary Meal* (New York: Collier, 1988), 20.

6. Margaret Visser, *The Rituals of Dinner: The Origins, Evolution, Eccentricities, and Meaning of Table Manners* (New York: Grove Weidenfeld, 1991), 80.

7. Christine D. Pohl, *Making Room: Recovering Hospitality as a Christian Tradition* (Grand Rapids: Eerdmans, 1999), 30.

8. Winifred Gallagher, *Rapt: Attention and the Focused Life* (New York: Penguin, 2009), 88.

9. See Maggie Jackson, *What's Happening to Home? Balancing Work, Life, and Refuge in the Information Age* (Notre Dame, IN: Sorin Books, 2002), 119.

10. Lianne George, "It's Not Just a Car Anymore . . . It's a Home," *Maclean's*, February 27, 2006, 22.

Chapter 4 Focal Centering and Orienting Power

1. Douglas V. Steere, *Together in Solitude* (New York: Crossroad, 1982), 25.

2. Albert Borgmann, interview with the author, September 2007.

3. Albert Borgmann, Missoula Consultation, University of Montana, March 2001.

4. David Weale, *Chasing the Shore: Little Stories About Spirit and Landscape* (Alexandra, PEI: Tangle Lane, 2007), 30.

5. Linda Underhill, *The Unequal Hours: Moments of Being in the Natural World* (Athens: University of Georgia Press, 1999), 1.

6. Barry Lopez, "Introduction," in *The Best American Spiritual Writing 2005*, ed. Philip Zaleski (New York: Houghton Mifflin, 2005), xix.

7. Gerald May, *Will and Spirit* (San Francisco: HarperSanFranciso, 1982), 55.

8. Ibid., 64.

9. Erazim Kohák, *The Embers and the Stars* (Chicago: University of Chicago Press, 1987), 185.

10. Bill McKibben, *The Age of Missing Information* (New York: Random House, 2006), 93.

11. Albert Borgmann, *Crossing the Postmodern Divide* (Chicago: University of Chicago Press, 1993), 97.

Chapter 5 Going on the ALERT

1. Edward Tenner, *Our Own Devices: How Technology Remakes Humanity* (New York: Vintage, 2004), ix.

2. Alain de Botton, *The Pleasures and Sorrows of Work* (Toronto: McClelland & Stewart, 2009), 212.

3. As quoted in Richard Lischer, *The End of Words: The Language of Reconciliation in a Culture of Violence* (Grand Rapids: Eerdmans, 2005), 17.

4. Jared Diamond, *Collapse: How Societies Choose to Fail or Succeed* (New York: Viking, 2005), chap. 16.

5. Ronald Wright, *A Short History of Progress* (Toronto: House of Anansi Press, 2004), 129.

6. See, for example, Matt Richtel, "Driven to Distraction: Drivers and Legislators Dismiss Cellphone Risks," *New York Times*, July 19, 2009, www.nytimes.com/2009/07/19/technology/19distracted.html?_r=1.

7. Julie Scelfo, "The Risks of Parenting While Plugged In," *New York Times*, June 9, 2010, www.nytimes.com/2010/06/10/garden/10childtech.html?_r=1.

Chapter 6 Attenuated Attention and Systemic Distraction

1. Simone Weil, *Waiting for God*, trans. Emma Craufurd (New York: Harper Colophon, 1951), 71–72.

2. Jerry Mander, *Four Arguments for the Elimination of Television* (New York: Quill, 1978), 303.

3. Robert Kubey and Mihaly Csikszentmihalyi, *Television and the Quality of Life: How Viewing Shapes Everyday Experience* (Hillsdale, NJ: Lawrence Ehrlbaum Associates, 1990), 140.

4. William McNamara, *Earthy Mysticism: Contemplation and the Life of Passionate Presence* (New York: Crossroad, 1983), 87.

5. Weil, *Waiting for God*, 105.

6. Robert Farrar Capon, *The Supper of the Lamb: A Culinary Reflection* (New York: Harcourt Brace Jovanovich, 1969), 19.

7. "Systemic distraction" is from Sharon Daloz Parks as cited by Nancy M. Malone, *Walking a Literary Labyrinth: A Spirituality of Reading* (New York: Riverhead, 2003), 72.

8. Maggie Jackson, *Distracted: The Erosion of Attention and the Coming Dark Age* (New York: Prometheus, 2008), 14.

9. Mihaly Csikszentmihalyi and Eugene Rochberg-Halton, *The Meaning of Things: Domestic Symbols and the Self* (Cambridge: Cambridge University Press, 1981), 9.

10. Michael Posner, "Breaking through the Information Overload," *Globe and Mail*, April 17, 1999, C8.

11. "Tom Vanderbilt Talks with John Intini about the Link between Corruption and Driving, and Why a Little Road Rage May be Good," *Maclean's*, August 25, 2008, 16. Also see Tom Vanderbilt, *Traffic: Why We Drive the Way We Do (and What It Says About Us)* (New York: Knopf, 2008) 51, 77.

12. Walter Kirn, "Here, There and Everywhere" *New York Times Magazine*, February 11, 2007, 17.

13. Csikszentmihalyi and Rochberg-Halton, *The Meaning of Things*, 5.

14. Ruth Conway, *Choices at the Heart of Technology: A Christian Perspective* (Harrisburg, PA: Trinity Press International, 1999), 19.

15. Marva J. Dawn, *Unfettered Hope: A Call to Faithful Living in an Affluent Society* (Louisville: Westminster John Knox, 2003), 7.

16. David Ehrenfeld, *Becoming Good Ancestors: How We Balance Nature, Community, and Technology* (New York: Oxford University Press, 2009), 51, 52.

17. Stephen Levy is cited in Naomi S. Baron, *Always On: Language in an Online and Mobile World* (New York: Oxford University Press, 2008), 219.

18. Nicholas Carr, *The Shallows: What the Internet is Doing to Our Brains* (New York: W. W. Norton & Company, 2010), 221.

19. Information about the Pearson study is from Christine Pearson, "Sending a Message That You Don't Care," *New York Times*, May 16, 2010, Business, 9.

20. Sherry Turkle, *Alone Together: Why We Expect More from Technology and Less from Each Other* (New York: Basic Books, 2011). See especially part 1 of this book.

21. As quoted by Michelle Swenarchuck's "Introduction" in Ursula Franklin, *The Ursula Franklin Reader: Pacifism as a Map* (Toronto: Between the Lines, 2006), 25.

22. Winifred Gallagher, *Rapt: Attention and the Focused Life* (New York: Penguin, 2009), 2.

23. Jonathan Rosen, *The Life of the Skies: Birding at the End of Nature* (New York: Farrar, Straus and Giroux, 2008), 11, 156.

24. Anthony Ugolnik, *The Illuminating Icon* (Grand Rapids: Eerdmans, 1989), 57. On the multiplication of images, see Jacques Ellul, *The Technological Bluff* (Grand Rapids: Eerdmans, 1990), 214–15.

25. Henri J. M. Nouwen, *Behold the Beauty of the Lord: Praying with Icons* (Notre Dame, IN: Ave Maria Press, 1987), 13.

Chapter 7 Eliminating Limits and Endangering Taboos

1. John Palfrey and Urs Gasser, *Born Digital: Understanding the First Generation of Digital Natives* (New York: Basic Books, 2008), 87, 88.

2. Peter Nowak, *Sex, Bombs and Burgers: How War, Porn and Fast Food Shaped Technology as We Know It* (Toronto: Viking Canada, 2010).

3. Daniel J. Lohrmann, *Virtual Integrity: Faithfully Navigating the Brave New Web* (Grand Rapids: Brazos, 2008), 13.

4. David G. Myers, *The American Paradox: Spiritual Hunger in an Age of Plenty* (New Haven: Yale University Press, 2001), 214.

5. Harlan Coben, "The Undercover Parent," *New York Times*, Week in Review, March 16, 2008, 14.

6. Thomas de Zengotita, *Mediated: How the Media Shapes Your World and the Way You Live in It* (New York: Bloomsbury, 2005), 227.

7. Ibid., 243.

8. Donald Kraybill, Elkhart Consultation, Associated Mennonite Biblical Seminary, 2008.

9. Quoted in William L. Hamilton, "Rip Van Winkle Awakens to a Flat-Screen Life," *New York Times*, Week in Review, December 24, 2006, 3.

10. Jacques Ellul, *The Technological Bluff* (Grand Rapids: Eerdmans, 1990), 337.

11. Albert Borgmann, *Technology and the Character of Contemporary Life: A Philosophical Inquiry* (Chicago: University of Chicago Press, 1987), 141.

12. Albert Borgmann, interview with Ken Myers, "Albert Borgmann on the Necessity of Deliberate Reflection about How Technology Shapes Everyday Life," *Mars Hill Audio Journal* 63 (July/August 2003).

13. Kraybill, Elkhart.

14. Matt Richtel, "Thou Shalt Not Kill, Except in a Game at Church," *New York Times*, October 7, 2007, 1, 20.

15. The "punctured flesh" quote is from Mark Slouka, *War of the Worlds: Cyberspace and the High-Tech Assault on Reality* (New York: Basic Books, 1995), 13.

16. Dacher Keltner, *Born to Be Good: The Science of a Meaningful Life* (New York: W. W. Norton & Company, 2009), 166. Keltner is alluding to a study by Craig Anderson and Brad Bushman in C. A. Anderson and B. J. Bushman, "Effects of Violent Video Games on Aggressive Behavior, Aggressive Cognition, Aggressive Affect, Physiological Arousal, and Prosocial Behavior: A Meta-Analytic Review of the Scientific Literature," *Psychological Science* 12 (2001): 353–59.

17. Jacques Ellul, *Perspectives On Our Age: Jacques Ellul Speaks on His Life and Work*, ed. William H. Vanderburg (Toronto: Anansi, 1997), 99.

18. Christine Rosen, "The Age of Egocasting," *New Atlantis* (Fall 2004–Winter 2005): 72.

19. Chellis Glendinning, "Technology, Trauma, and the Wild," in *Ecopsychology: Restoring the Earth, Healing the Mind*, ed. Theodore Roszak, Mary E. Gomes, and Allen D. Kanner (San Francisco: Sierra Club Books, 1995), 41–54.

20. Palfrey and Gasser, *Born Digital*, 187.

21. Benjamin R. Barber, *Consumed: How Markets Corrupt Children, Infantilize Adults, and Swallow Citizens Whole* (New York: W. W. Norton, 2007), 243.

22. David Shenk, *Data Smog: Surviving the Information Glut* (New York: HarperEdge, 1987), 43.

23. Sherry Turkle, *Alone Together: Why We Expect More from Technology and Less from Each Other* (New York: Basic Books, 2011), 227.

24. See Stephen K. Spyker, *Technology and Spirituality: How the Information Revolution Affects Our Spiritual Lives* (Woodstock, VT: Skylight Paths Publishing, 2007), 137–41.

25. Naomi S. Baron, *Always On: Language in an Online and Mobile World* (New York: Oxford University Press, 2008), 228–29.

26. The sociological study is cited by Ellul, *Technological Bluff*, 339.

27. Tara Parker Pope, "An Ugly Toll of Technology: Impatience and Forgetfulness," *New York Times*, June 6, 2010, www.nytimes.com/2010/06/07/technology/07brainside.html.

28. As cited in Roger Cohen, "Turkey Tune-Out Time," *New York Times*, November 22, 2007, www.nytimes.com/2007/11/22/opinion/22cohen.html.

29. Bill McKibben, *Enough: Staying Human in an Engineered Age* (New York: Henry Holt and Company, 2003), 209.

30. Daniel Lohrmann writes about accountability software in *Virtual Integrity*, 145–66.

31. Dennis Linn, Sheila Fabricant Linn, and Matthew Linn, *Sleeping with Bread: Holding What Gives You Life* (Mahwah, NJ: Paulist Press, 1995), 17.

Chapter 8 Eroding Engagement

1. Brian Ladd, *Autophobia: Love and Hate in the Automotive Age* (Chicago: University of Chicago Press, 2008), 181.

2. Jacques Ellul, *The Technological Bluff* (Grand Rapids: Eerdmans, 1990), 43.

3. Albert Borgmann, *Crossing the Postmodern Divide* (Chicago: University of Chicago Press, 1993), 15.

4. John Palfrey and Urs Gasser, *Born Digital: Understanding the First Generation of Digital Natives* (New York: Basic Books, 2008), 91.

5. Daniel Goleman, "E-Mail Is Easy to Write (and to Misread)," *New York Times*, October 7, 2007, www.nytimes.com/2007/10/07/jobs/07pre.html. See also Kristin Byron, "Carrying Too Heavy a Load? The Communication and Miscommunication of Emotion by Email," *Academy of Management Review* 33, no. 2 (2008): 311, 312.

6. Shane Hipps, *Flickering Pixels: How Technology Shapes Your Faith* (Grand Rapids: Zondervan, 2009), 117.

7. Clay Shirky, *Voices from the Net* (Emeryville, CA: Ziff-Davis Press, 1995), 43–44.

8. Goleman, "E-Mail Is Easy to Write."

9. As cited by Janet Kornblum, "Cyberbulling grows bigger and meaner with photos, video," *USA Today*, July 15, 2008, www.usatoday.com/tech/webguide/internetlife/2008-07-14-cyberbullying_N.htm.

10. Richard Mahler, *Stillness: Daily Gifts of Solitude* (Boston: Red Wheel, 2003), 15–16.

11. Naomi S. Baron, *Always On: Language in an Online and Mobile World* (New York: Oxford University Press, 2008), 226. See also 7–8.

12. See Melissa Seligman, "One Husband, Two Kids, Three Deployments," *New York Times*, May 25, 2009, www.nytimes.com/2009/05/25/opinion/25seligman.html.

Chapter 9 Remote Relationships

1. Stephen L. Talbott, *The Future Does Not Compute: Transcending the Machine in Our Midst* (Sebastopol, CA: O'Reilly & Associates, 1995), 140, emphasis mine.

2. Christine Rosen, "Our Cell Phones, Ourselves," *New Atlantis* 6 (Summer 2004): 43.

3. Tom Vanderbilt, *Traffic: Why We Drive the Way We Do (and What It Says about Us)* (New York: Knopf, 2008), 16.

4. Normal Wirzba, *Living the Sabbath: Discovering the Rhythms of Rest and Delight* (Grand Rapids: Brazos, 2006), 109.

5. Jane Jacobs, *The Death and Life of Great American Cities* (New York: Vintage, 1961), 56; Jacobs, *Dark Age Ahead* (New York: Vintage, 2005), 36–37.

6. David G. Myers, *The American Paradox: Spiritual Hunger in an Age of Plenty* (New Haven: Yale University Press, 2001), 178.

7. John L. Locke, *The De-Voicing of Society: Why We Don't Talk to Each Other Anymore* (New York: Simon & Schuster, 1998), 118.

8. Richard Stivers, *Shades of Loneliness: Pathologies of a Technological Society* (Lanham, MD: Rowman & Littlefield, 2004), 41.

9. Summarized in John T. Cacioppo and William Patrick, *Loneliness: Human Nature and the Need for Social Connection* (New York: W. W. Norton, 2009), 247.

10. Statistics Canada data is from Shannon Proudfoot, "Face Time Decreases as Pace of Life Accelerates," *Vancouver Sun*, January 17, 2009, www.vancouversun.com/Technology/Trends%20Social%20networking/1185242/story.html?id=1185242.

11. John Freeman, *The Tyranny of E-Mail: The Four-Thousand-Year Journey to Your Inbox* (New York: Scribner, 2009), 95.

12. Nie is quoted in ibid., 133.

13. Lianne George, "A High-Tech Ghost Story," *Maclean's*, September 20, 2004, 32.

14. Chicago heat wave quotes and information are from Jacobs, *Dark Age Ahead*, 81–85.

15. Malcolm Gladwell, *Outliers: The Story of Success* (New York: Little, Brown and Company, 2008), 3–11.

16. Lianne George, "It's Not Just a Car Anymore . . . It's a Home," *Maclean's*, February 27, 2006, 25.

17. Edward Tenner, *Why Things Bite Back: Technology and the Revenge of Unintended Consequences* (New York: Vintage, 1997), 231.

18. Ursula Franklin, *The Ursula Franklin Reader: Pacifism as a Map* (Toronto: Between the Lines, 2006), 85.

19. On studies about compassion and information overload, see Charles Korte, Ido Ypma, and Anneke Toppen, "Helpfulness in Dutch Society as a Function of Urbanization and Environmental Input Level," *Journal of Personality and Social Psychology* 32 (1975), 996–1003; D. Sherrod and R. Downs, "Environmental Determinants of Altruism: The Effects of Stimulus Overload and Perceived Control on Helping," *Journal of Experimental Social Psychology* 10 (1974), 468–79. Cited by David Shenk, *Data Smog: Surviving the Information Glut* (New York: HarperEdge, 1987), 38, 222.

20. Douglas Quenqua, "Friends, Until I Delete You," *New York Times*, January 28, 2009, www.nytimes.com/2009/01/29/style/29iht-29facebook.19771424.html.

21. Stivers, *Shades of Loneliness*, 41.

22. Albert Borgmann, *Holding On to Reality: The Nature of Information at the Turn of the Millennium* (Chicago: University of Chicago Press, 1999), 5.

23. Christine Rosen, "Romance in the Information Age," *New Atlantis* 4 (Winter 2004): 6.

24. Stivers, *Shades of Loneliness*, 28, 55.

25. William Deresiewicz , "The End of Solitude," *The Chronicle of Higher Education: The Chronicle Review*, January 30, 2009, http://chronicle.com/free/v55/i21/21b00601.htm.

26. Shenk, *Data Smog*, 127.

27. Quoted in Maggie Jackson, *Distracted: The Erosion of Attention and the Coming Dark Age* (New York: Prometheus, 2008), 55.

28. Hal Niedzviecki, "Facebook in a Crowd," Lives Column, *New York Times Magazine*, October 26, 2008, 114, www.nytimes.com/2008/10/26/magazine/26lives-t.html.

29. Kenneth J. Gergen, *The Saturated Self: Dilemmas of Identity in Contemporary Life* (New York: BasicBooks, 1991), 214.

30. Christine Rosen, "The Age of Egocasting," *New Atlantis* 7 (Fall 2004–Winter 2005): 68.

31. Ursula Franklin, *The Real World of Technology* (Toronto: House of Anansi Press, 1999), 46.

32. Ibid., 45.

33. Vartan Gregorian is cited in Martin E. Marty, "Virtual Spirituality," M.E.M.O. Column, *Christian Century*, April 5, 2005, 63.

34. Jackson, *Distracted*, 54, 59–60.

35. David Lyon, *Surveillance Society: Monitoring Everyday Life* (Philadelphia: Open University Press, 2001), 8.

36. Talbott, *Future Does Not Compute*, 74.

37. Heidi B. Neumark, *Breathing Space: A Spiritual Journey in the South Bronx* (Boston: Beacon, 2003), 18.

38. Bodil Jönsson, *Unwinding the Clock: Ten Thoughts on Our Relationship to Time*, trans. Tiina Nunnally (New York: Harcourt, 2001), 52.

39. Albert Borgmann, interview with the author, September 2007.

Chapter 10 Taxed Time

1. Donald Nicholl, *Holiness* (New York: Seabury, 1981), 62.

2. Roy Romanow and Tony Gagliano, "Modern Time Crunch Hijacked 'Leisure Society,'" *The Toronto Star*, June 20, 2010, A13.

3. Barbara Righton, "How We Live," *Maclean's*, July 1, 2006, 39.

4. Jim Forest, *The Road to Emmaus: Pilgrimage as a Way of Life* (Maryknoll, NY: Orbis, 2007), 142–43.

5. Phil Cousineau, *The Art of Pilgrimage* (Boston: Comari, 1998), 56–57.

6. Mumford is interpreted by Neil Postman, *Amusing Ourselves to Death: Public Discourse in the Age of Show Business* (New York, Penguin, 1986), 11–12.

7. Neil Postman, *Technopoly: The Surrender of Culture to Technology* (New York: Knopf, 1992), 15.

8. John P. Robinson and Geoffrey Godbey, *Time for Life: The Surprising Ways Americans Use Their Time* (University Park: Pennsylvania State University Press, 1997), 30.

9. Rebecca Solnit, *River of Shadows: Eadweard Muybridge and the Technological Wild West* (New York: Penguin, 2004), 59, 62.

10. Matt Richtel, "Attached to Technology and Paying a Price," *New York Times*, June 6, 2010, 3, www.nytimes.com/2010/06/07/technology/07brain.html.

11. Juliet B. Schor, *The Overworked American: The Unexpected Decline of Leisure* (New York: Basic Books, 1991), 258.

12. Malcolm Gladwell, *The Tipping Point: How Little Things Can Make a Big Difference* (New York: Little, Brown, and Company, 2002), 163–66.

13. The Milgram studies observations are from Benedict Carey, "Decades Later, Still Asking: Would I Pull That Switch?" *New York Times*, July 1, 2008, www.nytimes.com/2008/07/01/health/research/01mind.html.

14. Nicholas Carr, *The Shallows: What the Internet Is Doing to Our Brains* (New York: W. W. Norton, 2010), 220.

15. Cited by Judith Shulevitz, *The Sabbath World: Glimpses of a Different Order of Time* (New York: Random House, 2010), 26.

16. W. Paul Jones, "Love as Intrinsic Living," *Weavings* (January/February 1998): 30.

See also Jeffrey Kaplan, "The Gospel of Consumption: And the Better Future We Left Behind," *Orion* 27, no. 3 (May/June 2008): 40–47.

See Benjamin Kline Hunnicutt, "The New Economic Gospel of Consumption," chap. 2 in *Work without End: Abandoning Shorter Hours for the Right to Work* (Philadelphia: Temple University Press, 1988).

17. The story is told and analyzed in Benjamin Kline Hunnicutt, *Kellogg's Six-Hour Day* (Philadelphia: Temple University Press, 1996).

18. Schor, *Overworked American*, 2.

19. Sean McCluskey and Patricia Treble, "The Plugged-In Price," *Maclean's*, August 1, 2005, 58.

20. See Andrew Coyne, "Stuck in Traffic," *Maclean's*, January 17, 2011, 16.

21. Ivan D. Illich, *Energy and Equity* (New York: Harper & Row, 1974), 18–19.

22. Tom Vanderbilt, *Traffic: Why We Drive the Way We Do (and What It Says about Us)* (New York: Knopf, 2008), 9.

23. Linda Breen Pierce, "Time by Design," in *Take Back Your Time: Fighting Overwork and Time Poverty in America*, ed. John de Graaf (San Francisco: Berrett-Koehler, 2003), 198.

24. Christine Rosen, "Bad Connections," *New York Times Magazine*, March 20, 2005, 18. See also Rosen's "Age of Egocasting," 61, 64.

25. Ralph Keyes, *Timelock: How Life Got So Hectic and What You Can Do About It* (New York: HarperCollins, 1991), 63.

26. Geert Mak, *De Eeuw Van Mijn Vader* (Amsterdam: Uitgeverij Atlas, 1999), 15.

27. Thomas de Zengotita, *Mediated: How the Media Shapes Your World and the Way You Live in It* (New York: Bloomsbury, 2005), 202.

28. Randall Stross, "Caution: Driver May Be Surfing the Web," *New York Times*, August 24, 2008, Business, 3.

29. Jennifer Steinhauer and Laura M. Holson, "As Text Messages Fly, Danger Lurks," *New York Times*, September 20, 2008, www.nytimes.com/2008/09/20/us/20messaging.html.

30. Steve Lohr, "Slow Down, Brave Multitasker, and Don't Read This in Traffic," *New York Times*, March 25, 2007, A1, 25.

31. Winifred Gallagher, *Rapt: Attention and the Focused Life* (New York: Penguin Press, 2009), 152.

32. Thich Nhat Hanh, *The Miracle of Mindfulness! A Manual on Meditation* (Boston: Beacon Press, 1976), 4–5.

33. Maggie Jackson, *What's Happening to Home? Balancing Work, Life, and Refuge in the Information Age* (Notre Dame, IN: Sorin Books, 2002), 50.

34. Naomi S. Baron, *Always On: Language in an Online and Mobile World* (New York: Oxford University Press, 2008), 215.

35. Christine Rosen discusses Microsoft ads in "The Image Culture," *New Atlantis* 10 (Fall 2005): 39.

36. Cited in Jackson, *What's Happening to Home?* 30.

37. See Michelle M. Weil and Larry D. Rosen, *TechnoStress: Coping with Technology @ Work @ Home @ Play* (New York: John Wiley & Sons, 1997), 161–62.

38. Keyes, *Timelock*, 97–98.

39. See ibid., 67.

40. Abraham Joshua Heschel, *The Sabbath* (New York: Farrar, Straus and Giroux, 1979), 3, 28–29, emphasis mine.

41. William Powers, *Hamlet's Blackberry: A Practical Philosophy for Building a Good Life in the Digital Age* (New York: HarperCollins, 2010).

42. Cited in Judith Shulevitz, "Creating Sabbath Peace Amid the Noise," *New York Times*, Sunday Styles, July 18, 2010, 2.

43. See www.sabbathmanifesto.org.

44. Heschel, *Sabbath*, 13.

Chapter 11 Sundering Space

1. James Howard Kunstler, *The Geography of Nowhere: The Rise and Decline of America's Man-Made Landscape* (New York: Free Press, 1994).

2. G. Benko, cited in John Inge, *A Christian Theology of Place* (Burlington, VT: Ashgate, 2003), 17.

3. Maggie Jackson, *Distracted: The Erosion of Attention and the Coming Dark Age* (New York: Prometheus, 2008), 30.

4. Ibid., 31.

5. Heschel speaks of "conquering space" in Abraham Joshua Heschel, *The Sabbath* (New York: Farrar, Straus and Giroux, 1979), 3. Rebecca Solnit uses "annihilation" in *River of Shadows: Eadweard Muybridge and the Technological Wild West* (New York: Penguin, 2004), 11.

6. E. B. White, *One Man's Meat* (New York: Harper Colophon, 1983), 3.

7. Ursula Franklin, *The Real World of Technology* (Toronto: House of Anansi Press, 1999), 45.

8. Quoted in Eric Reece, "Moving Mountains: The Struggle for Justice in the Coalfields of Appalachia," in *The Future of Nature: Writings on a Human Ecology from Orion Magazine*, ed. Barry Lopez (Minneapolis: Milkweed Editions, 2007), 95.

9. Thomas Michael Power, "Trapped in Consumption: Modern Social Structure and the Entrenchment of the Device," in *Technology and the Good Life?*, ed. Eric Higgs, Andrew Light, and David Strong (Chicago: University of Chicago Press, 2000), 277.

10. As cited in Scott Russell Sanders, *Writing from the Center* (Bloomington: Indiana University Press, 1997), 5.

11. As cited in Richard Louv, *Last Child in the Woods: Saving Our Children from Nature-Deficit Disorder* (Chapel Hill, NC: Algonquin, 2005), 39.

12. Joel Kotkin, *The New Geography: How the Digital Revolution Is Reshaping the American Landscape* (New York: Random House, 2001), 147.

13. Erik Reece, "Happiness Grows Out of Tiny Parks, Not Huge Televisions," *Lexington Herald-Leader*, January 11, 2009.

14. Louv, *Last Child in the Woods*, 3.

15. Jonah Lehrer, "How the City Hurts Your Brain: . . . And What You Can Do about It," *Boston Globe*, January 2, 2009, www.boston.com/bostonglobe/ideas/articles/2009/01/04/how _the_city_hurts_your_brain/.

16. Louv, *Last Child in the Woods*, 43–47.

17. Ibid. See also Theodore Roszak, Mary E. Gomes, and Allen D. Kanner, *Ecopsychology: Restoring the Earth, Healing the Mind* (San Francisco: Sierra Club Books, 1995).

18. See Albert Borgmann, *Crossing the Postmodern Divide* (Chicago: University of Chicago Press, 1993), 87–97.

19. Paul Wells, "In Ottawa, at the Berlin Opera, Live," *Maclean's*, April 20, 2009, 71.

20. Kotkin, *New Geography*, 6.

21. Shane Hipps, *Flickering Pixels: How Technology Shapes Your Faith* (Grand Rapids: Zondervan, 2009), 115. Christine Rosen notes trends not only of "giving up face-to face for virtual contact" but also, "in some cases, a preference for the latter." Rosen, "Virtual Friendship and the New Narcissism," *New Atlantis* 17 (Summer 2007): 30–31.

22. Kenneth J. Gergen, *The Saturated Self: Dilemmas of Identity in Contemporary Life* (New York: Basic Books, 1991), 61–62, 55, 175–77.

Chapter 12 Finding and Funding Focal Fundamentals

1. As cited by Eric Metaxas, *Bonhoeffer: Pastor, Martyr, Prophet, Spy* (Nashville: Thomas Nelson, 2010), 176.

2. On the Purdue study see Stefan Klein, *The Secret Pulse of Time: Making Sense of Life's Scarcest Commodity* (New York: Marlowe & Company, 2007), 164.

3. "Peace, Love and Tech," *Maclean's*, October 29, 2007, 9.

4. David Wood, "Prime Time: Albert Borgmann on Taming Technology," *Christian Century*, August 23, 2003, 23.

5. Ibid.

6. Albert Borgmann, *Technology and the Character of Contemporary Life: A Philosophical Inquiry* (Chicago: University of Chicago Press, 1987), 140.

7. Ibid., 205.

8. Bill McKibben, *Enough: Staying Human in an Engineered Age* (New York: Henry Hold and Company, 2003), 118.

9. Albert Borgmann, Missoula Consultation, University of Montana, March 2001.

10. From the *Letters of William James* as quoted by Warren Bennis, *On Becoming a Leader* (New York: Basic Books, 2009), 49.

11. David Kline, *Great Possessions: An Amish Farmer's Journal* (San Francisco: North Point Press, 1990), xv.

12. Arlie Hochschild cited in Catherine M. Wallace, *Selling Ourselves Short: Why We Struggle to Earn a Living and Have a Life* (Grand Rapids: Brazos, 2003), 171.

13. Albert Borgmann, *Real American Ethics: Taking Responsibility for Our Country* (Chicago: University of Chicago Press, 2006), 172.

14. Jacques Ellul, *Reason for Being: A Meditation on Ecclesiastes*, trans. Joyce Main Hanks (Grand Rapids: Eerdmans, 1990), 3.

15. J. Parker Palmer, *The Courage to Teach: Exploring the Inner Landscape of a Teacher's Life* (San Francisco: Jossey-Bass, 1998). This discussion and these quotes are found on pp. 166–71.

16. Curtis Almquist, "A Letter from the Superior," *Cowley* 31, no. 3 (Pentecost 2005): 3.

17. Mihaly Csikszentmihalyi and Eugene Rochberg-Halton, *The Meaning of Things: Domestic Symbols and the Self* (Cambridge: Cambridge University Press, 1981), 9.

18. Palmer, *Courage to Teach*, 166.

19. The Christakis and Fowler study discussion is found in Clive Thompson, "Are Your Friends Making You Fat?" *New York Times*, September 13, 2009, www.nytimes.com/2009/09/13/magazine/13contagion-t.html.

20. Albert Borgmann, *Crossing the Postmodern Divide* (Chicago: University of Chicago Press, 1993), 111.

21. Ibid.

22. Summarized, not quoted, by Walter Earl Fluker, *Ethical Leaderships: The Quest for Character, Civility, and Community* (Minneapolis: Fortress, 2009), 65.

23. Haruki Murakami, *What I Talk about When I Talk about Running: A Memoir*, trans. Philip Gabriel (New York: Knopf, 2008), 50.

24. Stefan Klein, *The Science of Happiness: How Our Brains Make Us Happy—and What We Can Do to Get Happier* (New York: Marlowe & Company, 2006), 166.

25. Robert Kubey and Mihaly Csikszentmihalyi, *Television and the Quality of Life: How Viewing Shapes Everyday Experience* (Hillsdale, NJ: Lawrence Ehrlbaum Associates, 1990), 141.

26. Borgmann, *Technology and the Character of Contemporary Life*, 208.

27. Ibid., 221.

28. Cited by Browne Molyneus with Randall Fleming, "Without a Car: Going Bipedal in the Fossil-Fueled City of Angels," *Orion* 30, no. 3 (May–June 2011): 28.

29. Wendell Berry, "Why I Am Not Going to Buy a Computer," in *What Are People For?* (San Francisco: North Point Press, 1990), 171–77.

30. Anne Fadiman, "Mail," in *The Best American Essays 2001*, ed. Kathleen Norris and Robert Atwan (New York: Houghton Mifflin, 2001), 55.

31. Albert Borgmann, interview with the author, September 2007.

32. Christine Pearson, "Sending a Message That You Don't Care," *New York Times*, May 16, 2010, Business, 9.

33. Christine Rosen, "Our Cell Phones, Ourselves," *New Atlantis* 6 (Summer 2004): 41.

34. Judith Shulevitz, *The Sabbath World: Glimpses of a Different Order of Time* (New York: Random House, 2010), 17. Later she has an intriguing discussion on the erosion and eventual elimination of blue laws, 190–94.

35. Borgmann, *Technology and the Character of Contemporary Life*, 168.

36. Borgmann, *Real American Ethics*, 159–60.

37. Borgmann, *Technology and the Character of Contemporary Life*, 221.

38. Ibid., 225.

Conclusion

1. Thomas Hylland Eriksen, *Tyranny of the Moment: Fast and Slow Time in the Information Age* (Sterling, VA: Pluto Press, 2001), 157.

2. Thich Nhat Hanh, *Peace Is Every Step: The Path of Mindfulness in Everyday Life* (New York: Bantam, 1992), 16.

3. Thich Nhat Hanh, *The Long Road Turns to Joy: A Guide to Walking Meditation* (Berkeley: Parallax, 1996), 51.

4. Nhat Hanh, *Peace Is Every Step*, 29.

INDEX